A Traveller's History of England

FOURTH EDITION

CHRISTOPHER DANIELL

Series Editor   DENIS JUDD
Line drawings   JOHN HOSTE

THE WINDRUSH PRESS · GLOUCESTERSHIRE

First published in 1991 in Great Britain by
The Windrush Press,
Little Window,
High Street,
Moreton-in-Marsh,
Gloucestershire GL56 0LL

Telephone: 01608 652012 & 01608 652025
Fax: 01608 652125
Email:windrush@Netcomuk.co.uk

Reprinted 1993, 1996, 1999

British Library Cataloguing-in-Publication-Data

Daniell, Christopher
    A traveller's history of England.
    1. England. history
    I. Title
    942

ISBN 1–900624–28–1

Typeset by DP Photosetting, Aylesbury, Bucks
Printed and bound in Great Britain by
Biddles Ltd, Guildford

Contents

Preface

England is far more than a geographical expression. Throughout much of the world the term 'England' is still taken to mean 'Britain,' or at least the 'United Kingdom'. The patience of the Celtic inhabitants of the British Isles on being addressed and described as 'English' whenever they go abroad is something to marvel at, for the one thing that Scotland and Wales and Ireland are *not* is 'England'. Nor is it easy to get the English to think of themselves as British first and English second; moreover there are still many English people who deny that they are Europeans, let alone British.

This confusion is not helped by the tendency of other nations, notably the French, to describe the inhabitants of the United Kingdom, and indeed the United States, as 'Anglo-Saxons'. The underlying source of these muddied waters is, however, quite clear: the English came to dominate the British Isles and, by 1900, an Empire which comprised nearly a quarter of the human race. Although the Celtic peoples collaborated, with varying degrees of enthusiasm, in the establishment and administration of the British Empire they did so on English terms: English, not Welsh or Gaelic, was the language of the rulers, and became the language used by many of the ruled; it was English common law, an English based administration, the English public school ethic, predominantly an English export trade and much more, which shaped the imperial system.

The next problem is, who were the English and how did they achieve their local and global supremacies? In this well structured and detailed book Christopher Daniell leads us patiently through the obscure origins and tangled history of the English. Kipling once wrote 'Saxon and

Norman and Dane are we.' Today, however, he would have needed to add at least 'Jewish, Afro-Caribbean, and South Asian' to the list, and after 1992 perhaps 'French, German, Italian, Turkish' and so on. The truth is that despite the abiding insularity, the self-congratulatory definitions of an 'English' sense of humour or of the 'English' insistence on fair play, the English are a people endlessly distilled over centuries of invasion, migration and expansion.

It is no surprise that England has always been perceived as a desirable place to live, despite its unpredictable and sometimes foul weather. It is a fertile country with huge expanses of rich agricultural land; just stand at Offa's Dyke on the border between Wales and England and look to the east, or scramble over Scottish mountains, and you will see which part of the United Kingdom is rooted in prosperity and easy living. Even England's hill country is benign, somewhere to frolic and picnic, rather than to struggle for survival. Her river systems are small scale and often navigable; it is difficult to get lost on English moors, and her woodlands, even when wolves roamed, were not the great illimitable forests found elsewhere in the world.

The massive urbanisation of the English population during the nineteenth and early twentieth centuries changed the fair face of a predominantly rural England for ever. But even though life in the cities and towns was often, and still can be, grim and unrelenting, urban expansion was largely the product of the Industrial Revolution which offered relative prosperity to the countless numbers of country people who left their homes in search of better pay and prospects.

England's industrial supremacy enabled her to stamp her mark on the world as never before: the Empire expanded rapidly, many non-Empire countries became client states, the Royal Navy dominated the high seas and, along with the goods from Birmingham's factories, Lancashire's cotton mills and Yorkshire's wool and steel industries, the English exported less tangible products, that had matured over hundreds of years. Thus the English language, English culture, English concepts of democracy, English standards of public and private rectitude, English sport, and much else, were presented to, and sometimes thrust upon, a world that was both resentful and receptive.

Despite its industrial landscapes and its sprawling cities and towns,

England remains a beautiful country, from the rocky coast of Cornwall to the finely preserved wool villages of Suffolk, from the Sussex Downs to the wild border country of the north. The traveller will discover the essential history of the shaping of England, and the English, from this informative and thorough book.

Denis Judd
London, 1991

CHAPTER ONE

Early England: From Hunter-Gatherers to the Romans

Geography

TERMINOLOGY

England is one of three countries which make up Great Britain. The others are Scotland, which lies to the north of England, and Wales, which lies to the west. The union of England and Wales was formalised by two Acts of Parliament in 1536 and 1543. The union of England and Scotland was more complex: in 1603 James VI of Scotland became James I of England; to signify his sovereignty over the two kingdoms, he was the first monarch to use the title 'King of Great Britain' (see p. 117). Political unification occurred more than a century later in 1707 (see p. 145). The diverse history of England, Scotland and Wales has led to very different cultural traditions; the Scots and Welsh have a right to feel aggrieved whenever the term 'English' is used, wrongly, to mean all three.

To confuse the unwary, the term 'Britain' includes more countries than the term 'Great Britain'. A holder of a British passport may come from England, Scotland or Wales, or from Northern Ireland, which consists of the six northern counties of Ireland. The United Kingdom (UK) is virtually synonymous with 'Britain'; the official title is the 'United Kingdom of Great Britain and Northern Ireland'. Before 1922 the UK included Ireland in the definition, but when the Irish Free State ceased to be part of the Union in that year (see p. 214), the title was changed to include 'Northern Ireland'. The final name which needs to be explained is the 'British Isles'. This is a geographical term which includes Great Britain, the whole of Ireland, and all the offshore islands, most notably the Isle of Man which has its own parliament and laws.

If the terms 'Great Britain', 'Britain', 'United Kingdom' and 'British Isles' seem confusing, they are commonly misused within those regions as well. Nationalities, however, are never misused, and to call an Englishman a Scotsman, for example, or vice versa, can be treated as an insult or, at very least, an act of insensitivity.

THE EVOLUTION OF THE BRITISH ISLES

The present landscapes of Britain reflect the geological stages that have passed in the formation of the islands. The oldest rocks, dated to 2,700 million years ago, are mostly found in the Scottish highlands: they were caused by volcanic eruptions. Then 570 million years ago seas covered the south of Britain, leaving behind the deposits of Welsh slate. There was then an alternating pattern of flooding, followed by the development of dense forests and swamps. As the vegetation died and rotted, areas of peat were formed. When the peat was compressed the end result was coal. Such coal seams have been extensively mined, as in South Wales, Yorkshire, Kent and the North-East.

For a short time geologically, from 280 to 200 million years ago, Britain was a desert, but from 150 million years ago plants and animals once again appeared on land and in the shallow seas which covered low-lying areas. Seventy million years ago the seas had reached their greatest extent and Britain became blanketed by the fragments of algae, which have become chalk. The chalk is up to 500 metres thick in places and makes up the 'white cliffs' of the south coast.

The final major climatic change to affect Britain was the succession of ice ages, which started some 2.5 million years ago. In all there have been about twelve, and the average temperatures have ranged from –6° to –9° Centigrade. The earlier glaciations were the most extensive and ice sheets over 1000 metres thick moved as far south as London. All the mountain regions of Britain became centres of glacial activity and signs of ice erosion on the mountain-sides are still recognisable in the Lake District in Cumbria, Snowdonia in Wales, and in the Scottish Highlands.

GEOGRAPHY AND HISTORY

The two most important geographical features of British history are that

The British Isles Physical

Foula •

Shetland Is

• Fair Isle

ATLANTIC

OCEAN Cape Wrath

Orkney Is

Outer

Hebrides

North

West

Highlands

Moray Firth

Spey

Grampians

Clyde

Firth of Forth

Southern

Uplands

Firth of Clyde

Tyne

L Neagh

Solway Firth

Lake

District

Vale

of

York

Flamborough Head

Spurn Head

Ouse

I. of Man

IRISH SEA

Anglesey

Snowdonia

Peak

District

Trent

The Wash

Severn

Cotswolds

The Fens

Chilterns

Thames

Salisbury

Plain

N Downs

Exmoor

S Downs

Strait of Dover

Dartmoor

Portland

Bill

I. of Wight

Land's End

Start Point

Lizard

Inner

Hebrides

NORTH SEA

0   50 miles 100

0   50   100 kms

the British Isles are indeed islands and that they have a moderate climate. Separated from Europe by the English Channel and the North Sea, Britain was at times perceived as being on the edge of the world. But the seas around Britain also acted as barriers against attempted invasions – the Armada in 1588, the French in 1805 and Nazi Germany in 1940.

England's west coast was an ideal location for developing commerce with the New World; ports such as Liverpool and Bristol flourished. After the English loss of Calais to the French in 1558 (see p. 106), England was isolated from Europe. Much of the nation's energies became directed overseas, and the exploits of seafarers, explorers, merchants and adventurers over the centuries resulted in the building of the largest empire ever known. Possession of the empire further isolated Britain from the need to belong to Europe; this insular attitude survives to the present day, and finds expression in the reluctance to be fully committed to the European Community.

WEATHER

Technically Britain does not have a climate but is perpetually influenced by four major weather systems. The prevailing weather comes from the west with the Atlantic depressions which regularly sweep across the country; these are usually rain-bearing, even in summer. The second system comes down from the north, from the polar ice-cap, bringing cold clear air: it was an expansion of this colder air that caused the 'mini ice age' in the sixteenth and seventeenth centuries. To the east and south of Britain lies continental Europe, and east and south winds can bring very severe winters, especially if the weather comes from the Russian steppes, as in 1962. The final system comes from the south-west, with the high pressure of the tropics bringing warm weather and cloudless skies in summer, and cold sharp days in winter.

Between them the four systems produce a complex weather pattern which is generally mild and temperate, without the extreme conditions of the continent. This has allowed farming to flourish across the whole of the country, though there is a very general north/south divide running from the River Humber to the River Severn. To the north the land is generally less fertile, more rugged and wetter; to the south the landscape is generally flat or rolling, fertile and drier.

Old Stone Age (Paleolithic), 70,000–8000 BC

The Paleolithic Age was characterised by large variations in climate, alternating between warm and ice-age conditions. During the warm periods hippopotami, bison and horses roamed the country amongst forests of birch, pine and oak. In the colder eras, woolly rhinos, wolves and reindeer wandered amongst grasses and sedges.

For most of the Old Stone Age Britain was glaciated. As massive amounts of water was locked into the ice-sheets, the sea was considerably lower than present-day levels and land-bridges still existed between England and Europe. People could walk to England from Ireland, France and, across the present North Sea, Scandinavia. Even today trawlers fishing up to thirty miles off the Norfolk coast occasionally dredge up artefacts lost by Paleolithic man hunting on land. Despite these finds, the evidence for Paleolithic man is very meagre.

What is clear is that Britain was used as a hunting ground by small bands of hunter-gatherers. Most of the known base-camp sites for Paleolithic man are in caves. In Kent's Cavern, Devon, bones of horse, woolly rhinoceros, deer and bison were found, indicating the likely rewards of hunting expeditions. Unfortunately Britain has no cave art, possibly because the caves were not sealed off as in France, Italy and Spain. The only evidence which remains comprises a few scratched carvings on bone from caves in Derbyshire. The main evidence for Paleolithic man's existence consists of stone implements, such as flint axes and tools. Human remains are very scarce, but the burial site of a young man was found at Paviland caves, Dyfed, Wales, in 1823. It seems that he died whilst hunting and was buried at the base camp. Apparently a burial rite was carried out as the body was sprinkled with red ochre and mammoth bones were carefully laid beside the corpse in the grave. The dead man was buried during a period of glaciation when the base camp was only 6 km away from the ice-sheet itself.

Middle Stone Age (Mesolithic), 8300–3500 BC

In the Mesolithic era the climate grew warmer, the glaciers retreated and the land-bridges with Europe were overrun by the sea. Great Britain became an island. The combination of these factors meant that by 8000 BC hunter-gatherers began to settle for longer periods in England. The most remarkable site is at Star Carr in Yorkshire, from which it is possible to reconstruct the life of Mesolithic people. There were probably about twenty-five people occupying the site at any one time. Discarded bones indicate that they had a diet of red deer, roe deer, elk, ox and pig, as well as smaller animals such as hare, hedgehog, badger, fox and beaver. Bones of domestic dogs were also found and it may be deduced that they were being used to hunt the larger animals. Several curiosities have still to be adequately explained: the first is a wooden 'paddle' which implies that boats were in use; the second is a group of deer skulls and antlers which have been shaped. The possible reasons for these changes are that they were used as a disguise in hunting, or for ceremonial purposes before or after a hunt.

Nearly forty archaeological sites from around 7000 BC have been discovered. They indicate that the communities were beginning to hunt in localised areas. As each group became more settled, regional trends can be identified for the first time.

New Stone Age (Neolithic), 3500–2500 BC

The evidence for Neolithic man becomes very plentiful, from flint tools to standing remains. The major impact on the environment was the introduction of agriculture. Sheep, goats and pigs were domesticated, and wheat was grown as a cereal crop. These changes had a profound impact, for whereas the hunter-gatherers worked alone or in small, highly mobile groups, the agriculturalists depended on a communal effort and relied on a single harvest for the year.

The move to agriculture led to more permanent settlements, trade and the clearance of forests. The now bare and spartan slopes of the Lake District and the North York Moors were caused by deforestation in the Neolithic Age. In Somerset, trackways of hazel and willow were built across the marshy levels. In the quest for pieces of flint with which to make tools, mines were dug; the most impressive are dotted across the landscape at Grimes Graves, near Thetford. There are over 300 mine shafts over an area of 15 hectares and some are up to 12 metres deep. In one abandoned shaft, which seems to have been turned into a shrine, the figure of a 'Venus' or 'Mother Figure' was found.

During the Neolithic era a cult of the dead, or ancestor worship, became increasingly important. Elaborate monuments were built for communal burials, either menhirs (standing stones) or dolmens (flat stones resting on menhirs) or long barrows. Menhirs and dolmens still remain in large numbers in Cornwall and parts of Wales. The long barrows and dolmens contained burial chambers with more than one person inside and needed a major communal effort to construct, for a medium- to large-size tomb may have taken between 7,000 and 16,000 hours to build. The largest barrow, at West Kennet, is 350 feet long.

From examining the skeletons excavated by archaeologists, statistics about the population can be given. The average height of males and females was only slightly shorter than today, males ranging from 5 foot 1 inch to 5 foot 11 and females from 4 foot 11 to 5 foot 5. The evidence from skeletons shows that tooth loss, abscesses, and arthritis in the back, hands and feet were common.

Bronze Age, 2500–700 BC

The Bronze Age was marked by increasing inequality between those with wealth and those without. Communal burials were abandoned and replaced by smaller, but still impressive, round barrows for important individuals. At the same time a new object appears in graves, a finely finished red-patterned beaker, causing those who used them to be called the 'Beaker People'. The beakers might indicate a new migration of people from the continent, or alternatively increased trade between England and Europe. Over time a few individuals inevitably gained greater power and status. Chiefdoms emerged and with them the ornaments of power. In a few magnificently rich graves in Wessex the grave goods have shown trade links with the Mediterranean (Mycenae in Greece) and Germany. Other ornate burials have been discovered from this era: an individual buried at Mold, in Clwyd, had a cape of beaten gold and amber beads.

One of the great mysterious remains of this age may have symbolised power. Silbury Hill in Wiltshire is the largest prehistoric mound in

Europe, covering 5½ acres and rising to 131 feet (40 metres). Despite the terrific labour involved (it would have taken 500 people ten years to build it) no obvious explanation of its purpose has been given: it contains no burials and has no obvious practical use.

On a more mundane level farming continued to develop. Fields were laid out for cattle, sheep, pigs or for cereal crops. On farm and village sites pits for storing grain have been found, along with weaving combs indicating the manufacture of textiles. From about 1000 BC the first evidence for horse-riding equipment has been found. Some of the harnesses show that wagons may have been in use: the first indirect evidence of the introduction of the wheel into England. As there were no definite roads even a humble wagon may have been both practical and a status symbol.

STONE CIRCLES

There are over 900 stone circles in the British Isles, and while those in Scotland and Ireland were primarily for burials, the original purpose of the English and Welsh circles is less clear. They were possibly used for ceremonial occasions, or as trading places, but probably only rarely for astronomical observation. There are several major groups of stone circles scattered around Britain. In England there are concentrations in the Lake District and the Land's End peninsula. But the most celebrated of all are on the Wiltshire Downs which provide an incredibly rich archaeological landscape. A few hours walk from Avebury, where the stone circle is so large that it incorporates a village and fields, there are eight long barrows, Silbury Hill (see p. 7), over 400 round barrows, and the most famous stone circle in England, Stonehenge.

STONEHENGE

Despite many theories, no satisfactory explanation has been given as to why Stonehenge was built. In the Middle Ages it was thought that Merlin built it, in the seventeenth century it was considered a druidic meeting place, and later a place of sacrifice. In the 1970s and 1980s the prominent theory was that it was used for astronomy, but apart from the Heel Stone, which is directly in line with the rising of the soltice sun, there is no evidence for this.

Stonehenge

Even if the intended purpose of Stonehenge remains a mystery, the stages of its construction are less problematic. The first phase was during Neolithic times and resulted in a henge (circular ring and ditch) with a stone portal and the Heel Stone. It is likely that it had wooden buildings inside. The second phase occurred in the Bronze Age and involved the transportation of eighty-two bluestones, each weighing four tons, from Preseli in Wales to the site of Stonehenge. By the shortest route, the journey was over 200 miles. No satisfactory reason has been given as to why the stones were moved to Stonehenge. The puzzle increases since, after the stones had been put into position, the plan changed and the bluestones were dismantled. It has been inferred, from reworking marks, that the bluestones were then set up as a monument elsewhere. The final phase involved bringing the seventy-five main stones now standing, each weighing 50 tons, from the Marlborough Downs twenty miles away. The bluestones were dismantled from their second site and once again became part of the present structure of Stonehenge.

That a structure of such great antiquity and complexity is mysterious is not surprising. The number of man-hours needed to bring the stones and construct the monument have been estimated at three million. Through the centuries it has slowly disclosed its secrets to scientific and archaeological observation, but also as a result of chance and random observation. In the 1950s a huge scientific survey was undertaken, but it was a ten-year-old boy who spotted two carvings of prehistoric daggers etched into the stones.

The Iron Age, 700–100 BC

The history of the Celts is inextricably bound up with the Iron Age for they exploited iron to its full potential. Originating in Eastern Europe, the Celts migrated westwards in search of land. Evidence for their development and westward migration has been found in two remarkable archaeological sites. The first is at Hallstatt in Austria. Here salt had been mined as a valuable commodity, and at the same time had preserved a large number of Celtic objects. There was also a grim reminder of the dangers of mining when the bodies of some Celtic miners were also found. The second and later site is in Switzerland at La Tène ('the shallows'), where votive offerings had been thrown into a lake.

The first signs of Celtic influence in England occurred in the Hallstatt era. Some small settlements of the new migrants have been discovered, but more often individual items of Celtic design have been found, indicating trade with the continent. Later the number of Celtic settlers increased and they brought with them new methods of making swords and shields. These were elaborately decorated with beautiful swirling patterns, used as much for ceremony as for warfare. Such objects were highly prized and their designs were often imitated by the native English smiths. Many fine examples of Celtic metalwork have been found in rivers where the owners threw them as an offering to the water spirits. Two of the most spectacular are the Battersea Shield, found in the River Thames in 1857; and the only horned bronze helmet to survive in Europe, found near Waterloo Bridge in the heart of London (both can be seen in the British Museum).

The best evidence for Celtic migration from the continent to England occurs in Yorkshire. The newcomers, who were known as the Parisi to the Romans, had strong links with similar people around Paris. They are recognised as a separate people by their distinctive burial customs: the chiefs were often buried with wheeled vehicles (either chariots or carts) and a range of other grave goods. One woman was buried with a side of pork, an iron mirror, a dress pin and a workbox of bronze.

At the same time as the Celtic immigration and settlement, hill-forts became numerous in Britain. At first vast numbers of small forts were built, estimated at 3,000, but gradually a few dominant hill-forts emerged and the smaller ones fell into disuse. The reasons for the spectacular development and growth of the hill-forts have been a source of much debate. Some archaeologists have argued that the Celtic invaders settled and had to protect themselves; others that the native petty chiefdoms needed defence from each other, or that the hill-forts served as religious meeting places. The hill-forts were just one element of a growth of small communities and settlements. Field systems which can still be seen today were laid out: in one parish, Zennor, in Cornwall, about 80 per cent of the present-day field boundaries were laid out in the Iron Age. One of the more unusual settlements was at Glastonbury, where the village was built upon very marshy ground or a lake and contained workshops, storehouses and kennels.

For some reason as yet unexplained, after the initial Celtic migrations, which included the Parisi, the level of contact with the continent dropped dramatically for 200 years (350–150 BC) and strong localised traditions became dominant.

The Dawning of English History, 150 BC to AD 50

After a lull, the continental influence reasserted itself from 100 BC onwards. A major factor was the rapid expansion of the Roman Empire, which swept through France and Belgium and along the Rhine. Frontier posts were established along the French and Belgian coasts, but Britain remained free from Roman attack for over a century although the Romans made their presence felt through trade. One of the main ports on the English south coast was Hengistbury Head, Dorset, where evidence has been found of wine from Italy, pottery and coins from northern France, and glass from the Mediterranean. The main exports from Hengistbury were metals, such as tin, copper, iron and lead.

With the advance of Rome, classical writers began to take an interest in the Celts. The single most important source is *The Gallic War* by Julius Caesar (100–44 BC). He wrote that the Britons wore their hair long but shaved the rest of their bodies and dyed themselves blue with woad. In battle he noted how the Celts effectively used chariots by riding into the fighting, jumping off the chariot, and then, if forced to retreat, leaping back onto the chariot and riding swiftly away. Celtic customs were also occasionally recorded by classical writers: 'Hares, fowl and geese they think it unlawful to eat, but rear them for pleasure and amusement.' Unfortunately the classical sources are difficult to assess in terms of 'facts' for the writers almost certainly included propaganda which portrayed the Celts as 'barbarian' in contrast to the 'civilised' Romans.

One of the facts that Caesar did record was the movement of a Celtic tribe, the Belgae, from Belgium to Britain. The Belgae of Britain undoubtedly offered assistance to their allies on the continent against Roman attacks. To cut off these links and establish trade, Julius Caesar invaded Britain in two consecutive years (55 and 54 BC). He gives an account of the invasions and describes how in 55 the Roman soldiers were so fearful of the fearsome Celtic warriors that they refused to disembark from their ships until inspired by the standard-bearer of the Tenth Legion, who leapt into the sea. The campaigns were short-lived, but one result was the emergence of the first British historical figure, the Celtic chief Cassivellaunus, who ruled the Catuvellauni tribe north of London, probably at Verulamium (St Albans), and fought against the Romans.

Following Caesar's brief invasions, Britain was free from direct Roman rule for a hundred years. Further invasions of Britain were planned by a succession of Roman emperors, notably Augustus (27 BC–AD 14) and Caligula (AD 37–41), but more urgent considerations diverted their efforts elsewhere. During this period the politics of the tribes of south-east England appear complex and confused. Contacts with Rome continued via trade and it has even been suggested that some local chiefs sent their sons to Rome to be educated. Possibly because of this contact the political nature of the tribes began to change. Previously power seems to have been given to those with prowess in war, but increasingly a hierarchy was established where the leadership of each tribe became inherited. This often led to fear or jealousy amongst other family members, and a feud with such origins gave the Romans the excuse for a further invasion.

The British king of the Catuvellauni tribe, Cunobelinus, had increased his territory throughout the south-east of England. He expelled one of his sons, who fled to Rome and made a public act of submission to the Emperor Caligula. Caligula took this as a formal act of surrender and began to prepare an invasion. It was cancelled at the last minute because of a mutiny in the army, but the process of preparation had been completed. When Cunobelinus eventually died his other two sons, who were hostile to Rome, took over in his place. There was therefore a threat to the valuable trade between England and the Roman Empire; it was also possible that the Catuvellauni might help Rome's enemies.

The Romans, AD 43–45

THE CONQUEST OF BRITANNIA

At the same time as these troubles arose, Claudius (41–54) became the new emperor. His political weakness meant that he needed a military victory and he looked to Britain to secure his reputation and power – not even the mighty Julius Caesar had conquered Britain. As well as serving to confirm Claudius in power, the annexation of Britain would bring commercial benefits, as the island exported metals, corn, slaves and valuable hunting dogs. In AD 43 40,000 Roman soldiers were landed from Gaul at Richborough, Kent, and quickly secured south-east England. There is archaeological evidence of native Celtic hill-forts being rapidly strengthened, but inexorably the Romans continued their conquest. In the summer of 43 Claudius arrived and received the surrender of twelve English kings.

The early years of Roman rule were marked by further conquest and rebellion. The huge Celtic hill-fort at Maiden Castle in Dorset was taken after heavy fighting, and the stronghold of the Druids on the island of Anglesey was attacked and destroyed. Whilst the Anglesey campaign was in full swing (AD 60), the most serious uprising against Roman rule in the province took place, led by Boudicca, the queen of the Iceni. The Iceni had previously been loyal, but maladministration, greed, and the dishonour brought upon Boudicca and her daughters, turned the Iceni against Rome. From their lands in East Anglia, Boudicca's forces swept through the towns of Camulodunum (Colchester), Londinium (London) and Verulamium (St Albans). The official number of dead was 70,000 and several cities lay in smouldering ruins.

Roman reinforcements were hurriedly despatched from the campaign in Anglesey and when the two armies faced each other – at a place now not known – the Roman estimate was that Boudicca had an army twenty-three times as large as theirs. In the following battle, however, they routed her. It was reported that 80,000 British fell, for the loss of only 400 Roman soldiers. It was the last serious rebellion by the native tribes of south-east England.

Scotland and the north of England were not so easily conquered. The theory that the northern tribes annihilated the Roman Ninth Legion has now been discredited, but they remained restless under Roman rule and may have rebelled in 119. In 117 Hadrian had become emperor, and, as part of his policies of controlled frontiers and peace, he ordered a turf and stone wall to be built from the Tyne to the Solway. The wall was probably begun in AD 122 when Hadrian visited Britannia, and took about six years for the majority of the wall to be constructed. Large sections of the wall can still be seen as it runs across the often barren landscape from Newcastle to Carlisle. At regular intervals forts or mile-castles were built to station troops; Housesteads and Chesters are two of the most famous of these. Despite partial destruction and rebuilding, the wall has pretty well stood the test of time over 2,000 years.

Twenty years after the building of Hadrian's Wall, the frontier was pushed further north. A second wall, built of turf and running from the Firth of Clyde to the Firth of Forth, was called the Antonine Wall after the Roman emperor, Antoninus Pius, (138–161) who ordered its construction. Building had begun by AD 143, although thereafter its history appears highly confused. The Antonine Wall was probably abandoned about 164 when troops were needed elsewhere. Hadrian's Wall then became the limit of Roman expansion northwards into Scotland.

BRITANNIA: THE IMPERIAL PROVINCE

By the third century Britannia was secured by Hadrian's Wall to the north, shore forts around the coast, and internal garrisons. Behind such defences the province flourished.

THE ROMANISATION OF BRITANNIA

Cities and Towns

The Roman historian Tacitus described the policy of Romanisation that his father-in-law, Agricola, the governor of Britannia, used:

> [Agricola] urged people privately, and helped them officially, to build temples, public squares with public buildings, and private houses ... Moreover he had the children of the leading Britons educated in the civilised arts ... Roman dress, too, became popular and the toga was frequently seen. Little by little there was a slide toward the allurements of degeneracy: assembly-rooms, bathing establishments and smart dinner parties. In their inexperience the Britons called it civilisation when it was all part of their servitude.

The most Romanised areas were the towns. They contained public baths, and markets where luxury goods from the continent could be bought. The forum, as at Verulamium, was the administrative centre of the town, and for amusement people could go to amphitheatres like those in London and Durnovaria (Dorchester) to see gladiators or acrobats. Education was considered important and Latin became the official language; a few learnt it formally in schools, others more informally from merchants and soldiers.

Towns were introduced into Britannia by the Romans. The first, at Colchester, was specifically set up for veteran Roman soldiers, probably in an attempt to impress the native inhabitants. The towns were designed on a grid pattern for maximum ease of movement of troops or goods. The two premier cities of Britannia were London and York (Eboracum). London was the most important centre of administration in the province. In AD 53, ten years after the invasion, it was a thriving centre for trade and commerce. It quickly became the capital of the whole province, and also became the most Romanised city in Britannia, with large buildings for judicial and commercial business, bath houses, a forum, and fine works of art imported from the continent. In the third century walls were built around the city and the area they enclosed, 325 acres, was larger than most cities north of the Alps. The history of London is not one of continual growth and expansion, for it was destroyed by the

Boudiccan rebellion of AD 60 and by a massive fire *c*. 125, but after both occurrences London rose from the ashes.

Though London was the main capital city, other 'provincial' capitals grew up: the most important, after London, was York. The main military garrison of the north, it supplied troops for duty on Hadrian's Wall. Two Roman emperors died there after campaigning against the tribes of the north (Septimus Severus, 193–211, and Constantius, 292–306), and Constantine the Great (see p. 18) was first proclaimed emperor there. By the early fourth century Lincoln (Lindum), and Cirencester (Corinium) had also achieved provincial-capital status.

The development of cities was not, however, restricted to the provincial capitals. Others offered specialist attractions, such as the hot springs at Aquae Sulis (Bath), which have recently been excavated to show the magnificent Roman baths. Colchester had been the original capital of Britannia before London had risen to prominence; after the Claudian invasion the imperial cult had been established there and, though no longer a capital, it continued to be important for the local area. In other regions important cities or towns acted as the focal points for the various tribes: Caistor by Norwich for the Iceni; Verulamium for the Catuvellauni; Wroxeter for the Cornovii; and Exeter for the Dumonii.

Agriculture and Trade

In the countryside the Romans continued the clearing and draining of the land. The Fens were drained by a series of channels to allow large-scale farming, and the peat-cutting in East Anglia formed the wide expanses of water known as the Norfolk Broads. The new agricultural lands were controlled from estates, or villas. These varied in size, from the palatial and luxurious Lullingstone in Kent, to small dwellings. Villas tended to be characterised by stone buildings, underfloor heating, glazing, baths and, for the very rich, mosaics showing Roman myths and symbols. Unlike the Iron Age dwellings built of perishable wood, the Roman villas and buildings were constructed of durable stone.

Whilst little remains of Roman buildings, many of the plants and implements introduced by the Romans are still in evidence today. New agricultural tools included the iron-tipped spade, rake and scythe, and among the new building implements were the chisel and the carpenter's plane. New plants were cultivated for the first time, including rye, oats, flax, cabbage, turnips, carrots and celery. Roses, lilies, and poppies were imported Roman flowers, as well as apple, walnut and mulberry trees. Trade and industry flourished, with pottery and glassware being brought from the continent in bulk, as well as wine from Bordeaux and the Moselle valley. Exports from the province included woollen goods, corn, pearls – and bears. The local metals of lead and bronze were much in demand, and the major iron-fields of the province included the Weald area of Kent and the Forest of Dean.

Religion and Language

Roman policy never intended that native customs should be destroyed, unless the customs or religions were antagonistic to Roman rule. The Druids, based on Anglesey, had been massacred in AD 60 for disloyalty and for alleged human sacrifice. Elsewhere the Romans were very tolerant of regional traditions, including the local gods. New cults were

Stone head of Medusa, from the Roman temple of Sulis-Minerva at Bath

introduced, such as the worship of emperors, but often native and Roman cults became combined. At Bath the baths were dedicated to Sulis-Minerva, who was a combination of the Celtic water-goddess and the Roman Minerva. In rural areas, away from Roman centres, the native Iron Age culture and languages were stronger. In the upland zones, Latin was spoken in the forts and amongst traders, whilst the natives continued speaking Celtic.

Constantine the Great, 306–337

The rule of Constantine the Great has been described as the 'Golden Age' of Roman power in Britannia. The third century had seen two men establish breakaway empires which included Britannia (Carausius between 287 and 293, and Allectus between 293 and 296). Constantine's father, the Emperor Constantius I, reunited the island with the Empire and died in York. The German troops garrisoned there immediately proclaimed Constantine the new emperor. A new period of stability arrived.

Britannia seems to have been favoured by Constantine. He encouraged a major mint to coin money at London and during his reign the province prospered. New fortress walls were built, as at York, and a new phase of villa building and repairing took place. The administration of the provinces and the army in England were both reorganised to allow for greater flexibility and a better control of resources.

CHRISTIANITY

Constantine is best remembered as the first Roman emperor to have been converted to Christianity. Christian merchants and traders had probably arrived in England in the first century AD but had made little impact. In the next century Christianity slowly spread and was noted for its first English martyrs, especially St Alban who was executed at Verulamium in 208. In 314 three bishops from the province went to the Council of Arles, and the new religion continued to increase in the towns and spread into the countryside.

When Constantine was converted, attention began to shift from the multitude of local deities to the monotheistic religion of Christianity, which demanded belief in just one godhead, albeit a trinity. Pagan practices were tolerated for a while, but were then made illegal. In England the remaining evidence for Christianity in later Roman times is patchy. A definite Christian grave has been found at Dorchester; it is possible that churches were sometimes built over the graves of martyrs, as at St Albans; and in the countryside some villas included Christian symbols and portraits within mosaics – indeed a mosiac showing an unbearded Christ has been found at Hinton St Mary, Dorset.

The End of Britannia

With the death of Constantine the Great in 337, the security of the island quickly vanished. From the 340s to the ending of Roman rule in Britannia in *c.* 410, the history of the province was one of military rebels proclaiming themselves emperor (in 383, 406, 409) and invasions from Scotland (in the 340s, 350s and especially between 365 and 368). However, these disturbances were temporary phenomena and recovery was quickly achieved after each disruption. How much these events affected local populations is unknown, but it seems that the countryside and towns continued to enjoy a considerable prosperity in the last part of the fourth century, despite looming threats to the province's security.

One such threat came from the increasing attacks by Saxon pirates. They had threatened the east and south coasts since the third century and a series of garrisons and forts, stretching from Norfolk to Hampshire and known as the Saxon shore, had successfully defended the coastline. However the Roman military strength was weakened when troops were recalled to the continent in the early years of the fifth century to defend against Saxon attacks there. This left Britannia itself open to invasion by the Saxons, who attacked in increasing numbers. The mainly civilian inhabitants were left to combat the invaders alone.

The depleted militia tried to cope with increasingly dangerous Saxon raids, and the internal administration of the province began to crumble. The year 410 stands as a convenient date for the separation of Britannia from Roman rule. Barbarians pushed east from Asia Minor, crossed the Rhine, 'and attacked everywhere with all their power'. Rome itself was threatened and this caused a dislocation of central government. Saxons also attacked Britain in great force. The desperate Britons appealed to Rome several times, but each time without success. The last known appeal came in about 446, when the Britons sent a letter for assistance to the consul, Aetius: 'The groans of the Britons . . . the barbarians drive us to the sea, the sea drives us to the barbarians, between these two means of death we are either killed or drowned.'

The plea went unheeded. Roman rule in Britannia had ended.

THE LEGACY OF ROMAN RULE

The Romans had occupied the province for 400 years: one-fifth of recorded English history. Roman and Greek historians chronicled some episodes in detail, but generally the archaeological evidence is all that remains today. The physical legacy of the Romans is most evident in roads and towns. Roman roads are characterised by their straightness over long distances. Over 5,000 miles of roads were built and many radiated from London. Ermine Street ran from London to Lincoln, the present A5 road is based upon the Roman road from London to Chester and others lead from London to York and London to Exeter. The origins of Roman towns can often be recognised today by the Roman place-name element of '-chester': Winchester, Colchester and, of course, Chester.

These are the long-term legacies, and for the new invaders and the local populations it is unlikely that they considered that Roman influence had been abruptly ended. Rather, the evidence suggests that the new invaders rapidly adopted Roman customs to increase their own prestige and power. In later centuries an Anglo-Saxon king carried a 'tufa', which was a replica of a Roman standard. Even so, that desperate letter to Aetius shows that the central Roman administration from the continent had been effectively destroyed.

CHAPTER TWO

The Anglo-Saxons and Vikings, 450–1066

The Dark Ages, 450–595

After the decline and collapse of the Roman Empire in England the picture of what happened becomes blurred and confused. Pin-points of light in these dark and troubled times are given by a few written sources and archaeological sites. Occasionally the pin-points can be joined together, but what happened around the whole country is subject to much debate.

THE SOURCES

The two greatest historical sources for the period are *The History of the English Church and People*, written by the Venerable Bede (d. 735), and the *Anglo-Saxon Chronicle*, started *c.* 892 in the reign of King Alfred. Bede is proclaimed as the father of English history as his work has helped more than any other to determine the early years of the Anglo-Saxon kingdoms. He was chiefly interested in the religious aspects of the times, but also included political and kingly information. One miracle he gives is of Caedmon, who is credited as the first English poet. The *Anglo-Saxon Chronicle* starts from AD 1 and continues until 1154.

Archaeology can fill some gaps. Human burials are frequently found, either singly or in large cemeteries; in some cases the bodies were buried with jewellery or weapons. The most famous site is at Sutton Hoo in Suffolk, where a kingly burial was uncovered in 1939. The finds are magnificent (they can now be seen in the British Museum) and show all the paraphernalia of kingship. It is thought it is the burial of the East Anglian King Redwald who died in 624 or 625.

A shoulder clasp from the Sutton Hoo ship burial

Angles, Saxons and Jutes

The decline of Roman authority left a vacuum of power in England which was rapidly filled by three European tribes: the Angles, from Schleswig–Holstein in Germany; the Saxons, from the Saxony region of Germany; and the Jutes from Jutland. Gildas, a contemporary monk (*c.* 550), recorded – simplistically and with very dubious factual accuracy – how the Angles and Saxons had at first been invited to England by the remaining Romano–British population to defend the country from attacks by the northern Picts. The Anglo-Saxons quickly realised their power and made impossible demands: when these were not met they turned on the native population and devastated the towns and countryside. The Romano–British formed an army under the leadership of Ambrosius Aurelianus and crushed the Anglo-Saxons at Badon Hill. This victory did not win the war and many of the native population either fled across the Channel (hence the name 'Brittany' in France) or into the the mountain regions of Wales. Even today the Welsh and Breton languages are very similar.

After the initial raids, the Angles, Saxons and Jutes settled in England: the Jutes in Kent, the Angles in Norfolk and Suffolk (hence its regional name of East Anglia) and westwards, and the Saxons settled from Essex to Wessex. From these bases, the Angles and Saxons pushed inland using the river systems, colonising areas as they went.

THE ARTHURIAN MYTH

It is from this era that the legend of King Arthur arises. Arthur was supposed to have been the native leader, much in the role of Ambrosius Aurelianus. Many areas claim him as their own; the most renowned sites are situated in the West Country – Tintagel Castle in Cornwall, the legendary site of the Round Table; and Glastonbury Tor, associated with Avalon. Elsewhere are Arthur's Seat, just outside Edinburgh and many more: Badon Hill, where Arthur is supposed to have fought, may lie in Lincolnshire, the Midlands or Dorset.

All that has ever been written about him – and the amount is enormous, with thousands of books produced over the centuries – rests upon a few stories written hundreds of years after the events. Gildas and Bede, the earliest authorities, make no mention of him. The first reference to Arthur comes in a Welsh poem of *c.* 600, when a hero is compared to Arthur, but this may have been added later. The first written account was by a monk writing *c.* 900 (i.e. 450 years later) who says that Arthur fought at Badon and he carried a cross for three days and nights on his shoulders. From this time the myth began to grow, with the addition of the Knights of the Round Table and Camelot, along with Merlin, Guinevere and Mordred. Any connection these people have with Arthur – if he existed at all – is purely coincidental.

However, the Arthurian stories are far from worthless. Many of them contain important themes from different cultures and religions: the sword in the lake has been seen as an echo of Iron Age religions which offered gifts of armour to water deities. As the legends became more popular they were expanded; in the thirteenth and fourteenth centuries the chivalrous deeds and courtly love themes of Arthur and his knights were embellished to fit in with the activities of the court. The Arthurian legends therefore act as a guide to the times in which they were written, rather than revealing the Dark Ages.

KINGS AND KINGDOMS

Although the early history of the Anglo-Saxon kingdoms is obscure, by the seventh century three kingdoms, Northumbria, Mercia and Wessex, were the most important. Northumbria dominated the others at first, but slowly through the centuries the balance of power shifted southwards, first to Mercia, then to Wessex.

With the multiplicity of kingdoms, some of them tiny, England is estimated to have had over 200 kings between the Roman Empire and the Norman Conquest. Only a handful stand out as truly great individuals, and for the most part they are mere names in lists. Despite being newcomers, the early kings were aware of the Roman past and to increase their own power tried to copy Roman customs. King Ethelbert of Kent established laws 'after the manner of the Romans'. Nevertheless, the new peoples were pagan with a distinct past, and each king linked his ancestry to either powerful kings or pagan gods to increase his own prestige. The most popular pagan god was Woden, the god of war (hence Wednesday, meaning Woden's day), for kingship demanded bravery, valour, and strength of personality. Yet acquiring land and goods was not enough, for a king was also judged on his generosity: if warriors did not receive valuable gifts for bravery or a successful war the king's fame and reputation was diminished.

THE COMING OF CHRISTIANITY

The break with Rome had caused Christianity in England to decline to the point of extinction. From being civilised and partially Christian, England was now seen as pagan and barbaric. In some remote regions of north-west England, Wales and Ireland small Christian communities had survived and they began a campaign of conversion which spread into northern England. One of the most famous missionaries, St Columba, founded a monastery on the Scottish isle of Iona which became a major missionary centre.

However, the situation changed when Pope Gregory I sent a missionary expedition from Rome to England. The mission, headed by Augustine, was at first reluctant to cross the Channel because of the savage reputation of the English. Eventually they crossed and arrived in 597 at the court of King Ethelbert of Kent, who had a Christian wife. He was won over to Christianity and Augustine and his companions were given authority to preach and convert. Pope Gregory had known of England through Roman documents and chose London and York as the two archbishoprics. As Ethelbert's capital was Canterbury, Augustine altered the original plan and established an archbishopric at Canterbury instead.

The missionaries from Rome were not welcomed by the Celtic missionaries from Ireland and with each side secure in their beliefs they attempted to convert as many people as possible. The huge kingdom of Northumbria proved to be a key area. First of all the Roman missionary Paulinus converted the king, and then later the Celtic missionaries, led by St Aidan, founded the missionary centre and monastery of Lindisfarne on the Northumbrian coast. By 670, after seventy-five years of proselytising, every English king was Christian. Some of these conversions appear to have been an insurance policy in case the magic of the pagan gods did not work: one king, King Redwald, was recorded as having set up two altars, one for his pagan gods and another for the Christian god.

THE PEACE OF THE MISSIONARIES

Despite both being Christian, the Celtic and Roman Churches had differing theologies, which meant that Easter, the crucial Christian festival, was often not celebrated on the same day (in 631, for instance, the Roman Easter fell on 24 March and the Celtic on 21 April). Sometimes a king could be converted by one faction and his wife by the other. Eventually the situation became so confused that in 664 an ecclesiastical meeting, or synod, was called to decide the issue. The Synod of Whitby proved to be a turning-point: a lively debate led to heated argument on both sides, but it was finally decided when King Oswy, who was judging the issue, declared Roman Christianity the accepted religion. A group of Celtic missionaries rejected this decision and left for Iona.

Any differences that remained between the two factions were reconciled by the next archbishop, Theodore of Tarsus, and the missionary work among the nobles and peasants continued. Several great figures emerged. St Wilfrid became as wealthy and image-conscious as any king, whilst at the other extreme St Cuthbert lived as a hermit before becoming Bishop of Lindisfarne. He retired to the Farne isles, and died in his hermitage after surviving for days on half an onion kept under his blanket; his remains now lie at Durham Cathedral.

MERCIA

Little is known of England in the eighth century. Bede had written about the seventh century in detail but he died in 735 and had despaired of the times in which he lived. What is clear is that Mercia became the prominent kingdom, with two of its kings reigning for forty years each. The first was Ethelbald, who has been described as a 'ruthless barbarian' and established Mercia as the greatest kingdom of the age. Offa, who took over after Ethelbald's murder in 757, shared many of his predecessor's qualities, being both determined and ruthless. His conquests stretched from Kent to Northumbria and in later years he styled himself 'King of the whole land of the English': for the first time one king ruled over the greater part of England. Little else is known about his reign, but his power was recognised on the continent: he was the only western monarch whom the Frankish king Charlemagne treated as an equal.

The largest archaeological monument in Britain is attributed to Offa. Offa's Dyke was a combination of a ditch 6 feet deep and a rampart 25 feet high, stretching for over 150 miles along the English-Welsh border (80 miles are still extant). It was apparently built to stop Welsh raids upon the rich Mercian lands and, if the archaeological record is correct, it succeeded for over 200 years. The dyke was probably planned as a whole, although differences in technique show that local officials controlled the building. The huge labour force involved and the energy expended shows what could be achieved with the power and might of Offa's kingdom.

ANGLO-SAXON SOCIETY

Whilst Bede and the *Anglo-Saxon Chronicle* describe the historic events of the times, the law codes describe the structure of the society. The fullest surviving codes are for Kent and Wessex. They show a society with slaves, freemen and nobles. People were valued depending upon their social class: the family of a Welshman who was killed, for instance, would receive 60 shillings if he was a slave or at the opposite extreme 200 shillings if he was a horseman in the king's service.

PLACE-NAMES AND TRADE

The invaders brought with them new languages, which affected place-names as well as ideas and thought. 'Tun' or 'ton' is the commonest Anglo-Saxon word for a settlement (Southampton, Northampton), and 'leah' (now 'leigh' or '-ley') means an open woodland or clearing (Bletchley). Place-names were also connected with trading towns. The most common was 'wic' (now '-wich') meaning a market or trading centre, in such towns and cities as Norwich and Ipswich (originally Gip's wick). The most important trading centre was London, which Bede described as 'an emporium of many peoples coming by land and sea'.

The Vikings

The Vikings were Scandinavian people who, because of population increase and political instability, sought their fortune throughout Europe. Vikings were observed in Constantinople and Russia, founded a colony in Greenland and reached Newfoundland in North America. Around the coast of Britain they settled in Ireland, the Isle of Man and the Scottish islands of Orkney and Shetland. The wealth of England proved an attractive lure, particularly since the internal dissent in England between the warring kingdoms meant there was no effective nationwide resistance.

The alleged portents of impending disaster – whirlwinds, storms and fiery dragons – were borne out on 8 January 793 when a Viking raid took place at the island missionary church of Lindisfarne. The church was destroyed, valuables robbed and men killed or enslaved. A succession of such raids followed, by ruthless men out for what they could get. Gradually the length of time the Vikings remained in England each year increased and in 851 they stayed over the winter for the first time.

The tide of war ebbed and flowed. After subduing East Anglia in 865, the Vikings marched north and installed a king at York, and then returned to East Anglia where in 869 they killed King Edmund of East Anglia by shooting him full of arrows 'like a hedgehog'. (Edmund was later canonised, and the town of Bury St Edmunds was named after him.) With the whole of the North of England, the Midlands and East

Anglia under Viking control, and Mercia subdued, the Vikings prepared to strike Wessex.

The Rise of Wessex

With the death of Offa in 796 the power of Mercia began to wane and the kingdom of Wessex, covering the southern counties of England, began to emerge. The two kings responsible were Egbert and his son Ethelwulf who between them subdued Cornwall, defeated the Mercians and heavily defeated the Vikings in 851. By the time of Ethelwulf's death, the king of Wessex ruled all of southern England, south of the Thames.

Ethelwulf's three eldest sons, Ethelbald, Ethelbert and Ethelred ruled in quick succession. In 871 Ethelred won a great victory against the Vikings at Reading, but the war continued and, when Ethelred died in the same year his twenty-three-year-old brother, Alfred, became king over a kingdom fighting for its existence. He became one of the greatest English kings.

King Alfred the Great, 871–899

DEFEAT AND RECOVERY

Nine battles are recorded in 871 between Alfred and the Viking host but by the end of the year an unstable peace was made. Apart from the occasional raids Wessex remained untouched until 878. Instead the Vikings turned their attentions once again to Mercia and Northumbria. The Viking army divided and one portion settled in Yorkshire; the *Anglo-Saxon Chronicle* records that they were 'ploughing and providing for themselves'. Gradually the invaders became integrated with the local population.

The other main section of the Viking army was still avid for war and in a lightning raid almost destroyed Alfred in 878. The *Chronicle* records that the Vikings came upon Alfred at Chippenham 'in midwinter, after Twelfth Night' – a traditional time of feasting and peace. Taken by surprise, Alfred and a small company fled and 'with difficulty went through the woods on to the inaccessible moors' to Athelney in Somerset. (It was from this time that the well-known story of Alfred and the bread supposedly occurred although it was only recorded centuries later. In return for refuge he was requested to mind some bread cooking; becoming engrossed in mending his weapons, he let the bread burn; the woman returned and scolded Alfred. True or not, the story illustrates the humiliating position the king had been reduced to.) For three months Alfred and his followers hid at Athelney. After Easter a network of loyal nobles was activated and an army raised which defeated the Vikings, forcing them to retreat to Chippenham. After a fourteen-day siege their leader Guthrum surrendered; he was obliged to accept Christianity, with Alfred acting as his godfather at the baptism. The Viking army next withdrew to Cirencester, and then to East Anglia where they settled. A further Viking raid in 885 failed, and in 886 Alfred took London by storm.

A key element of Alfred's success after 878 was the instigation of defended towns, or 'burhs'. These were located so that nowhere was more than twenty miles away – the equivalent of a day's march. Some were based on existing towns, for instance the fort at Portchester, and others were designed and built from new, as at Wallingford. They were garrisoned by the people of the town and surrounding areas and provided refuge if a Viking army raided the region. The walls at Wareham are still impressive.

Alfred's victories led to a formal treaty between Alfred and Guthrum by which England was divided into two parts. The fixed border between the Anglo-Saxon and Danish areas ran diagonally across the country from the mouth of the Thames to Staffordshire, giving Alfred the south and west and the Vikings the north and east, called the Danelaw. This division can still be seen by the differences between place-names: the Danish endings of '-by' (Derby, Whitby) or '-thorpe' (Scunthorpe) are still very numerous in the Danelaw areas, but are virtually non-existent in the Wessex-controlled areas where the English '-ton' (Taunton, Islington) or '-ley' names are more common.

ALFRED AS KING

As well as being a brilliant and inspiring military leader, in peacetime too Alfred deserved the appellation 'the Great'. He was magnanimous to his enemies, as demonstrated by his acting as godfather to Guthrum, and he encouraged learning throughout the kingdom during the years of peace (887–93). He became concerned about the lack of priestly education and stated that there was not a priest who could translate a Latin letter into English. To counter this, schools were founded in monasteries and even in his own household. At the age of thirty–eight Alfred started to learn Latin, and in the following years Bede and some of St Augustine's writings were translated into English under his direction. He also produced a new set of law codes based on those which had gone before.

As well as attacks by the Vikings, Alfred's 'many tribulations' included a severe physical disease which caused him great distress. In a translation of St Augustine's *Soliloquies* there is a passage about men living in peace and calm and Alfred has added, 'as I have not yet done'. The last years of his reign saw a resumption of the Viking raids and invasions, but the position of Wessex was much stronger than it had been previously and the Vikings were defeated in battle.

Alfred died on 26 October 899. He had created a strong Wessex and also reigned as overlord in Mercia. A silver penny describes him as 'Rex Anglor[um]' (King of the English), a title which only King Offa had used before him.

THE VIKINGS IN ENGLAND

The history of England at this time was apparently dominated by Wessex, an impression enhanced by the wealth of historical sources for the kingdom. The Vikings, however, left no equivalent to the Wessex-inspired *Anglo-Saxon Chronicle* and so for centuries were portrayed as ruthless raiders and pillagers who came, slaughtered and left. This was probably true of the early raiders, but many of those who later settled were skilled craftsmen. Archaeology has shown the outstanding workmanship that could be produced by the Viking settlers. In York an excavation on one of the main Viking streets (Coppergate) revealed workshops and elaborate craftsmanship. (The street name ending '-gate' is indicative of Scandinavian influence and comes from the Scandinavian *gata*, meaning street, as found in many northern towns.)

England in the Tenth Century

STRATHCLYDE

LOTHIAN

NORTHUMBRIA

Bamburgh

NORTH SEA

Carlisle

English Frontier 927

KINGDOM

York

OF YORK

Isle of Man

Manchester

LAND

English Frontier 920

Dublin

OF THE

Lincoln

Chester

FIVE

ENGLISH Stafford

BOROUGHS

English Frontier 917

Tamworth

EAST

MERCIA

Thetford

Bedford

ANGLIA

Buckingham •

Cambridge

Wallingford

Hertford

Maldon

Bath

Malmesbury

London

WESSEX

Canterbury

Winchester •

Portchester

Southampton

Chichester

Wareham

Exeter •

Hastings

| Norse settlements |
| Danish settlements |
| Boundary of Guthrum's Kingdom |

ENGLISH CHANNEL

| 0 | 25 | 50 | miles | 100 |
| 0 | 25 | 50 | 100 kms |

The Heirs of Alfred

Alfred's descendants continued to rule Wessex or England until 1016, more than a century after his death. Many were glorious and able rulers who stood supreme in their own day, but none – with the exception of Athelstan – matched the vision and breadth of interest that Alfred achieved. In the tenth century three great kings ruled Wessex: Edward, Athelstan and Edgar.

After Alfred's death his son Edward the Elder (899–924) became king and his sister Aethelflaed, who ruled Mercia, was known as the Lady of the Mercians. Between them they set about enlarging their territory with spectacular military successes. Edward conquered East Anglia and later the five principal Danish towns of Derby, Leicester, Lincoln, Nottingham and Stamford. When Aethelflaed died in 918 Edward was left as king of all of England south of the River Humber. The height of his power came in 920 when he received the recognition of overlordship from the English, Danes, Britons, Scots, Norsemen and the kings of York and Strathclyde.

Edward died in 924, leaving the kingdom to his son Athelstan (924–39). Like his father and grandfather before him, Athelstan was an excellent military leader and pushed the boundaries of the kingdom still further, capturing the city of York and occupying Northumberland. In 937 the Norwegians, who had settled in Lancashire, and the Scots retaliated by marching far into England, but were defeated by Athelstan; five kings and seven earls of the invading forces died. As the *Anglo-Saxon Chronicle* says, 'The Northmen went off in nailed ships, sad survivors of spears . . . over deep water seeking Dublin again, Ireland again, ashamed in their hearts.'

Athelstan was well aware of his enormous military power and even styled himself 'Basileus' – the Byzantine word for emperor. His continental links were strong, especially after he gave three of his sisters in marriage to the duke of the Franks, the king of Burgundy and Otto, the future Holy Roman Emperor. As a man, Athelstan was a great collector of art and relics, and his collection included Constantine the Great's sword and what was claimed to be a piece of the Holy Cross embedded in crystal. He was also a generous benefactor. The *Chronicle* calls him a 'ring-giver to men' and he was the patron of many religious houses.

Athelstan died in 939. His successors, Edmund (939–46), Edred (946–55) and Eadwig (955–9), were forced to fight longer and harder to maintain overlordship of England against the increasingly menacing Vikings and Norwegians.

EDGAR AND ARCHBISHOP DUNSTAN

Edgar (959–75) was the last of the powerful monarchs of Alfred's line. He ruled England with a firm hand, and the tranquillity he brought earned him the title of Edgar the Peaceful. The peace was the result of his subjugation of other kings, and legend records that he was rowed across a river by six lesser British kings. His strength allowed him to be generous to potential enemies and he permitted his Danish subjects to keep their own laws and customs.

The most noted event of Edgar's reign was the monastic revival spearheaded by Edgar and the Archbishop of Canterbury, Dunstan (*c.* 909–88). Dunstan had been forced into exile to Flanders in the previous reign but on his return he put into practice the ideas he had learned on the continent. With Edgar's wholehearted support, a strong programme of ecclesiastical reform, which came to be known as 'The Tenth Century Reformation', was set in motion. The most important reform was to implement and enforce the Benedictine Rule which governed how monks in the monasteries lived. Within a decade this strict rule was observed at Glastonbury, Winchester, Canterbury, Worcester and a host of smaller monasteries.

The Reformation included a revival in education and art. Parts of the Bible were translated into Anglo-Saxon, beautiful illuminated manuscripts were produced, and continental glaziers and builders were invited to England to glorify churches. In 973, at the height of the reforms, Edgar was crowned at Bath Abbey. Dunstan devised the glittering ceremony and it was made into a religious occasion: previously the high point had been the placing of the crown upon the monarch's head, but now the most important aspect was anointing the king with holy oil as God's chosen representative on earth. The hereditary right of kingship had now been sanctified by the power of divine choice.

Edgar died two years later. The chroniclers wrote glowingly of his reign because of the reforms but conveniently forgot his numerous illegitimate children.

Treachery and Decline

ST EDWARD KING AND MARTYR

Edgar was succeeded by his eldest son, Edward (975–9). He quickly became unpopular because of his objectionable speech and manner, and on a visit to Corfe Castle in Dorset he was stabbed to death. The outcome was twofold: his half-brother Ethelred (978–1016) succeeded to the throne, and soon Edward's unpleasantness was forgotten as miracles began to occur at his tomb. He was later canonised as St Edward the Martyr.

ETHELRED THE UNREAD

Ethelred's name means 'good counsel', but in the thirteenth century a monk added 'unread' which means 'no counsel' or 'ill counsel'. An alternative meaning is 'a treacherous plot', which would act as a constant reminder of his half-brother's death. In the sixteenth century this was wrongly translated as 'unready' and the misleading name of Ethelred the Unready has stuck. Far from being unready, Ethelred reorganised the English fleet into the largest yet seen, and tried to raise armies to repel the Viking raids. He was constantly hindered by the treachery of some of his followers who either welcomed the invaders, refused to raise troops, or mutinied.

In Ethelred's reign the Vikings, or Danes as they came to be called because of the direct involvement of the Danish king, resumed their attacks on the coasts of Kent and East Anglia. An incident at Maldon in 991, where a Viking raiding party defeated the men of Essex, is recounted in the famous Anglo-Saxon poem 'The Battle of Maldon'. Raiding became increasingly intense. The south coast was attacked, London was besieged and it was rumoured that some Essex nobles were willing to welcome Swein, the Danish king.

Around 994 Ethelred set a disastrous precedent when he agreed to pay the Norwegian king, Olaf Tryggvason, who was fighting with the Danes, money to keep the peace. This became known as the Danegeld and the Danes quickly realised that a high price could be asked for peace: £24,000 was given in 1002, rising to £36,000 three years later and £48,000 in 1012. To try to repel the invaders Ethelred gathered a large fleet together, but in 1009 one of its leaders rebelled and in pursuing him the rest of the fleet 'were beaten and dashed to pieces' by a storm. Treachery and incompetence were also evident on land. In 1009, the *Chronicle* recorded, the army had been hindered by the English noble Eadric, adding pointedly 'as it always was'. The next year the *Chronicle* entry recorded how the English army was constantly outwitted by the Danes: 'When they were in the east, the English army was kept in the west, when they were in the south our army was in the north.' Perhaps the worst single event of the raids was the capture of Aelfheah, the Archbishop of Canterbury, and his murder in 1012 by Vikings in a drunken rage.

Between 1012 and 1016 the history of England was one of confusion. In 1013 King Swein of Denmark landed and quickly overran London and the south of England. Ethelred was forced to flee to Normandy with his wife, Emma, and their children. During the same winter Swein died leaving the throne vacant. The English magnates asked Ethelred to return, 'if he would govern them better than he did before'. He accepted the throne but his son, Edmund Ironside, fled north and was recognised as ruler by Utred, the powerful Northumbrian nobleman. In the south Swein's son, Cnut, attacked Wessex and was joined by the men of Mercia. Edmund Ironside attempted to raise an army against Cnut, but a large portion refused to fight unless led by Ethelred. As Ethelred, an ill and broken man, lay dying in London, his kingdom was being torn apart by his son in the north and Cnut in the south. Edmund went to London to see his father, but whether they were reconciled is unknown. Ethelred died on 23 April 1016, and Edmund was assassinated later in the same year.

The success of a king's reign often depends on luck, of which Ethelred had none. Yet perhaps Ethelred's greatest misfortune was the sixteenth-century mistranslation which declared him 'unready' when he had worked hard for almost thirty years to repel the Danes amidst the treachery of his friends and family.

Cnut, 1016–1035

By the end of 1016 Cnut (the English spelling is Canute) was unchallenged as king of England. He showed both expediency and strength: strength in the way he killed or expelled his political enemies; expediency by being married to two wives at the same time. Cnut's wife in the eyes of the Church was Ethelred's widow, Emma, who had been queen of England for more than a dozen years. His second wife was Aelfgifu, a Mercian noblewoman from Northampton; she and her son, Swein, were sent to govern Norway in 1028. Thus Cnut was able to minimise hostility and lessen rivalry, and his policies gave England nearly twenty years of peace.

Even though Cnut was king of England, he still collected vast sums of Danegeld to pay off Danish warriors: £83,000 was given in 1018 to part of the navy; the remaining fleet was estimated to cost £4,000 a year. Other taxes were levied, such as the 'heregeld' or army tax. The enforcement of taxation was strict: if a landowner's payment was over three days late, the estate was forfeit to anyone who could produce the money.

As England became prosperous and peaceful, Cnut continued to expand his empire. In 1019 he went to Denmark to claim the throne after the death of his brother. In 1028 he became king of Norway and its dominions of Greenland, Shetland, Orkney, Hebrides and the Isle of Man. He was one of the greatest figures in the northern world and for a while ruled an area greater than any other medieval English king. In 1027 he was present at the coronation of Emperor Conrad II in Rome; whilst there he persuaded Pope John XIX to reduce the fees of the English archbishops when they went to Rome, and wrote joyfully home that the princes of the empire 'all received me with honour, and honoured me with lavish gifts'.

Even in his own lifetime Cnut became a legend, both as a splendid Viking and as a pious man who fostered the Church. He was remembered for his courage and military prowess: 'Gracious giver of mighty gifts . . . you will lose your life before courage fails.' In Christian terms he was a devout and pious man: he went on a pilgrimage to Rome, allowed himself to be counselled by bishops, and was a generous benefactor to the Church. Once more England became peaceful, with Cnut looking back to Edgar's reign for inspiration and avoiding the anarchy of Ethelred's rule. His legend has also passed down to the present day for the possibly apocryphal story of Cnut and the waves is well known. He ordered his throne to be brought down to the water's edge and commanded the waves to stop advancing. This was not because of his arrogance, but rather to show his advisers that even a king had limits to his authority.

The End of Danish Kingship, 1035–1042

Cnut ruled England with a small group of sixteen 'earls', who were all-powerful in their own regions. Ten of the sixteen earldoms were in Danish hands and it is noticeable that during Cnut's reign the Danish word for a noble, 'earl', became more common than the Anglo-Saxon word, 'ealdorman'. The king was able to hold them in check, and in return for their loyalty they gained land and immense wealth from him.

After Cnut's death in 1035, Harold Harefoot, his second son by Aelfgifu, became king of England in 1037. Harthacnut, Cnut's only son by Emma, was too busy defending Denmark from the Norwegians to claim what he saw as his rightful throne. Harold died in 1040, and Harthacnut's reign in England was short (1040–2). Technically the next in line was Magnus of Norway, for in 1038 a treaty had been signed with the curious clause that Magnus should become Harthacnut's heir, and vice versa, if either died without an heir. When Harthacnut died the English nobles supported his half-brother, Ethelred's son Edward, who had recently arrived from Normandy. Attention now switched from the Scandinavian countries to Normandy.

Edward the Confessor, 1042–1066

Edward's mother, Emma, was the daughter of Richard I of Normandy and in 1013 Ethelred, Emma and their son had fled across the Channel to

Normandy. Edward remained there until 1041 and after Harthacnut's death was proclaimed the undisputed king. Yet in many ways he was a stranger to England, for his speech, background, friends and customs had all been acquired from the Norman court.

The English faction was represented by the ambitious English noble, Earl Godwin. Godwin had risen rapidly to power under Cnut, from reputedly humble origins, to become the Earl of Wessex with major estates across the south of England. Relations between him and King Edward had been damaged in 1036 when Godwin murdered Edward's brother. Until 1053, when Godwin died, Edward and he battled for control, but Edward's position was not made any easier by his marriage to Godwin's daughter, Edith. At first Edward actively encouraged links with the Norman court of Duke William, promoting Normans to the most prominent positions: in 1051 a Norman, Robert of Jumièges, was appointed Archbishop of Canterbury. Slowly Godwin's influence was being eroded, and an attempt to exile him in 1052 succeeded for six months. But by the end of the year Godwin returned stronger than ever. In 1053 he died and his eldest son Harold took over his position and power: one chronicler called him the 'under-king'.

Relations between Edward and Harold seem to have been good, with Harold leading the army and organising hunts for the king. Gradually over his reign Edward devoted more and more of his time to pious works. It was popularly believed that his marriage to Edith was never consummated. His life's work became the the rebuilding of Westminster Abbey. A biographer writing shortly after his death attributed miracles to him, and Edward later became known as 'the Confessor'. (Almost a hundred years after his death, in 1161, Edward was canonised.)

1066

Edward died on 6 January 1066, and by the end of the year the course of English history had been changed for ever. Three powerful claimants fought for the English throne: Harold, Earl of Wessex; William, Duke of Normandy; and Harold Hardrada, king of Norway. Earl Harold was declared king by the English, and immediately he had to deal with the double threat of Harold Hardrada and William. In May Tostig, Harold's brother, landed on the south-east coast and fought his brother before being ousted from England. Harold mobilised his militia and throughout the summer kept watch along the Channel coast. By September it was becoming clear that William would not invade, so the southern coast militia was disbanded. Suddenly Harold Hardrada and Tostig landed in Northumbria and defeated the northern earls and militia. Harold was drawn away from the south to deal with this attack, and on 25 September took the Norwegian army by surprise at Stamford Bridge just outside York. Both Tostig and Harold Hardrada were killed.

BATTLE OF HASTINGS

In Normandy William had collected an army and had been patiently waiting for the wind to change. Finally on 27 September he sailed to England. Unhindered, as the local militia had been disbanded, he marched inland whilst Harold force-marched his troops from the north.

A scene showing the death of King Harold from the Bayeux Tapestry

The armies met just outside Hastings, at the spot later called Battle. The speed of Harold's march meant that his army was about the same strength as William's – each had about 3,000 men. The English were situated on a small hill with a forest to the rear.

As dawn came up on 14 October, the Normans attacked and the day-long battle began. The English used the tactic of building a shield wall, which the Normans found impossible to penetrate: it was only broken when the English rushed headlong after the Normans who retreated, either in panic (the French version) or as a tactical move (the English version). Twice more the tactic was repeated and the English were again cut down. At the end of the day the Normans launched a major attack and Harold was killed. Whether he died from an arrow in the eye or being killed with a sword is debatable, for either could be true as shown in the magnificent Bayeux Tapestry (see pp. 39, 44). This chronicles the events of the times, including the Norman army building the ships and sailing across the Channel and the Battle of Hastings itself. Whichever version is true, however, Harold and two of his brothers died in the battle and the path was open for William to claim the crown.

LITERATURE AND EDUCATION

Looking back over the Anglo-Saxon period we can see that the monasteries had been the centres of learning. The Church language (Latin) was taught to override the heathen language of Anglo-Saxon, and the transmission of holy writings needed literacy and the ability to copy manuscripts accurately. It was only rarely that education and literacy were promoted at court. A major exception was King Alfred, but the kings found uses for literacy in the growing numbers of law codes, legal documents, chronicles and royal biographies.

The works that survive are of four major types. The vast bulk is in Latin and concerns the interpretation of the scriptures. In a lesser category are the numerous saints' lives and miracle stories that were popular; perhaps to a modern audience they seem ridiculous, but to the medieval mind the actions of God were beyond the laws of nature. The third type could be described as administrative, such as charters, or the *Anglo-Saxon Chronicle* itself. The fourth type could be classed as 'pagan'. These writings are mainly found in four large Anglo-Saxon books, and for centuries there has been much debate as to how Christian or pagan they really are. They probably represent oral tradition, which was spoken or sung in the halls of both kings and ordinary people and finally written down in the monasteries. By far the most famous Anglo-Saxon work is the magnificent epic poem *Beowulf*. Whilst Bede emphasises Christianity and holiness, *Beowulf* is set in Denmark and is a story of a hero in combat with two monsters, and in later years with a dragon guarding a horde of treasure. It is full of 'pagan' images of the hall, wealth, strength and kingship although Christian images are also prevalent. Above all what the poet stresses is the warrior's search for glory and renown.

ART

The artwork produced is often breath-taking in its colour and imagination. The Celtic influence is strongly felt in the *Book of Kells* and the *Lindisfarne Gospels*, books which have dragons, animals, men and swirling interlace in the margins, along with full-page pictures of people and designs. They are intricately coloured and have an amazing richness in quality. These books are very early – pre-Viking – manuscripts. From the later Anglo-Saxon centuries, increasing numbers of manuscripts and artwork have survived. Traditional themes still predominated, such as Christ on the cross, flanked by Mary and St John, but more unusual themes also occur, such as Noah's Ark or the pictures of kings.

Much sculpture still survives, especially in areas settled by Danes, and can still be seen in some old north-country churches and graveyards. Many of these have become eroded over the years but may show scenes from Scandinavian myths and legends (Nunburnholme), armed warriors (Middleton), or interlaced patterns.

ARCHITECTURE

The surviving architecture of the period consists almost exclusively of churches. Some of these only have a few stones of an original Anglo-Saxon church, whilst others have hardly been altered. St Gregory's Minster, Kirkdale in North Yorkshire still has a sundial which declares that 'Orm, Gamel's son, bought St Gregory's minster when it was all broken down and fallen and he let it be made anew . . . in the days of

King Edward and Tostig the Earl'. Substantial remains of larger Anglo-Saxon churches can be seen at Barton-upon-Humber; Sompting (built *c.* 1070) and Earls Barton. The church at Escomb has been in continual use, and is almost unaltered, since the late eighth century, but the Anglo-Saxon church of St Lawrence at Bradford-on-Avon was only rediscovered a century ago. Before this it was being used as a cottage and a school. It is known that elaborate palaces existed in the countryside, such as those at Yeavering and Cheddar, as well as the court at Winchester, but there are no standing remains.

CHAPTER THREE

The Normans and Plantagenets, 1066–1272

The Background to the Norman Invasion

In 1035 William's father, Robert I of Normandy, left on a pilgrimage to Jerusalem from which he never returned. Even though William was technically illegitimate – hence the English chroniclers were able to call him William 'the Bastard' – at the tender age of eight he inherited his father's estates in Normandy. He faced a multitude of dangers: his advisers were murdered and there were several attempts on his own life; he survived them all and proved to be a strong and ruthless king.

Exactly when William began to think of winning the English throne is unknown. In 1053 he married Matilda, a descendant of Alfred the Great, and he may have been promised the English crown whilst Edward the Confessor was at the Norman court (see p. 37). William had to wait until 1064 before an amazing stroke of luck occurred. The story is confused, but he managed to capture Harold who had sailed to France. The encounter culminated (as shown in the Bayeux Tapestry) in Harold swearing an oath to William. The oath is the crucial unknown factor. Did Harold swear away his right to the English crown or not? That Harold was released suggests he did. When Harold declared himself king in 1066, William acted. The contemporary opinion was that the invasion of England 'was too difficult, far beyond the strength of Normandy'. Undeterred, William received a papal blessing for his invasion, gathered together a fleet, sailed across the English Channel, and killed Harold at Hastings (see p. 39).

William the Conqueror, 1066–1087

The death in battle of his principal enemy left William unopposed and he marched slowly to London. On Christmas Day 1066 he was crowned in Westminster Abbey. During the ceremony there was such shouting that the guards outside became fearful and in panic burnt down several surrounding houses. Despite the inauspicious start, the history of England had been changed for ever. At the beginning of 1066 there had been three possible kings, now there was one; a new royal dynasty had been founded.

For the first few years William's position was insecure. Between 1068 and 1070 the most serious rebellion of the reign took place in Yorkshire. William marched north and destroyed the opposition in an operation known as the 'harrying of the North'; almost twenty years later much land was still described as 'waste' and in some areas it was not re-colonised until a hundred years later. Wessex and Mercia continued guerrilla warfare under such leaders as Hereward the Wake, who was based in the marshland around Ely and was only finally defeated in 1071. William now consolidated his power and in 1075 the last uprising was easily defeated. The rest of his reign in England was peaceful, but in France William's territorial neighbours had been plundering Normandy. He returned to France in 1086 and attacked the town of Mantes. One account states that as the flames rose, his horse stumbled and William was thrown against the iron pommel of his saddle. He died soon afterwards of internal injuries on 9 September 1087.

DOMESDAY BOOK AND BAYEUX TAPESTRY

Two unique documents survive from William's reign: the *Domesday Book* and the Bayeux Tapestry. The *Domesday Book* is actually two huge volumes, one concerned with East Anglia and the other for the rest of England. It is so called because the evidence it contained could not be disputed; just like the Final Judgement at the Day of Doom. The *Anglo-Saxon Chronicle* records its inception when at Christmas 1085 William had 'important deliberations . . . about this land [England], how it was peopled and with what sort of men'. Commissioners collected details from every English village of the landowners' taxable wealth and landholdings. The details were then sent to Winchester where the final version was compiled. Despite its errors, inaccuracies and omissions, the scale of the project and the details it includes make it the envy of continental scholars. Although William the Conqueror is best known for being the last successful invader of England, the Domesday Book stands as a more fitting tribute to his enterprise and vision.

The second 'document' is a huge piece of embroidery: 230 feet (70 metres) long and 20 inches (50 cm) high. It vividly depicts the background to the Norman Conquest, the battle of Hastings and William's subsequent enthronement at Westminster. The 'Tapestry' was probably commissioned by Odo of Bayeux (William's half-brother) and this explains why it is now in Bayeux in Normandy. There are many uncertainties over its origin, but the evidence suggests it was designed by a single man and then sewn by a group of nuns at Canterbury. It is a remarkable achievement and makes a spectacular visual record of the time. It even shows Halley's comet, which appeared at the time of the Conquest and was assumed by many to be an omen of great events.

THE IMPACT OF THE CONQUEST

Much has been written about the impact of the Conquest. Some historians see an abrupt change in laws, policies and even social customs in England, while others argue that the Normans continued trends which had already started.

In some cases, certainly, the change was dramatic. The Normans introduced castles with the classic plan of a 'motte and bailey': the motte was the mound upon which the fortifications stood and the bailey was a large walled area in front of the motte (an impressive motte still remains in York). At times the Conqueror used square central keeps as strong points and these may still be seen at the Tower of London and Colchester Castle. These castles were symbolic of the fact that England had been conquered, for the Norman lord and his family now lived securely within the castle, safe from attack. Previously the defences of England had been communal, with whole towns lying protected behind the town walls.

The Normans also had an impact upon the structure of English society. A social and military system known as 'feudalism' was established, whereby a person's rank was determined by the amount of land he held. In theory the feudal system worked as a pyramid, with the king at the top owning virtually all the land. Below him were a group

The White Tower, the Tower of London, which was begun in 1078

of barons who were granted substantial areas of land, and below them were the lesser nobles or tenants. Each person had a military commitment to the king, and William reckoned that England could support 6,000 'knights', who were in effect heavily armed cavalry and formed the backbone of his army. The Domesday Book records some of the changes imposed by the development of the feudal system, for 4,000 English landowners were replaced by less than 200 Norman nobles. Feudalism worked well when a strong king was on the throne, but if the king was weak, or only a child, over-mighty subjects manipulated him or rebelled.

A less obvious change was in relation to language: Norman French now became the language of the court and upper-classes, whilst Anglo-Saxon survived amongst the peasantry. This often resulted in two words for the same object: for example, the Normans ate 'mutton' and 'poultry', whereas the Anglo-Saxons looked after and ate 'sheep' and 'chicken'. For the first time a Germanic-based language of Northern Europe, Anglo-Saxon, and a Romance language from Southern Europe, Norman French, coexisted and slowly became combined to form a language of great flexibility and potential.

Sons of the Conqueror

WILLIAM RUFUS, 1087–1100

William I had three sons. He gave the eldest, Robert, the Normandy homelands, and so his second son, William Rufus – known as such because of his ruddy complexion – was granted England. The third son, Henry, was landless but given 5,000 pounds of silver, which he characteristically weighed on receipt. Even as William the Conqueror lay dying William Rufus left his father's bedside, sailed to England and was crowned within two weeks.

The religious chroniclers of the reign detested Rufus. According to them he was 'hateful', injustice was rife, and he was 'very harsh and fierce with his men, his land and all his neighbours, and very much feared'. William II viewed the Church as a source of wealth: in some instances the taxation was so severe that church treasures had to be melted down to pay them. The taxes were used to finance expeditions to capture Normandy from his elder brother. In the end Robert decided to go on the First Crusade and pawned the duchy to the king for 100,000 silver marks. By 1100 William Rufus was confident of expanding his empire deep into France.

But William died on 2 August 1100, at the peak of his power. His death has caused speculation ever since: during a hunting expedition in the New Forest he was shot dead by an arrow, rumoured to have been fired by Walter Tirel, although he of course strenuously denied it. Several theories have been given to explain William's death: that he was sacrificed for a devil-worshipping sect; that heretics had arranged his death; and that it was part of a plot by his brother Henry, who was in the hunting party. The truth will never be known, but immediately afterwards it was believed that his death was a simple accident, and this seems the most likely explanations: such accidents were not uncommon in hunting expeditions. Even so, Henry acted with great speed. Without waiting to see William's body removed for burial he galloped to Winchester and seized the Treasury. Three days after William's death he was crowned king.

HENRY I, 1100–1135

Henry was of moderate height and thickly set, with black hair and a soft expression in his eyes. The expression was misleading for he could be ruthless and unforgiving when necessary – on one day he ordered forty-four thieves to be hanged. However Henry was seen to be fair and he became known as the 'lion of justice': the strength of his kingship is perhaps illustrated by the lack of rebellions in his reign. He was also highly pragmatic, had a scandalous private life and only paid lip service to religion (it was said that his chaplain was chosen for the speed at which he could say mass). His pragmatism stretched to politics and war. In 1100 Robert, who had returned from the Crusades with high prestige, invaded England and forced Henry to pay him an annual sum of £2,000. Henry did so for several years but in 1106 himself invaded Normandy and captured Robert at the Battle of Tinchebrai. Henry was now king of England and Normandy, and Robert was to spend the last twenty-eight years of his life as Henry's prisoner.

THE COURT AND THE BEGINNINGS OF GOVERNMENT

The chroniclers warmly praised Henry for his wisdom and his ability to gain military victories; in contrast, he was also noted for his insatiable quest for money. To satisfy this need an accounting system was developed to calculate the dues owed to the king. This involved moving counters about a large chequered cloth and the department became known as the Exchequer. (A chequered cloth and counters were used because the Roman method of using letters for numbers, V for 5, X for 10 and so on, had not yet been replaced by Arabic numerals, which included zero. Arabic numbers were first introduced into England in the fourteenth century.) Not surprisingly the exchequer was the first department which became too large to travel with the king and court and therefore remained at either Winchester or Westminster. The king still travelled about the kingdom a great deal and his usual retinue of followers included great men and small, from the chancellor and treasurer to the fruiterers, tent-keepers and wolf-hunters.

THE SUCCESSION

Despite his twenty known illegitimate children and two marriages he only had two legitimate children, William the Aetheling (the Anglo-Saxon for prince) and Matilda. The succession seemed secure until William died in a shipwreck; only a butcher survived who reported that everyone had been drunk. Henry was devastated and the succession became uncertain. His only other legitimate child, Matilda, had married the Emperor of Germany, and then Geoffrey, Count of Anjou. The second marriage was deeply unpopular amongst the English barons, even though Henry had taken the expedient measure of ensuring that they took an oath to recognise Matilda as Lady of England if he died without male heir. Her husband had other ideas and, eager for the English crown, went to war against Henry. The two were still at war when Henry died, probably after eating too many eels, in December 1135.

THE CHURCH

One result of the Norman Conquest was that the corrupt Anglo-Saxon Archbishop of Canterbury was replaced by Lanfranc. Lanfranc had come originally from Italy and was full of the reforming zeal then sweeping the continent. He barred married priests from high office and halted the practice of simony (the buying and selling of church offices for money). He was also keen to extend the power of his own position and for the first time established the primacy of Canterbury over York, though the disputes between the archbishoprics continued.

As well as being the spiritual leader of England, the Archbishop of Canterbury was an important statesman and diplomat who worked closely with the king. After William's death, Lanfranc successfully placed William Rufus on the throne, carrying out to the letter his old master's wishes. Rufus expected the same loyalty from Anselm, the next archbishop. Anselm was a man of charm and a fine philosopher, whereas Rufus was violent, ruthless and given to outbursts of rage. Anselm thus compared his position to that of a 'weak old sheep being yoked to an

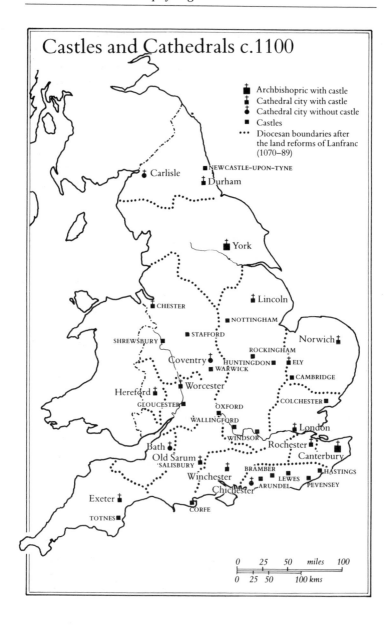

Castles and Cathedrals c.1100

† ■ Archbishopric with castle
† ■ Cathedral city with castle
† ● Cathedral city without castle
■ Castles
••• Diocesan boundaries after
the land reforms of Lanfranc
(1070–89)

● ‡ Carlisle

■ NEWCASTLE–UPON–TYNE

‡ ■ Durham

† ■ York

† Lincoln

■ CHESTER

■ NOTTINGHAM

■ STAFFORD

SHREWSBURY ■

Norwich ‡ ■

ROCKINGHAM ■

Coventry ● ‡ HUNTINGDON ■ † ■ ELY
WARWICK ■

■ CAMBRIDGE

Hereford ‡ ■ ‡ Worcester

GLOUCESTER ■

COLCHESTER ■

OXFORD ■

WALLINGFORD ■

† London

WINDSOR ■   Rochester ■ ■

Bath ‡ ● Old Sarum ■

Canterbury † ■

'SALISBURY

Winchester ‡ BRAMBER ■ ■ HASTINGS

Chichester † ● LEWES PEVENSEY ■

Exeter ‡ ■ ARUNDEL ■

TOTNES ■ CORFE ■

```
0     25    50    miles   100
0   25  50      100 kms
```

untamed bull'. Eventually Anselm was forced to flee to the continent, but even there he argued the king's cause and saved him from excommunication. After Rufus died, Henry was content to pocket the revenues of the archbishopric and Anselm finally returned to Canterbury in 1107 and died a year later.

MONASTIC GROWTH

The twelfth century saw a remarkable growth of monasteries, not only in England but throughout Europe. Between 1066 and 1154 the number of monastic houses in Europe rose from forty-eight to nearly 500, the number of monks from about 900 to well over 5,000. Many new monastic orders were started, but the only purely English order was the Gilbertines, founded by St Gilbert of Sempringham in 1131. Sixty years later they had twelve houses and some influence, for they were looked upon with favour by Henry II.

The most dramatic growth took place among the Cistercians. Founded in 1098 by a monk who led some followers into the wilderness of the French forests, by 1152 the order had 328 monastic houses throughout Europe. Their phenomenal early appeal rested to some extent on the personality of a particularly fiery abbot, St Bernard of Clairvaux, but the order's harsh conditions of poverty, simplicity and withdrawal from the world satisfied a need amongst a segment of the population. The Cistercian monks deliberately founded monasteries in the forests and wastes well away from towns and cities; over the centuries huge estates were laid out and the Cistercians achieved great wealth. The remaining ruins which still dot the English landscape, as at Fountains Abbey and Rievaulx, still bear testimony to their power and influence.

King Stephen, 1135–1154

The death of Henry I precipitated a civil war between his daughter, Matilda, and his nephew, Stephen, the younger son of Adela, William the Conqueror's daughter. Although Stephen had two older brothers, he took the initiative. He sailed across the Channel and was quickly crowned king by his brother, Henry, Bishop of Winchester, and thereafter Matilda had to fight as a contender for the throne. Stephen produced two reactions amongst the chroniclers of his reign. For most of them he was a mild man, generous, likeable, exceptionally brave and chivalrous, but he could be obstinate and rash. He fought tirelessly at the battle of Lincoln in 1141 instead of retreating and so was eventually captured. His chivalry could also be misplaced, for when he had Matilda at his mercy in 1139 he gave her safe conduct to Bristol and thus prolonged the war. Not all the chroniclers, however, were flattering; some said he was sly and shifty, and one that he was 'a good knight, but otherwise a fool'.

In 1138 Matilda invaded England to claim the crown and began a time of war known as the 'Anarchy'. The fighting went back and forth across the country. In 1141 Matilda captured Stephen but her arrogance turned many of her former friends against her. A powerful counter-attack by forces led by Stephen's queen led to the capture of Matilda's half-brother, Robert, Earl of Gloucester. Each side had a crucial hostage, and so an exchange was arranged, Stephen for Robert. This marked the beginning of the end for Matilda, and by 1148 she gave up the struggle, leaving Stephen in comparative peace.

Stephen had won control in England, but the question of the succession and the power of the barons immediately arose. Many barons had land in both England (ruled by Stephen) and France (ruled by Matilda and Geoffrey). If a baron openly supported one side his land could be forfeited across the Channel. The major landholders were therefore keen to negotiate peace and to settle the problem of the succession. Stephen attempted to crown his son Eustace as his successor, but the archbishop of canterbury fled rather than co-operate and the pope, who had been influenced by the nobles supporting Matilda, forbade the coronation.

A new player emerged on the stage, Henry of Anjou, son of Matilda and Geoffrey. In 1147 and 1149 he raided England, and landed with an army in 1153. He marched to Wallingford, where Stephen met him and an agreement was reached that Henry rather than Eustace would succeed to the throne after Stephen's death. Fortunately for Henry Eustace died, and after Stephen himself died in 1154, Henry II was crowned by the now-returned Archbishop of Canterbury on 19 December of the same year.

The Plantagenets

The surname 'Plantagenet' first came to be used by Henry II's father, Geoffrey of Anjou, who wore a sprig of broom (French: genet) in his helmet. The alternative name for the line of kings was Angevin, so called because Geoffrey was the Count of Anjou.

Henry II, 1154–1189

Henry impressed his contemporaries. He was broad-shouldered, tall and strong, and preferred to wear the informal dress of a huntsman; he had a sense of humour and was charming, but equally possessed a legendary temper. Both friends and enemies were exasperated by his unpredictability. The chronicler Peter of Blois wrote about the difficulties of living with the king and his sudden changes of mind:

> . . . and if the king promises to spend the day anywhere . . . you may be sure that the king will leave the place bright and early . . . You may see men rushing madly about . . . a perfect portrait of hell. But if the prince has announced that he is setting off early to reach a particular place, beyond doubt he will change his mind and sleep until noon. You will see the pack horses loaded, the wagons silent . . . and everyone grumbling.

Before becoming king, Henry had hurriedly married Eleanor of Aquitaine, or rather she had hurriedly married him. Eleanor had been previously married to the monk-like French king, Louis VII; their obvious incompatibility had led to a divorce being granted on 21 March 1152. Eleanor, who knew what she wanted, immediately made contact with Henry and they were married in France less than two months later on 18 May. Eleanor brought with her the territory of Aquitaine (which ran from the Pyrenees to Bordeaux in France), so Henry now controlled land running from the Scottish border, through England and France, to the Pyrenees. Just holding the territory together involved constant travelling and, fortunately, Henry had immense energy. Peter of Blois reported that Henry's legs were constantly sore from being in the saddle. Despite his keen love of hunting, Henry loved intellectual debate and was the first king since the Conquest to be fully literate.

HENRY AND BECKET

When Henry came to the throne Theobald was Archbishop of Canterbury, and the relations between the two men were cordial. However, Henry disliked the Church's power and independence and sought a more worldly and co-operative archbishop as Theodore's successor. Thomas Becket seemed the perfect man as he held the position of royal chancellor, and in this role had shown a mixture of efficiency and glamour. He had also been loyal to Henry when disputes arose with the Church. Henry planned that Becket would combine the roles of archbishop and chancellor and that his duties would include organising the court and maintaining its pageantry, at the same time as being subservient to the king.

Through Henry's influence Becket became archbishop in 1162. However, to the king's bewilderment Becket's attitudes totally changed. He rejected the court and became a monk and a prophetic spiritual leader. The more Henry tried to push him to co-operate, the more Becket reacted against him. By 1164 Henry was determined to break the archbishop, and promulgated the Constitutions of Clarendon, which recorded the customs and privileges of the king over the Church. Becket at first bowed to the pressure; the king had won. Then suddenly Becket refused to acknowledge the Constitutions and fled into exile.

Deprived of his Archbishop of Canterbury, Henry tried to usurp his authority by having his own son crowned as successor in 1170 by the Archbishop of York. Becket reacted strongly and issued an order to close all the churches in the kingdom. This time Becket won and on 1 December 1170 he returned to England. The atmosphere was electric, and three weeks later the storm broke. Becket set about punishing Henry's supporters and excommunicated the archbishop of york. When Henry heard he flew into a rage and said, 'Will no one rid me of this turbulent priest?' Four knights took the statement literally and rode to Canterbury Cathedral. They found Becket in front of the altar of St Benedict and killed him by four blows to the head. Christendom was outraged. William FitzStephen, who wrote a life of Becket, described how apparently even nature reacted to his death: 'A terrible storm cloud overhung the firmament, sudden and swift fell the rain and the thunder rolled round the heavens. After this the sky turned a deep red in token of the blood which had been shed and the horror of the outrage.'

The results of the murder were varied. The intense outcry was such that Henry walked barefoot through Canterbury and was then flogged by the monks as a penance. At Becket's tomb in the cathedral miracles were said to occur, and it quickly became the popular destination of pilgrims in England. From the gifts made at the tomb Canterbury Cathedral increased its wealth and influence. In 1172 the pope canonised Becket. The long-term effects upon the king were negligible, for Henry continued to follow his policies and quarrels still broke out between future archbishops and kings. In church politics, however, the effects were more marked. Canterbury had gained a martyred saint and the revenue generated from pilgrims, but the other archbishopric, York, had no comparative advantage; its saint, St William, never rivalled Becket in popularity. Thus Becket's martyrdom and his subsequent reputation helped to confirm Canterbury's supremacy over York.

KING AND COURTS

Under Henry's strong kingship the country began to enjoy the peace and prosperity that had existed before the Anarchy. Many disputes were still unsettled from the civil wars, especially those over the ownership of land. Henry developed the structure of jurisdiction and developed a system of national and local courts. Until his reign methods of testing guilt or innocence included trial by ordeal: a common ordeal was combat between the opposing parties. In 1179 Henry replaced trial by ordeal with trial by a jury of twelve men. The jury method was known as the 'grand assize' (the word 'assessment' comes from the same root). Whilst there was little refinement about it, it was essentially a sound system, and was the origin of the process in use today throughout the English-speaking world.

A BROOD OF EAGLES

Henry II compared his four sons, Henry, called the 'Young King',

Richard, Geoffrey and John to a brood of eagles. Each was desperate for power at any cost: to placate them Henry divided his lands between them but this only spurred them on. Queen Eleanor, too, turned against him. In 1173 Eleanor, the 'Young King', Richard and Geoffrey all rebelled against Henry, and after their defeat they fled. Eleanor was captured and Henry II kept his dangerous wife a closely-guarded prisoner.

By 1189 Geoffrey and the 'Young King' had died, but this left Richard and Eleanor to plot with the French king, Philip II, against Henry. Philip and Richard overran Normandy and Maine and forced an ailing Henry II to accept humiliating terms. On 6 July 1189 Henry died, 'heartbroken and alone', and was buried at Fontevrault in France.

Richard I 'The Lionheart', 1189–1199

Richard is often viewed as a legendary figure in English history: his romantic and dynamic image have caught the imagination, as have his brave and chivalrous exploits as a soldier throughout Europe and the Holy Lands. Other aspects of his character, such as his violence, vanity and selfishness, are often forgotten. His passion was warfare and he used England as a treasury from which to finance his European missions and crusades. During the ten years of his reign he spent a total of only five months in England.

Richard's coronation sparked off the most serious public disturbances of his reign when anti-Jewish riots erupted all over the country. Anti-semitism had increased because of the debts incurred by those who had borrowed heavily from the Jews, and because of the rhetoric used to get people to go on crusade. The most serious outbreak occurred in York: on the night of 16 March 1190 a group of 150 Jews sought refuge in the castle, and committed mass suicide by burning the castle down rather than falling into the hands of the mob. Richard quelled the disturbances and protected the Jews: they were, after all, an excellent source of money for the crown.

After the riots Richard left England for Europe, travelling far and wide. From England he sailed to Sicily (the other island kingdom captured by the Normans) and married Berengaria of Navarre. He then became leader of the Third Crusade and after many heroic deeds won a great victory over Saladin in 1191 at Arsuf. He was able to reach within twelve miles of the walls of the Holy City of Jerusalem before being forced to retreat. For his return to England he planned a route through Europe. Unfortunately he was deeply unpopular in many European courts and was captured by the Duke of Austria, an old enemy, and then passed over to Henry IV, the Holy Roman Emperor, who held him captive in Germany for a ransom of £100,000. England was taxed again and again by Richard's chancellor, William de Longchamp, and his efforts resulted in the payment of the ransom and Richard's release.

Richard eventually reached England in 1194, stayed just two months and then left again for France. Between 1194 and 1199 he waged a successful campaign against King Philip II of France. In a minor skirmish he was shot through the shoulder by an arrow. A few days later, on 7 April 1199, he died of the injury. He was buried at Fontevrault Abbey alongside his father. Later his mother and his brother John's wife, Isabella of Angoulême, were also buried there, making the French abbey a Plantagenet mausoleum.

ROBIN HOOD

It was while Richard was in capitivity in Germany that Robin Hood was supposed to have been active. The legend of an outlaw hiding in the forest and robbing the rich to give to the poor is a powerful one. The first mention of Robin Hood occurs in *Piers Plowman* (see p. 77), written about 1380, when a character states that he knows the 'rhymes of Robin Hood'. The earliest texts of the Robin Hood stories were written down around the 1450s. There are two problems which have been studied in detail: where does the action take place, and did Robin Hood exist? From the earliest texts there is little evidence for Robin Hood ever hiding out in Sherwood Forest. Indeed, it is likely that he never did battle with the sheriff of Nottingham, for the place most frequently mentioned in the texts is Barnsdale in Yorkshire. Gangs of outlaws did exist in the forests, but it is a matter of debate whether Robin Hood was one of them. Various people bearing the same name have been discovered around the country, though this proves little concerning the legend. It is safest to say that the stories and legends developed to satisfy the needs of the population, many of whom resented the almost unassailable power of the sheriffs and bishops.

King John, 1199–1216

John, Henry II's youngest son, now succeeded to the throne. He has been portrayed as a monster of cruelty, combining fits of lethargy with bouts of frenetic activity. One chronicler in particular, Roger of Wendover, hated John and wrote how the king split the noses of papal servants. Wendover wrote: 'Foul as it is, hell itself is defiled by the fouler presence of John.' Apart from this chronicler's lurid fantasies there is little to suggest that John was any more ruthless or cruel than his precedessors. What was significant was that he was seen as a failure. He lost lands in France, had a major dispute with the papacy, and was forced to agree to the barons' demands as encompassed in the Magna Carta.

All went well at first. Philip II of France, allied with John's enemies, attacked the English stronghold of Mirebeau in Anjou where his mother Eleanor of Aquitaine was trapped. In 1202 John won a spectacular victory over the besiegers, so freeing Eleanor, but his treatment of the prisoners was so cruel that numerous provinces turned against him. The catalogue of disasters in John's reign is remarkable. By 1205 he had lost the provinces of Anjou, Maine and Touraine (the homelands of the Plantagenet line), the wealthy province of Normandy (the homeland of the many Norman nobles) and, with the death of his mother in 1204, Aquitaine as well.

The chroniclers' hatred of John was also fuelled by a long-running dispute with Pope Innocent III. In 1205 the archbishop of canterbury died; John nominated his candidate, the monks of Canterbury chose another, and the pope, to the king's fury, decided upon his own choice, Stephen Langton. John was so angry that he forbade Langton to enter the country. The pope retaliated in 1208 by ordering all the churches of England to close. No church services, marriages or funerals took place between 1208 and 1213; only baptism and confession for the dying were formally allowed. To John it was a mixed blessing: on the one hand he was able to confiscate church revenue and thus increased his income dramatically, but on the other he was excommunicated by the pope in

1209. For the common man it was an intolerable situation and resulted in increased discontent with the king. Eventually in 1213 John relented, the churches reopened and Stephen Langton arrived in England.

THE MAGNA CARTA, 1215

By 1214 John had enough money to lead an expedition to France. No expense was spared, but disaster struck when John's allies were defeated by Philip II at the battle of Bouvines in 1214 and John's hopes for recovering the French lands were shattered. He returned downhearted and poor to England, where the treasury was empty and many discontented nobles nursed long-standing financial grievances. The French fiasco gave them the opportunity they needed: many nobles rebelled and the king quickly realised that he was beaten. A historic meeting took place in a meadow called Runnymede (near Windsor) between John and the barons, where John was forced to implement the Magna Carta, a document which stated the barons' demands.

Magna Carta means 'Great Charter'. It comprised sixty-three clauses, which described the privileges and rights of the nobles which the king agreed to preserve and honour. The clauses were wide-ranging, sometimes vague and sometimes precise, covering such subjects as the reduction in area of the royal forests and the abolition of certain taxes. The two most important were clause 39, which states that no one should be imprisoned without trial, and clause 40, that no-one could buy or deny justice. When the king assented to the Magna Carta a revolutionary principle was established: he had conceded that even a monarch was subject to the law. Although he signed the charter, John – and all subsequent monarchs down to Charles I – fundamentally disagreed with its principles, preferring to see themselves as the source of all laws and thus above the law. This basic conflict was only finally settled nearly 450 years later in the Civil War between King and Parliament.

TREASURE, RUIN AND DEATH

John lost no time in renouncing Magna Carta, and began to crush his enemies. The barons had the support of the king of France, who was delighted at the state of turmoil in England. John marched his army back and forth across England with little result, except that he suffered the disaster of losing his baggage train (which included jewels and relics) in the quicksand of the Wash on the Norfolk coast: they remain there to this day waiting to be found. John died in October 1216 at Newark, and was buried in Worcester Cathedral, near the tomb of St Wulfstan. The choice of Worcester rather than Fontevrault shows clearly how the centre of Plantagenet rule had shifted from France to England. It was a trend which continued in the next reign.

Henry III, 1216–1272

When John died he left a nine-year-old son, who was crowned Henry III. Apart from Gascony Henry had no French possessions, and was content with England alone. Two half-hearted attempts were made to recapture lands in France in 1230 and 1242, but they gained nothing and were not repeated. Henry's temperament was more suited to piety and peace. The chroniclers described how he preferred the 'delight and rest' of Westminster, and would stay for months in his favourite palaces rather than go on campaigns. His piety was shown by giving food to 500 beggars and hearing Mass four times a day. His holiness and love of England meant that he increasingly compared himself with the Anglo-Saxon king and saint, Edward the Confessor. Henry had a new church built at Westminster – Edward the Confessor had restored the old one – and when he died he was buried in the tomb from which the Confessor had been removed earlier.

Henry's English identity was shared by many nobles. One of the major undercurrents of the reign was the anti-foreigner feeling between the English lords and the French courtiers who came with Henry's wife, Eleanor of Provence. The English nobles slowly gained the upper hand in court and in 1234 ousted two of Henry's closest French advisers. Despite this political infighting, the years from 1227 (when Henry began to rule in his own right) to 1257 were mostly peaceful. However, the nobles were pressurising the king for reforms to the taxation system, administration and the government.

To deflect criticism and conflict at home, in 1250 a debt-burdened Henry had grasped at a phantom opportunity to extend his empire. The pope, who had been selling titles and lands across Europe, had offered

Henry the kingdom of Sicily. Henry accepted and made his second son, Edmund, king. Edmund had an enjoyable and extravagant time there for a few years, until the island fell into other hands. Unfortunately Henry was left with nothing permanent to show for this adventure except an immense debt, and many deeply suspicious barons. His visions of grandeur collapsed further in 1259 when he signed away his remaining rights in Normandy, Anjou and Poitou in return for money and promised future rights in France.

By 1258 the pressure from the barons had proved too much and Henry surrendered to their demands. In the Provisions of Oxford a Council of Fifteen was set up, with the king as a 'first amongst equals'. The council effectively ruled for seven years until Henry reasserted his power. Under the leadership of Simon de Montfort (1208?–65) the barons raised an army and captured the king at the battle of Lewes on 14 May 1264. De Montfort now became temporary ruler, but the ever-distrustful barons began to side with the king. Henry's son, Edward, raised an army and the two sides met at Evesham in 1265. De Monfort was killed and the king was reinstated, though Edward was the true ruler; within two years de Montfort's remaining supporters had been crushed.

Henry enjoyed his last years in peace, and fulfilled his ambition in 1269 when the new Westminster Abbey was consecrated and St Edward the Confessor's body reburied there. When Henry died in 1272 opinions about him differed; Dante described him as 'the simple King who sits apart'. His piety was undoubted but it often resulted in a lack of political judgement which led to the rebellions of the reign.

THE CHURCH: ARCHITECTURE, UNIVERSITIES AND FRIARS

Henry's reign spanned a time of great development in all aspects of the Church, not least in architectural design. The early Norman cathedrals were solidly built, with small windows and large pillars which made the interiors dark; the supreme example of Norman work is Durham Cathedral. Gradually the architects became more skilled and confident; the width of the walls and pillars decreased whilst the height of the walls and size of the windows increased. These characteristics formed part of the Gothic style of building and can be seen in the choir of Canterbury Cathedral (built for Thomas à Becket's shrine), Wells Cathedral, started

Salisbury Cathedral

in 1220, and above all at Lincoln Cathedral, begun in 1192.

Changes in other aspects of the Church were also noticeable during Henry's reign. The relative importance of the monasteries, and of the abbots who ruled over them, declined as the bishops grew more powerful. Many were able administrators, such as the Bishop of Salisbury who, in 1218, moved the site of his cathedral from the isolated but secure fort of Old Sarum to the lush and prosperous plain below. An entirely new cathedral was built incorporating the new and exciting styles of the times. The most remarkable bishop of all was Robert Grosseteste, Bishop of Lincoln from 1235 to 1253, who became Oxford University's first chancellor, wrote detailed works on theology, and incurred the pope's displeasure more than once. He was also very human: at a feast he told an over-formal friar to drink a glass of wine as a penance.

A new movement within the Church was also gaining prominence in

Henry's reign. The friars reacted strongly against the monastic ideal of isolation and deliberately worked in the towns amongst both the rich and poor. The most popular and famous order was the Franciscan; their founder was the nature-loving St Francis of Assisi and the order followed his example by concentrating on good works and charity. The next most important order was the Dominican; founded by St Dominic to counter heresy in southern France during the early 1200s, the Dominicans soon acquired a reputation for learning and theological debate. In Europe they formed the backbone of the greatly feared Inquisition which rooted out heresy, and in England they were the confessors to every king from Henry III to Richard II.

The Church also controlled the two universities of Oxford and Cambridge. Oxford was the larger and the older: by 1230 the student population was about 1,300 and the colleges became endowed with land and had halls of residence. Cambridge University had been founded in 1220, but little is known of its early history.

THE ECONOMY

In the late thirteenth century the English economy and society was much the same as recorded in Domesday. There had been some changes, of course: the population had grown and towns had got bigger. Some lords had planned new towns which could be taxed and so increase profits; Salisbury, Leeds, Liverpool, Hull and King's Lynn were all deliberately built for the extra revenues they generated. Throughout the period the main industries remained the same. Wool and cloth were predominant and these were exported to Europe, along with grain, salt and fish. In return, wine was imported from Gascony and finished cloth from Flanders. Whereas the towns were growing in size and number, in the countryside only the occasional technological advance, such as the introduction of windmills in 1200, changed the pattern of farming which had remained basically unaltered since the Conquest 200 years before.

CHAPTER FOUR

The Thistle, the Lily and Roses,
1272–1485

Edward I, 1272–1307

Edward I was born on 17 June 1239, the first son of Henry III. Before becoming king, he had aquired a reputation for deviousness by first supporting the barons and then siding with the king in their dispute. After the end of the Barons' War in 1265 Edward effectively ruled the country during Henry III's last years. Physically he was very tall, with noticeably long arms and legs (hence his nickname 'Longshanks'); he had immense strength and 'his breast swelled above his stomach'. He became fascinated by the legends of King Arthur and sought to associate himself with the mythical king. When his son, Edward II, was born in 1284, the feasting, tournaments and ceremonies were all inspired by the Arthurian legends.

By 1270 the country was peaceful enough for Edward to go on a crusade to the Holy Land. Little of substance was achieved, although his heroic feats enhanced his reputation. Whilst staying in Sicily he heard of his father's death in 1272. After a leisurely journey through the courts of Europe he finally returned to England in 1274.

During Edward's absence corruption had been rife amongst the royal and baronial officials in England. To reassert his own authority Edward instigated an enquiry to recover royal rights, disclose abuses and re-establish law and justice. Written replies were required to a series of detailed questions and it became the largest official undertaking since the Domesday survey nearly 200 years earlier. The answers revealed widespread malpractice. As a result Edward started a great reform and codification of the law, thus becoming known as the 'English Justinian', after the Roman emperor who had codified Roman law. Throughout his reign Edward acted vigorously against any misuse of authority, for example by exposing the Chamberlain of the Exchequer who had amassed a personal fortune of £50,000, while having an official salary of only eight pence a day.

THE WELSH CAMPAIGN

During Edward's early years the Welsh began to assert their independence. The antagonism between the Welsh, with their Celtic language and independent lords, and the English reached back to the Anglo-Saxon conquest of England. The Lord of Snowdonia, Llywelyn ap Gruffydd, (1225?–82), had steadily built up his power-base in the Snowdonian mountains, and was formally acknowledged as the Prince of Wales by Henry III in 1267. To counter Llywelyn's power as an independent lord and put pressure upon him, Edward captured de Montfort's daughter, Eleanor, on her way to marry the Welsh leader. Llywelyn, however, still refused to pay homage to Edward, so the king decided to use force to subdue him.

In 1277 an English army marched on Wales and cut off Llywelyn from his supply-base in Anglesey and captured him in the mountains of Snowdonia. The resulting peace treaty was mild in character, and he was allowed to marry Eleanor. The magnificent marriage ceremony took place at Worcester Cathedral in 1279 with the cost of the proceedings being met by Edward. In 1282 the Welsh again rose in revolt, led by Llywelyn's brother David. This time the fighting was harder and Edward had to call on the considerable power of England, along with many great nobles from Gascony, to destroy the Welsh. Llywelyn was killed in a skirmish, and David was betrayed and executed. There were two further Welsh uprisings in 1287 and 1294, but the English conquest had been effectively achieved by 1284. Edward seized Llywelyn's lands for himself: his son Edward was later given Llywelyn's title of Prince of Wales to demonstrate England's political dominance.

The greatest tangible residue of these events was the string of immense castles built around the Welsh coast. Even now they remind us of the permanence of English rule. The castles, as at Caernarfon, Beaumaris and Harlech represent the climax of castle-building. They were built around the design of a large open space surrounded by a very thick 'curtain' wall. The courtyard at Rhuddlan Castle held a fishpond, seating for the ladies of the court and enough space for 6,000 turves. Built into the curtain wall were a series of towers from which the enemy could be fired upon. The prohibitive expense of building and maintaining the castles meant that never again were so many built on such a large scale.

A TURNING POINT

The year 1290 proved to be a turning-point in Edward's reign. Until then he had been successful in love and war, and he planned to fulfil his ambition of going on a second crusade. Wales was peaceful and firmly under English control, his English subjects were contented, and he was contentedly married to Eleanor of Castile whom he had married at the age of fifteen; although the match had been politically contrived, it proved to be very happy. Eleanor died in 1290 and a grief-stricken Edward wrote, 'My harp is tuned to mourning, in life I loved her dearly, nor can I cease to love her in death.' His affection is shown by the series of twelve 'Eleanor crosses' which marked the route of her funeral cortège from Lincoln, where she died, to Westminster, where she was buried.

In the same year Edward expelled the Jews from England. They had always been disliked by the Christian community for their religion and money-lending; they were also accused of various crimes, like the supposed killing of Christian children. Persecution of the Jews took several forms, including: having to wear a distinctive 'badge of shame' (two strips of yellow cloth six inches long and three wide); not being allowed to eat with, or employ, Christians; and being forbidden to go out of doors at Easter. They had previously been allowed to live in England because kings and nobles had found them to be an excellent source of money. They were taxed excessively, and in the early 1200s they provided nearly a seventh of the monarchy's total income. As the century progressed they continued to pay exorbitant taxes and endured diminished rights – from 1275 they were even forbidden to lend money at interest. By 1290 they were impoverished, and Edward decreed they should be expelled. This was the first banishment of the Jews from a European country in the medieval period; in 1306 France followed

England's example, and Spain persecuted and expelled them in the 1490s.

THE HAMMER OF THE SCOTS

In 1286 King Alexander III of Scotland died leaving his three-year-old granddaughter Margaret as heir to the throne. She was the child of Alexander's daughter and the king of Norway but Edward's carefully arranged plans to marry her to his son, Edward, collapsed when Margaret died on her way from Norway to Scotland. Thirteen nobles came forward to claim the Scottish throne as their own. In an attempt to avoid a civil war and an English attack, the Scots acknowledged Edward as overlord and he decided the succession in favour of John Balliol. However, the new King John became increasingly caught between Edward's demands and the growth of Scottish nationalism. In the end John's advisers persuaded him to defy Edward, and Scotland allied itself in 1295 to England's old enemy, France.

The first phase of the resulting war was quickly over when Edward invaded Scotland in 1296, captured Berwick-upon-Tweed and defeated the Scots at the battle of Dunbar. Yet Edward had stirred up a hornet's nest and the Scottish rebellion continued long past the end of his reign. The tide of war ebbed back and forth. During the campaigns two great Scottish heroes emerged. The first was William Wallace (1272?–1305?), who led the Scottish forces to a great victory over the English at Stirling Bridge in 1297. The following year Edward defeated him at the battle of Falkirk; this victory was the first where the long bow was used to great effect – a new, and very successful, English tactic. Archers using long bows could shoot up to twelve arrows a minute over a range of 220 yards which enabled them to decimate the approaching cavalry. After the onslaught foot soldiers and archers then killed or captured the struggling knights in armour. In the next century the results of these tactics would reverberate throughout Europe.

Edward proceeded to mount further invasions of Scotland in 1300, 1301, 1303 and 1304, but only in 1305 was William Wallace finally captured. Yet a year later the second Scottish hero, Robert Bruce (1274–1329), had himself crowned king at Scone by the Bishop of St Andrew's. Edward reacted swiftly and heavily defeated Robert, who was forced into hiding. Robert Bruce's recovery is enshrined in a famous legend. The story is told that he hid in a cave to escape the English; desperate and hungry he was about to surrender when he noticed a spider trying again and again to build a web. The spider, through instinct and determination, succeeded and gave Robert Bruce the inspiration to carry on.

THE LAST YEARS

After remaining nine years a widower, in 1299 Edward married Margaret, sister of Philip II of France. Edward has often been portrayed as a monarch whose only ambition was grimly, almost obsessionally, to crush the Scots. But there was a livelier side to him as well: he could be affectionate and amusing. In 1284 it is recorded that he paid 10s. 4d. for a boat for his son, and he also persuaded the royal laundress to ride in a horse-race. The war to conquer Scotland, however, continued. In 1307 Robert Bruce gathered his forces and Edward, determined finally to crush the Scots, marched north to meet them in battle. By this time it was also apparent that Edward, aged sixty-eight, was dying, and he died at Burgh-on-Sands, within sight of the Scottish border, on 7 July 1307. One of his last wishes was for his son to continue the fight until the Scots were subdued.

Edward II, 1307–1327

After the stern and essentially successful overlordship of Edward I, the reign of Edward II came as a sad contrast. Edward II was twenty-three when he became king, and in the plain words of a contemporary chronicler 'he did not realise his father's ambitions'. The political struggles of Edward II's reign centred on his passion for his male favourites and the barons' hostility towards them. The first love of Edward II's early years was the Gascon knight Piers Gaveston. Edward I had expelled him because of his influence on his son, but he was recalled by Edward II and given the title of Earl of Cornwall. Edward favoured Piers with power and gifts; even at the king's marriage to Isabella of France in 1308 he received the bride's finest jewels and some wedding presents. Piers's arrogance – he gave nobles nicknames, and then beat them in duels – and the exclusion of the nobles in his favour led to his murder in 1312.

Unlike his father, Edward II had no love for war or for military leadership. After a minor campaign in Scotland to fulfil his father's wishes, Edward quickly returned to the scandalous delights of his court. But by 1314 Robert Bruce had become strong enough to pose a real threat, and an English army marched into Scotland to destroy him. Although the English forces were three times as large as the Scottish, they were wiped out at Bannockburn. A chronicler described the day as one of 'utter loss and shame, evil and accursed'. As a result of Bannockburn Scotland remained independent, and Edward's already low standing plummeted still further.

England seemed set for ruin. The Scots invaded the border areas constantly, the harvests failed in 1315 and 1316, and new favourites Hugh Despenser and his son became prominent at court. Various nobles, led by the Earl of Lancaster, formed an opposition against Edward and the Despensers, but they were defeated at the battle of Boroughbridge in 1322.

The next four years remained relatively peaceful. In 1325 Edward's wife and his young son Edward had arrived at the French court. Isabella immediately began to plot against her husband and the French court became the focus for English exiles. One of the most powerful, Roger Mortimer, became Isabella's lover. In 1326 Isabella, Mortimer and Edward landed in England with some mercenaries and were welcomed with open arms by many cities. The two Despensers were captured and Edward II was eventually persuaded to renounce the crown in favour of his son. The deposed king was seen as an embarrassment and a potential threat to the queen and Mortimer. He was killed by thrusting a red-hot poker into his bowels so no visible mark would be left on the body.

Edward III, 1327–1377

Edward III was crowned when he was fourteen and within a few years he had successfully restored the prestige of the English crown. Like his grandfather, Edward I, Edward III loved pageantry, was a born military leader and was even hailed as a new King Arthur. He was also contentedly married, to Philippa, the daughter of the Count of Hainault, and the couple had twelve children. Edward fostered the idea of chivalry, basing the conduct of his court upon those of Arthurian legend. In 1344 a 'Round Table' tournament was held at Windsor where Edward 're-established' the 'original' Arthurian order of knights. Thus did legend and myth shape reality.

Chivalry and knightly ideals were prominent in Edward's reign and they helped to strengthen the loyalty of the barons to the crown. In 1348, whilst dancing, Edward's mistress, Alice, Countess of Salisbury, lost her garter. Edward immediately picked it up and fastened it to his own leg with the words 'Honi soit qui mal y pense' (Shame on him who thinks evil of it). The prestigious Order of the Garter was born and the motto remains today on the coat of arms of the royal family.

The Hundred Years War

Edward's fifty-year rule was marked by a shift in external strategy, from a desire to conquer the Scots to an attempt to win the French crown. His reign saw the start of what historians have called The Hundred Years War. In some ways this is a misnomer, for the war was sporadic rather than continuous and lasted more than one hundred years, but even so it is a useful term for the wars between England and France over the next century. To complicate the issue the French became allied to the Scots, thereby creating two attacking fronts against England.

At first the war against Scotland continued successfully when in 1333 the Scots were thoroughly beaten at Halidon Hill. The final major battle of the reign against the Scots occurred in 1346 at Neville's Cross near Durham, when again the Scottish army was beaten and Robert Bruce's son, King David II, was captured by the English. But by now the emphasis of war had shifted to France.

When the French king Charles IV died in 1328 without a male heir, Edward had a strong claim to the French throne through his mother, who was Charles's sister. By 1337 Edward was ready to attack France. At first the war was one of attrition and the only early English success was a naval victory in 1340. The new French king, Philip VI, refused to fight open battles, and the cost to Edward of fighting on French soil began to mount. A breakthrough occurred in 1345 when Henry, Earl of Derby, gained most of Gascony. The next year Edward led an army to France; the English forces set about destroying the countryside, and the French finally gathered for battle at Crecy.

CRECY AND CALAIS

Crecy is one of the great English victories won against terrible odds. Edward had just managed a punishing crossing of the Somme when he was boxed into a defensive position by the huge French army. Even with the setting sun in their eyes, the French were keen for action and charged. The English archers fired so fast that the arrows were compared to snow falling; soon scores of French knights lay dead and dying before the English lines. The main battle continued until midnight, when the French finally fled the field, but even in the early morning mists the following day groups of Frenchmen attacked and were shot down. Moving amongst the dead the English heralds found the Count of Flanders, the blind king of Bohemia and 1,500 knights.

Despite the devastating French losses and the high English morale, the pace of the war was slow. Edward eventually captured the port of Calais after a gruelling eleven-month siege. The starving town burghers who surrendered were only spared because Queen Philippa pleaded for their lives. England now held both sides of the English Channel as well as an important trading gateway into Europe.

THE BLACK DEATH, 1348–1350

The Black Death was the most catastrophic outbreak of plague that Europe had ever seen. The disease occurred in two forms: the first was bubonic, which was carried in the bloodstream of the black rat and was transmitted to humans via fleas; and the second was pneumonic, which was transmitted by an infected person's breath. Death normally came within two to five days after high temperatures and large swellings in the groin or armpit.

It first reached England in June 1348 when a ship unwittingly carried black rats to the port of Melcombe Regis in Dorset. From the port it quickly spread inland and the towns began to take defensive measures – Gloucester, for instance, barred anyone from Bristol entering – but still the plague advanced; by the end of 1349 it covered all of Britain. Many saw the plague as a visitation by God upon the wickedness of humanity, but prayers and almost any evasive action was useless against the onslaught. It has been estimated that in some areas up to 50 per cent of the population died. A monk at Rochester wrote:

> The plague carried off so vast a multitude of people of both sexes that nobody could be found who would bear the corpses to the grave. Men and women carried their children and threw them into common burial pits, the stench from which was so appalling that scarcely anyone dared to walk beside them.

By 1350 the plague began to abate, leaving behind a greatly depleted population. Suddenly labour was very scarce and landlords, anxious to harvest the crops, offered labourers wages two or three times above the pre-plague level. Now, if a labourer's wage was kept low, he could simply move elsewhere. In 1351 Edward attempted to limit wages by setting them at pre-plague levels; this was strictly enforced for several years, but the laws of supply and demand eventually won. It was only by the middle of the sixteenth century that the population reached pre-plague levels once again.

THE BLACK PRINCE AND POITIERS

Edward III's son, Edward (1330–76), became known as 'The Black Prince' in the sixteenth century because of the colour of his armour. At Crecy Edward III's attendants had advised the king to withdraw his son, but Edward rebuffed them, saying, 'Let the boy win his spurs.' The Prince did so, and took as his motto 'Ich Dien' ('I serve'), from the standard of John, the blind king of Bohemia. (This motto is still used by the Prince of Wales and appears on the modern 2p coin.) In 1356 the prince led another expedition to France but the French king, John II, trapped his army near Poitiers. As at Crecy the French cavalry were cut down by arrows, but the battle became a desperate hand-to-hand fight for survival and the archers had to pull the arrows out of corpses for re-use. The French were finally defeated when the King John was captured; he was ransomed for £500,000.

Off the battlefield the Black Prince – the expected future king – was famed for his chivalry. He was 'the perfect root of all honour and nobleness, of wisdom, valour and largesse'; like his father and great-grandfather he was a natural leader and enjoyed war. Yet he never became king. During a stay in Spain he contracted a painful disease which prevented him from fighting again, and in 1371 he returned to England. He survived until 1376, but finally died on 8 June and was buried in Canterbury Cathedral.

EDWARD III'S LAST YEARS

Had Edward died in 1360 his reign would have been remembered as glorious, both for the elegance of his court and the glory of the battles won. Unfortunately, in his last years the familiar pattern of controversy aroused by favourites at court reappeared. The most influential of them was the king's mistress, Alice Perriers, and he was likened to a puppet in her hands. In 1376 the 'Good' Parliament subjected the crown to severe criticism and tried several of Edward's ministers.

Across the Channel the French were attacking England's newly-won territory, and at home the elegance and chivalry was crumbling around the court. After a long dotage, the king finally died in 1377, unloved by even his mistress, who wrenched the rings from his fingers.

THE GROWTH OF PARLIAMENT

From the 1230s a new term, Parliament (from the French: 'parley', to talk, discuss), had been increasingly used to describe an assembly of nobles and administrators who offered advice to the king. Edward I had summoned whatever lords he cared to see and consult, but by Edward II's reign the chief nobles insisted that they had a right to be summoned. At first Parliament's main duty was dispensation of justice, and it came to regard itself as the highest court in the land. Parliament considered that it could try any noble (a process known as 'impeachment') and, as we have seen, in 1388 even the king's advisers were successfully tried by Parliament.

Parliament had developed further in the later fourteenth century, when representatives from towns or counties were summoned. The king met them separately from the nobles and by 1399 the Commons always attended. It also became accepted practice that statutes agreed to by the Lords were passed on to the Commons. Parliament's status and power further increased with the idea that 'common consent' (i.e. the assent of Parliament) was needed if the king required extra taxes. The link between extra taxation and the assent of Parliament developed into a powerful principle which became a key factor in the growth of democracy and parliamentary power.

Richard II, 1377–1399

Richard was born at Bordeaux on 6 January 1367, son of the Black Prince, and at the age of ten, on the death of his grandfather, became king. He was in a weak position. The country was shackled by debt from the unrewarding French wars, and he had a potentially over-powerful council of nobles to govern for him. The supervisor of the council was Richard's uncle, John of Gaunt (a corruption of Ghent, where he was born). Gaunt's influence lies like a shadow over the reigns of Edward III and Richard II. Little is known about his activities but he was suspected of much, and rumours were rapidly spread by his enemies. However, Gaunt was always loyal to Richard and helped to build up the image of the English throne. Gaunt married three times. His first wife was Blanche of Lancaster, who brought to the marriage all the lands of the Duchy of Lancaster. Blanche died in 1368 and Gaunt's marriage to his second wife, Constanza of Castile, meant that his ambitions were directed to acquiring the Castilian throne in Spain.

THE PEASANTS' REVOLT

In 1381 the council of nobles supervising Richard was faced by the terrifying occurrence of a mass popular revolt. The underlying reasons of the revolt lay with the economic conditions following the Black Death, but the actual measure which sparked it off was the third collection of the poll tax in 1380 (the tax had also been levied in 1377 and 1379). There was widespread evasion, and so in 1381 tax collectors were sent to extract payment, forcibly if necessary.

The revolt against the poll tax was well timed and spread rapidly. The king's armies were abroad and there was little active resistance. In Kent

Rochester Castle and Canterbury were taken, and in high spirits the rebels marched to London. Meanwhile an army of peasants marched from Essex, creating a pincer movement upon the capital. Richard and his frightened council hid in the Tower of London and watched as the rebels set fire to property in the city including Gaunt's magnificent London palace. Against the advice of his council, Richard met the rebels twice. On the second occasion, on 15 June 1381, the charismatic leader of the rebels, Wat Tyler, was killed and the peasants started to string their bows. With great presence of mind the young king rode forward and said, 'Will you kill your king? I am your king, your captain and your leader. Follow me into the fields.' The rebels did so and then were dispersed.

The revolt sent a shock wave through the ruling classes. Property had been destroyed, jails broken into, and in Bury St Edmunds the heads of the Prior and Chief Justice had been cut off and stuck on poles. Although the leaders of the revolt were quickly executed the lessons lingered on, making the government more conciliatory and cautious. The poll tax was abandoned.

FAVOURITES, POWER AND DEFEAT

Following the peasants' revolt, dissatisfaction amongst the nobles simmered as Richard grew more extravagant towards his favourites. He looked with especial favour upon Robert de Vere. De Vere was given a foreign title, unused previously in England, of Marquis of Dublin, which was later converted into a dukedom in 1386. He was renowned for his greed and arrogance, and the opposition nobles, known as the Lords Appellant, included Henry Bolingbroke, John of Gaunt's son and heir to the Lancastrian estates, and Thomas Mowbray, Duke of Norfolk. The Lords Appellant demanded that Richard's friends should be tried by Parliament. De Vere raised an army, but this was defeated in 1387 at Radcot Bridge in Oxfordshire and de Vere deserted his troops, swam across the Thames and fled. He died in 1392 after being gored by a boar.

After this defeat the 'Merciless' Parliament of 1388 tried and executed many of the king's advisers and friends. Richard was outraged but bided his time. In 1389 he came of age and began to reign without a council. To his genuine sorrow his wife Anne died in 1394, but in 1396 he married

Isabella, the six-year-old daughter of Charles VI of France. The new marriage treaty included a secret agreement stating that the French would support Richard if so desired. At home he quietly built up his private army, at the centre of which were the fine Cheshire archers, who wore Richard's famous white hart emblem.

In 1397 Richard struck against Bolingbroke and Mowbray. A dispute concerning their loyalty to Richard broke out between them and it was decided that the outcome would be decided by a duel. In a piece of pure theatre Richard stopped them just as they were about to fight and banished them both. The king now had a completely free hand and became an absolute monarch. He imposed arbitrary taxes, showered gifts upon his favourites, terrorised his enemies, and even built a huge throne from which to survey people at courtly feasts. With his powerful personal army he appeared invincible. The king's increasing confidence and power encouraged him to covet the huge Lancastrian estates. When Gaunt died in 1399, Richard seized them and disinherited Henry Bolingbroke. It was a grave error of judgement which was to cost him his crown and ultimately his life.

Still sure of his power Richard went to Ireland to enforce his claim to be the overlord of the country and to extend English rule further than the small area around Dublin, later known as the 'Pale'. While the king was in Ireland, Henry Bolingbroke landed at Ravenspur, Yorkshire, in July 1399 to claim his inheritance, and marched down to the Midlands. While his following increased, Richard's army dispersed. Even the Cheshire archers slunk home. Richard returned from Ireland and took refuge at Conwy Castle in Wales, before being forced to abdicate before Parliament in 1400. Bolingbroke assumed Richard's place and was crowned Henry IV. Richard was first held prisoner in the Tower of London before being moved to Pontefract Castle in Yorkshire where he died, probably murdered.

LANGUAGE, LITERATURE AND THE ARTS

During the fourteenth century the English language gradually superseded French as the language of the court and literature. The evidence of its survival since the Norman Conquest is shown by a steady trickle of religious and devotional works written for those ignorant of Latin (the language of the Church) and French (the language of the court). The most famous examples of the English vernacular language are the mystery play cycles of Chester, York, Coventry and Wakefield. These plays probably originated in the last half of the fourteenth century and were performed from carts by members of trade guilds who travelled around the respective cities.

The political implications of the Hundred Years War with France helped the decline of the French language at court, for it was, after all, the language of the enemy. Edward III preferred to speak French, but in 1362 he addressed Parliament in English for the first time and decreed that English was to be used in the law courts. The flowering of English literature was marked towards the end of the century. William Langland (d. 1398), a poverty-stricken priest, wrote his famous religious work *The Vision of Piers Plowman* in English. At the same time Geoffrey Chaucer (1343–1400) was writing his masterpieces, though each was ignorant of the other's work. Whereas Langland was a poor cleric writing sympathetically of the downtrodden and the poor (leaders of the Peasants' Revolt cited *Piers*), Chaucer was a man of the court; his original patron was John of Gaunt. His most famous work is *The Canterbury Tales*, which was left unfinished. It is a literary masterpiece depicting in vivid detail fourteenth-century English life by describing a group of pilgrims on their way to Becket's shrine at Canterbury.

Court ideals of chivalry and the Arthurian legends also feature prominently in literature. In *Sir Gawain and the Green Knight* (Anon, *c.*1370) the poet described the court of Arthur and the adventures of one of his knights, Sir Gawain. This work continued the tradition of Arthurian literature and prompted the most famous Arthurian work of all, *Le Morte d'Arthur* (The Death of Arthur) by Sir Thomas Malory (d. 1471?) in 1469. Caxton printed Malory's work in 1485 and the vitality of the tradition led to the future Henry VII naming his son Arthur in 1486.

Henry IV, 1399–1413

Henry Bolingbroke was the eldest surviving son of John of Gaunt and was probably born in 1366. His youth was a glorious one; he was renowned both as a fighting man, and for his faithfulness to his wife,

Mary of Bohun. He cut a dashing figure and travelled to Lithuania, Jerusalem, Cyprus and Italy, during which time he had enjoyed the hospitality of many of the courts of Europe. In the event the overthrow of Richard had been surprisingly easy, due to the king's unpopularity, but making the throne secure was much more difficult. Henry's usurpation of the throne had set a dangerous precedent of an overmighty subject defeating the king.

Henry's reign as a whole was one of troubles overcome and power consolidated. His personal claim to the throne was relatively weak, and the constant challenges to his position meant that his reign was never easy. He was perpetually in need of money and in 1401 a court official despairingly wrote, 'There is not enough money in your treasury to pay the messengers.' Henry summoned several Parliaments to grant extra revenue, but the Commons, now freed from Richard's wrath, retaliated by constantly challenging the king over his expenses.

A series of rebellions were plotted and unleashed, but Henry withstood them all. The most serious occurred in 1403 when the Welsh nobleman, Owen Glendower, proclaimed himself king of Wales and seized castles and estates on the English/Welsh border. Henry's position became much more dangerous when the powerful Earl of Northumberland, who had been previously loyal to him, sided with Glendower. On 21 July two armies, one led by the king, the other by Northumberland, met at Shrewsbury. The king was victorious but the life of the Earl of Northumberland was spared. This act of clemency was rapidly forgotten by the earl, who organised another revolt which included the Archbishop of York, Richard Scrope. This too was successfully overcome by Henry, who then executed the archbishop, to the dismay of many. When Henry later became paralysed by illness it was widely reported to be God's just punishment for the archbishop's death.

From 1406 the king was frequently ill, and his death came seven years later on 20 March 1413 at Westminster Palace. He had successfully survived the many storms that had beset him and was able to pass on intact the throne he had won. It was an admirable achievement.

THE LOLLARD HERESY AND REBELLION

In the second half of the fourteenth century the Catholic Church had been making greater financial demands upon England. Edward III had employed a theologian named John Wycliffe (c.1330–84) as a propagandist against some aspects of the Church's theology, such as heavier church taxes, and the embarrassing Papal Schism (1378–1417), where there were two rival popes, one in Rome, the other at Avignon between 1378 and 1417. Wycliffe declared that many Catholic beliefs were in error, and that the Bible was the only true guide to faith. This teaching was heresy to the Catholic Church, which believed strongly in the validity of the traditions of the Church, and that the Bible could only be interpreted by priests. Wycliffe rejected this and supervised the first translation of the Bible into English – thereby making it more accessible to all. He died peacefully in 1384, but his ideas were kept alive by 'Lollard' preachers.

The Lollards (from the Dutch 'lolleard', meaning someone who mumbles) were so called by Catholics as a term of abuse. The Lollard preachers were generally humble in origin and travelled round the country expounding their beliefs. Different preachers had different ideas, but all condemned aspects of the established Catholic Church. Their converts tended to come from locally important men, such as merchants or knights, and a Lollard petition was even presented in Parliament in 1395. When Henry IV came to the throne, sterner measures were taken to combat religious dissent. In 1401 William Sawtry became the first Lollard to be burned as a heretic.

The most serious incident came in 1414 when Sir John Oldcastle, a personal friend of Henry V, organised a Lollard rebellion. Only 250 supporters assembled outside the walls of London – he had expected 25,000 – and Oldcastle was executed, but the memory of his challenge lingered on. Although he was vilified by Catholics, he was later treated as a martyr by sixteenth-century Protestants. The memory was so powerful that in 1598 (184 years later) Shakespeare had to change the name of Oldcastle to Falstaff in the two parts of his play *Henry IV*.

Henry V, 1413-1422

Henry V's reign was one of tremendous achievement. Within eight years he had conquered an empire, won the French throne and

Henry V

decimated the chivalric class of France. In many ways it was the Norman Conquest in reverse. The chroniclers record that he was a dissolute youth, associating with low company and robbing his own retainers. Once he became king, however, his character changed completely to that of a responsible and resolute ruler. Corruption was rooted out and feuds between nobles were suppressed by threats of hanging.

After the danger of the Oldcastle rebellion had passed, Henry's ambitions were directed towards France. He received a double parliamentary subsidy to finance an expedition, and on 11 August 1415 Henry set sail from Southampton. His first success, the capture of the French port of Harfleur, was obtained after a long siege. The price of success, however, was the loss of many men through illness.

AGINCOURT

With the few thousand remaining men, Henry decided to march across

France to Calais. Like Edward III at Crecy in 1346, Henry crossed the Somme and found the French army – 50,000 men to his own 6,000 – waiting on the other side. The battle took place on 25 October, St Crispin's Day, 1415.

Henry enjoyed war and had considerable tactical flair. He positioned sharpened stakes before his archers so that the French cavalry charge was effectively halted. The French knights became boxed in with little room to swing their weapons and so were easy prey for the English archers. Once unhorsed the heavily armoured French knights were unable to stand and many drowned in the marshy conditions. It was a stunning victory. The French death roll included three dukes, nine counts, ninety lords and over 5,000 knights. As at Crecy, the French were heavily defeated against all the odds. English morale soared, but strategically the battle achieved little and Henry had to return to France in 1417.

THE WAR, MARRIAGE AND DEATH

Henry's 1417 expedition to France marked a turning-point in his ambitions. From this time on he had the long-term aim of making France a permanent English possession rather than just raiding the country. Siege after siege took place and French cities surrendered because of starvation or the destruction of the city walls. The powerful French political faction of the Burgundian nobles supported Henry, and with their co-operation he became heir to the French throne, thereby disinheriting the Dauphin. In 1420 Henry married the French king Charles VI's daughter, Katherine of Valois, and on 1 December they entered Paris in triumph. The following year Katherine gave birth to a son, who was christened Henry. The succession was secure.

By 1422, however, it was obvious that the king was ill, and during July he had to be carried around on a litter. In the early morning of 31 August he died in France at Bois de Vincennes. After his death Katherine stayed in England and eventually married a Welshman, Owen Tudor. It was as a result of this marriage that their grandson, Henry Tudor, later claimed the throne of England as the legitimate Lancastrian heir.

Henry VI, 1422–1471

Henry V's son became king before he was a year old. By the time of his death in 1471 Henry VI had lost two kingdoms, his only son, and his sanity. Everything went wrong for him, partly through bad luck and partly because of his appalling lack of judgement. In France the situation went from bad to worse after 1429 when the English hold on the country began to crumble. A French peasant girl, Joan of Arc, was now inspiring and leading the French army as they recaptured towns and cities. To make matters worse the Dauphin, who had technically been disinherited by Henry V, was crowned as Charles VII.

By 1431 the English realised that they quickly needed to crown Henry as the king of France. Henry's uncle, the French regent and the Duke of Bedford arranged the ceremony, and on 16 December Henry's coronation took place. It was the first and only time the kingdoms of France and England were united in the person of a single king. Yet even the siting of the ceremony did not bode well, for it took place at Notre Dame, Paris, rather than the traditional coronation cathedral at Reims. The English party hurriedly left in January 1432 and Henry never again set foot in France. Unsurprisingly, the English continued to lose control of French lands.

After Henry came of age in 1437, neither the politicial situation in England nor the military problems in France improved. His own ineptitude was shown by the marriage treaty he accepted with the French princess Margaret of Anjou in 1444: she persuaded him secretly to give back the French province of Maine to the king of France. In the continuing conflict the English lost so much land that by 1453 the sole remaining territory in their hands was Calais. The Hundred Years War was effectively over.

Even in England the government was a shambles. A chronicler wrote: 'The realm of England was out of all good governance . . . for the King was simple, and led by a covetous counsel, and owed more than he was worth.' Henry's chief virtue was his holiness, which did nothing to enhance his authority as king. He pardoned criminals, hated bloodshed and spied upon his servants through a secret window in case they should 'fall' with any 'foolish' women.

In 1453 the king went mad. His insanity may have been inherited from his Valois grandfather, Charles VI, but whatever the cause such treatments as head-shaving, ointments and blood-letting predictably failed. The question arose as to who should rule. There were two main contenders. Queen Margaret had given birth just after the onset of Henry's madness to a son, Edward (1453–71), who was technically the legitimate heir. But instead, another contender, Richard, Duke of York – who was Henry's cousin and Margaret's arch-enemy – was chosen by a council of nobles and ruled effectively until 1455 when Henry's sanity suddenly returned. This left Richard in a difficult position, for he had become used to power and was reluctant to lose it. Challenging Henry's right to the throne, he marched with his army to St Albans where Henry and Margaret's forces were waiting for him. The Wars of the Roses had begun.

The Wars of the Roses

The Wars of the Roses were so called because Henry and Margaret were later associated with a red rose as the Lancastrian emblem, and Richard, Duke of York, adopted the white rose as a Yorkist badge. In the middle was Richard Neville, Earl of Warwick (1428–71). He became known as Warwick the Kingmaker as his power was the deciding factor in who became king. The wars were a heady and complex mixture of intrigue, factional hatred, loyalty and treachery.

The first battle took place in May 1455 at St Albans and the Yorkists won. From then on the pendulum swung back and forth. Queen Margaret forced Richard into exile (1459) and was then beaten at the battle of Northampton (1460) where Henry VI was captured. Richard then claimed the throne for himself, to the embarrassment of many of his followers who had been told they were fighting to rid Henry of evil counsellors. A compromise was reached whereby Richard, or his heirs, would reign after Henry's death. Margaret, who was described as a 'manly woman, used to rule and not be ruled', baulked at this. She marched from the north and killed Richard at the battle of Wakefield in 1460; Richard's head was cut off, decorated with a paper crown and displayed in York. Edward now took his father's place as the Yorkist leader. Margaret's luck continued, however, and at the second battle of St Albans in 1461 she recaptured Henry.

Despite Margaret's victory the city of London and many nobles strongly supported Richard's eldest son and he was duly crowned as King Edward IV in 1461. At one time Henry had ruled two kingdoms; now two kings ruled in England. It took the biggest and bloodiest battle of the war to decide the first stage. The Lancastrian forces were crushed in 1461 at the battle of Towton in which an estimated 100,000 men fought. A major factor in the result was a strong wind and driving snow which blew against the Lancastrian forces, causing their arrows to fall a long way short of the Yorkist lines. After this defeat Henry and Margaret fled to Scotland. Margaret strove to regain the throne and eventually went to France to further her ambition. Henry was abandoned and wandered about like a fugitive; he was eventually found in Lancashire in 1465 and imprisoned in the Tower of London.

In 1470 Margaret's luck changed when she and the Earl of Warwick, who had changed his allegiance, launched a joint invasion and forced Edward IV to flee. Henry, lodged unhappily in the Tower of London, was amazed to be suddenly called king again. Unsurprisingly his 'readeption' did not last long. Edward returned in early 1471, defeating and killing Warwick at the battle of Barnet in April. Three weeks later he defeated Queen Margaret and killed Henry VI's son Edward at the battle of Tewkesbury. Henry was executed in the Tower on 27 May.

HENRY VI'S REPUTATION

The religious chroniclers who wrote about Henry quickly realised that he had many saintly (though not kingly) qualities. He was interested in education – Eton College and King's College, Cambridge, were founded by him – and in people's souls. After his death rumours quickly spread that miracles had taken place at his tomb. His body was moved to Westminster Abbey and in the next decade Henry VII prudently commissioned a book of miracles about him and sought his canonisation from the pope.

Edward IV, 1461–1483

Edward first came to the throne aged eighteen and ruled for eight years (1461–9) before Henry VI's 'readeption'. His charming personality (which masked potentially despotic tendencies) and his military skills enhanced his kingship and because of these qualities his 'extreme' licentiousness towards both married and unmarried women was overlooked. All went smoothly for eight years until Edward married the beautiful Elizabeth Woodville. His council took the view that 'she was not his match . . . and he must know well himself that she was no wife for a prince such as himself'. This rash marriage turned the Earl of Warwick against Edward, as he had hoped to marry one of his daughters to the king.

The second period of Edward's reign (1471–83) after the execution of Henry VI, lacks the drama and colour of the Wars of the Roses period, but it ushered in a period of stability. One of the difficulties lay in the behaviour of Edward's brother, George, Duke of Clarence, who fomented political discontent and was executed, although later the tradition grew up that he was drowned 'in a butt of sweet wine'. Edward's real achievement during these years was to instigate financial reform to enable the king to live off his own revenue. These measures included 'voluntary' gifts and donations from employees of the crown. Such requirements were unpopular but successful and Edward IV was one of the few medieval kings to be solvent when he died. He was not always so successful: he attempted to capture the French crown, with no success whatever; he attacked Scotland but gained little from the expedition; and, most importantly, he failed to pass the crown on to his son. Edward died peacefully on 9 April 1483 after spending three days in a coma; the contemporary verdict was that he died as a result of excessive eating, drinking and debauchery.

Edward V

The reign of Edward V, for all practical purposes, is non-existent. He was the eldest son of Edward IV and was only twelve when his father died. At the time he was in the care of his maternal uncle, Earl Rivers, but on his way to London he was taken by his royal uncle, Richard, Duke of Gloucester, and along with his younger brother held captive in the Tower. Edward V's planned coronation on 22 June 1483 never took place, for he and his brother disappeared.

Richard III, 1483–1485

Before Richard's seizure of power there was nothing to indicate that he had any ambition to become king. He had fully supported his brother, Edward IV, during his reign and had been rewarded by many northern estates, especially around the city of York. Richard was styled 'Lord of the North' and he effectively ruled there whilst Edward ruled in the south. The north/south conflict in politics continued throughout the reign and in 1483 the southern supporters of Edward IV rose in revolt. Richard's attempt to rule England from the north failed when he died at the battle of Bosworth in 1485.

The two-year reign of Richard has generated a huge amount of historical research and controversy, nearly all of which can be summed up by the question: 'Did he have the Princes in the Tower murdered?' There are two opposing views. The standard version of events is that

Richard III

Richard did have the Princes murdered. This view was encouraged by the incoming Tudor monarchy which actively discredited Richard. His official portrait was retouched to give him a humpback, and for centuries his character was blackened; Shakespeare's *Richard III* portrays him as a deformed, power-mad and evil king who had the Princes killed. A different version of events sees Richard as the victim of Tudor propaganda, with Henry VII largely to blame for the death of the Princes. The issue can never be certain but there is probably enough circumstantial evidence to implicate Richard.

THE BATTLE OF BOSWORTH

On 7 August 1485 a contender for the throne, Henry Tudor, grandson of Henry V's widow, Katherine, and Owen Tudor, and descended from John of Gaunt on his mother's side, landed at Milford Haven in Wales. He had the support of several exiled Lancastrian nobles and as he marched through Wales his army grew. By 19 August Henry had reached Lichfield, which impelled King Richard to move from his base camp at Nottingham. The two armies met between the two cities at Market Bosworth on 22 August 1485.

The battle lasted two hours but the accounts of the conflict are confused. What does seem clear is that one of Richard's former supporters, Lord Stanley, took no part until he saw which side was going to win. At Richard's hour of need Stanley launched his forces against him. The king refused to flee to safety and fought to the last in the best tradition of medieval chivalry. How he died is not known, but one possibility is that he became unhorsed in a bog after a frenzied charge against Stanley, thus giving Shakespeare's line 'A horse, a horse, my kingdom for a horse', a basis in historical fact. After Harold's death in 1066, Richard was the only English king to die in battle. To prove beyond dispute that Richard had died, his body was stripped naked and taken to Leicester, where it was exposed to public view before being buried there. There could be no question now that Henry Tudor was king. A new dynasty had been founded.

CHAPTER FIVE

The Tudors,
1485–1603

Henry VII 1485–1509

When the crown of England was retrieved from the field of battle at Bosworth, Henry became the next king of England. The problems of the previous thirty years were not easy to resolve, and for a while his throne seemed very insecure.

HENRY'S CLAIM TO THE THRONE

Henry's hereditary claim was weak. His grandmother was Katherine of Valois who had married Owen Tudor after the death of her first husband, Henry V (see p. 81). Henry was also descended, via his mother, Margaret Beaufort, from John of Gaunt and his third wife, Catherine Swynford. This line of descent had little political importance until 1471, when both Prince Edward and Henry VI (see p. 84) died. Henry Tudor's descent from John of Gaunt now became important, as he was a possible Lancastrian contender for the throne. He was taken to Brittany at the age of four for safety and later went to the French court. Other exiles joined him and in 1485, aged 28, he landed at Milford Haven and went on to defeat Richard at Bosworth (see p. 87).

Rebellion, Marriage and Money

In 1486 Henry married Elizabeth of York, daughter of Edward IV, and thus attempted to unite the Lancastrian and Yorkist factions. (The symbol of the union was the 'Tudor Rose' with its red and white petals.) However, there was still a Yorkist threat as many nobles were fearful that the power and land granted to them by Edward IV would be reclaimed by Henry. In 1487 a carpenter's son, called Lambert Simnel, was pushed forward as the supposed Earl of Warwick, nephew of Richard III and Edward IV. Simnel became the figurehead for a Yorkist rising against Henry, but the rebellion was defeated at the Battle of Stoke on 16 June 1487. Rather than executing the 10-year-old Simnel, Henry sent him to work in the royal kitchens. Simnel eventually rose to be Royal Falconer.

A more serious rebellion was inspired by another imposter, Perkin Warbeck (1474-1499). Warbeck had been touring the royal courts of Europe, passing himself off as the younger of the princes who had died in the Tower (see p. 86). He received the support of the Scottish king James VI, and they advanced into England, but soon retreated. Warbeck next sailed to Cornwall in 1497. A few months before Warbeck's arrival 15,000 men from Cornwall and Devon had marched to London and camped on Blackheath before being defeated by Henry's forces. Warbeck took advantage of this unrest and landed in Cornwall, where he soon gained an army of 6,000 local followers. They attacked Exeter and fought their way into the city, before being repelled by the inhabitants. Warbeck's army began to melt away and he made a dash for the coast in an attempt to flee abroad. He was captured and sent to the Tower of London, where, after another escape attempt, he was executed in 1499.

To secure his position as king, Henry employed three main weapons to bring peace: the law courts, financial policy and marriage. During the Wars of the Roses the centre of government had shifted between southern support, under Edward IV, and the northern support of Richard III. Henry solved the problem by centralising government and reinvigorating two branches of the law. At the national level Henry revived various courts, notably the Court of the Star Chamber, so called because of the stars painted on the ceiling at Westminster where the court met. This court had between twenty and thirty members and was generally used to punish and discipline nobles, and to sort out problems effectively when the local courts were inadequate. Even though the previous thirty years had, at times, been lawless, the use of the Star Chamber soon calmed any lingering problems. On a local level Henry used JPs (Justices of the Peace) to keep control of towns and parishes.

Although their primary role was to keep local law and order, by the end of the century they had gained so much responsibility that many complained of the burdens. By centralising government and increased law and order, the national north/south divide in politics became fused in a national respect for the crown.

Henry's desire for money was renowned and he collected it with a single-minded zeal. Many statutes were passed in his reign to increase the flow of money into the royal coffers – such as the embargo upon exporting of unfinished cloth (finished cloth could have a higher tax put upon it). The efficiency of tax collection was dramatically increased, and with it the loathing for the tax collectors, especially the two most famous: Empson and Dudley. With the king's support they imposed fines for a variety of offences – some of which had happened decades before. Henry's most duplicitous method of increasing his revenue came when Henry asked Parliament for a grant to go to war with France. Parliament gave him two subsidies, but France had other ambitions in Europe and paid Henry not to go to war. Apart from the cost of some minor battles to keep up appearances, Henry had received three lots of income and spent little. Henry took a close personal interest in his finances, initialling every page of accounts. From a receipt of £17,000 in 1488, the annual sum rose to an average of £105,000 between 1502 and 1503. By these measures Henry made the crown solvent, although he did not amass a great fortune.

As has been seen, Henry strengthened his claim to the throne by his marriage to Elizabeth of York. Elizabeth gave birth to a son, named Arthur (1486-1502), a name of great historical significance. (Henry deliberately fostered the myth of the Tudor descent from King Arthur, as well as Tudor Welsh origins, to imply that the new dynasty was Arthur's return to restore the glory of the nation after the Wars of the Roses.) Great things indeed were expected from this future king, especially when, at the age of 15, he married the Spanish Princess Catherine of Aragon (1485-1536) in 1501. The pattern of English history would have been very different had not Arthur suddenly died five months later in 1502. The question as to whether Arthur and Catherine's marriage had been consummated would be a central one in the following years. The king was fearful of losing the dowry attached to the marriage and so he decided that Catherine should marry his younger son, Henry. As this was technically forbidden by the Catholic Church, Henry sought and received permission from the pope and the marriage took place. One other marriage had long-term consequences. Henry's daughter Margaret was married to King James IV of Scotland. As a result of this James VI came to rule over both England and Scotland in 1603.

By the end of his reign Henry had secured his position as king by firm and effective government while concurrently restoring the crown's finances. The country was at peace and trade was vigorously encouraged. It was during Henry's reign that John Cabot first discovered Newfoundland in North America and so gave England its first New World territory. Henry died on 21 April 1509.

Henry VIII, 1509–1547

Henry's reign is a pivotal one in English history. His desire for a divorce resulted in Henry breaking the thousand-year link between the Church in England and the pope (see p. 97), and later the destruction of the monasteries (see p. 99). Parliament, although still firmly under the control of the king, increased its importance, and included a group of Welsh MPs, whose country was legally incorporated into England by 1543 (see p. 100). By the end of Henry's reign England had been changed forever.

When Henry VIII came to the throne in 1509, he was different from his father in many ways, not least that he had been reared in security and wealth, whereas his father had been brought up in relative poverty and exile. Henry was a brash young man of eighteen, confident of his own skills and a Renaissance Prince. In 1515 a Venetian diplomat, Pasqualigo, described Henry as:

the most handsomest potentate I ever set eyes on; above the usual height, with auburn hair combed straight and short, . . . and a round face so very beautiful that it would become a pretty woman, his throat being rather long and thick. . . . He speaks French, English and Latin, and a little Italian, plays well on the lute and harpiscord, sings from book at sight, draws the bow with greater strength than any man in England, and jousts marvellously.

Henry also gained glory from two English military successes in 1513. In 1511 he joined the Holy League – which had been founded by the warlike pope, Julius II, and included Ferdinand of Aragon and Venice – to combat the power of France. The outcome was a brilliant cavalry action by the English which defeated the French at the 'Battle of the Spurs' (so called because the French spurred their horses to get away quickly) in August 1513. Three weeks later a Scottish invasion of England, intended to create a diversion from Henry's French campaign, was defeated at Flodden Field and the Scottish king, James IV died, along with a large number of Scottish nobles, a result of which was that the Scottish threat was curtailed for over thirty years.

Henry also preferred the pleasures of life – dancing, eating and the pursuit of women – to inspecting and initialling every page of accounts as his father had done. This left a gaping hole in the royal administration, which was filled by a succession of eminent men, of whom the greatest were Thomas Wolsey and Thomas More.

THOMAS WOLSEY

Thomas Wolsey (1472–1530), the son of an Ipswich butcher, rose through his career in the Church to hold some of the highest offices of both Church and State. He had been in the service of Henry VII and in 1509 he became a member of the new king's council. He was largely responsible for the French campaign and his efforts were rewarded by a rapid rise to some of the highest positions of Church and State. In 1515 Wolsey became Lord Chancellor and his power was such that he virtually ruled the kingdom. The Tudor historian, Polydore Vergil, wrote that 'Wolsey carried on all business at his own will, since no one was of more value to the King'.

Wolsey's rapid rise to power was equalled by his accumulation of preferments and church offices, which included: Archbishop of York (in 1514); Cardinal (in 1515); and Papal Legate (in 1518). These offices gave Wolsey an income of £50,000 and, as well as living in pomp and splendour, which allowed him to build three palaces, the most famous of which was Hampton Court. As the Venetian ambassador said of Wolsey in 1519, 'He rules both the King and the kingdom'. Henry allowed Wolsey to have this power, for the king was generally bored by affairs of state, satisfied with the results of Wolsey's diplomacy, and the latter could act as a scapegoat if need be.

WOLSEY'S FOREIGN POLICY

The shifts of Wolsey's foreign alliances were so frequent that historians have attempted to find a consistent policy behind them, although with little success. One suggestion is that Wolsey had ambitions for the papacy itself. The two major opponents in Europe were Francis I, the king of France, and the King of Spain, Charles V, who was elected Holy Roman Emperor in 1519. A key element in their rivalry was their desired domination of the papacy, both for its religious importance, and the ownership of the Papal States in central Italy.

In 1515 Francis won the Battle of Marignano which put northern Italy and the papacy under the shadow of the French. This was reversed in 1525 when Charles won the Battle of Pavia. In 1527 the unpaid imperial soldiers mutinied and savagely sacked Rome. The pope, Clement VII, became a prisoner of Charles V. This occurred just when Wolsey was most in need of papal support, for Henry VIII was determined to divorce Catherine, and only the pope could legally undo the marriage. The problem was that Charles was Queen Catherine's nephew, and Charles had the pope prisoner.

THE DOWNFALL OF WOLSEY

In the early years of Henry's marriage both he and the queen were happy. Slowly, however, things began to turn sour. Catherine of Aragon was a loyal, courageous and warm-hearted wife, but the succession became an increasing problem. In the first five years she gave birth to five children, all of whom died, and when finally she gave birth to a healthy child in 1516 it was a girl, christened Mary. Further miscarriages occurred, and Henry, now desperate for a son, looked about his female courtiers and his eye alighted on Anne Boleyn (1507–1536).

Within the court Anne Boleyn was disliked. Wolsey called her a 'night crow' and rumours spread that she was a witch, but these tales did nothing to dampen Henry's passion for her. Despite many gifts and much sweet talking, Anne Boleyn refused all Henry's amorous advances, and would only consider them if they were married. With his passion aroused, and a growing conviction that he should never have married Catherine in the first place, Henry made it plain to Wolsey that he demanded a quick divorce. With the pope under the control of Charles V, Wolsey predictably failed to gain papal consent. Henry banished Wolsey from court: Wolsey fled north, but was summoned to London to face a charge of treason. On his way from York to the Tower of London, he died on 29 November 1530 at Leicester Abbey. Just before his death he was reported as saying 'If I had served God as diligently as I have done the King, he would not have given me over in my grey hairs'.

CATHOLICISM, NON-CATHOLICISM AND PROTESTANTISM

In many countries, including England, there was widespread anti-clericalism. This was nothing new as the Lollards had attacked many practices of the Church (see p. 78), but anti-clerical sentiment became a prominent theme and Wolsey had been an easy target. He was in charge of several dioceses and religious houses, which he never visited, and gained an immense income from them – allowing him to have a lifestyle which rivalled the king's. At the other end of the ecclesiastical spectrum the parish clergy were often uneducated. In 1529 at the opening of Parliament, the members complained about the poor education of the clergy, with a statement that 'one priest being little learned, had ten or twelve benefices, and was resident on none'. Twenty-two years later in 1551, after the learning of the clergy had supposedly improved, a bishop examined 249 clergy and still found that 171 could not say the ten commandments, 10 could not say the Lord's Prayer and 27 did not know its author.

In reaction to the ignorance of the ordinary clergy, a small group of scholars, who were part of a European movement now known as 'humanism', began to emphasise classical learning and simple biblical piety. John Colet (1466–1519), the dean of St Paul's Cathedral, advocated reform of the Church from within, and also a literal approach to biblical texts. The most famous humanist was Erasmus of Rotterdam who taught for a time at Cambridge. His book *Praise of Folly* in 1514 was embarrassing for the leaders of the Church as it wryly mocked the abuses of the Church.

The strongest reaction against the corruption of the Church occurred in Germany. In 1517 a monk named Martin Luther had criticised the Catholic Church by nailing his Ninety-five Theses to the church door of Wittenberg Cathedral. These were rapidly printed and circulated, and almost unwittingly he found himself at the head of a movement protesting against the abuses of the Church. This movement became known as Protestantism. The Ninety-five Theses stimulated clerical and lay discontent, and soon the number of Protestant groups was rapidly increasing.

Henry had no love for Protestants: several were burnt at the stake and Henry supposedly wrote a pamphlet denouncing Lutheranism although the real author was probably Thomas More. The pope was so pleased with the king's ardent defence that he gave Henry the title of '*Fidei Defensor*' (Defender of the Faith): he was less pleased when Henry changed religion but kept the title. (The letters 'F.D.' still appear on British coins.) However, Protestantism was also emerging as a powerful influence at court. Anne Boleyn read the first English translation of the New Testament from the Greek (by William Tyndale (d. 1536)) and she persuaded Henry to read Tyndale's *Obedience of a Christian Man*. This work argued that the king of a country must be morally reponsible for the spiritual welfare of his subjects as well as their physical well-being. It was a useful weapon to have in his argument with the pope over the divorce of Catherine.

WEDLOCK, DIVORCE AND DIVISION

However, the pope was still a virtual prisoner of Charles V and in the Treaty of Barcelona in June 1529 he had vowed 'to become an imperialist and live and die as such'. Delaying tactics were used to prevent a decision and so Henry tried various policies to force the pope to grant his divorce. From August 1529 an attempt was made to win over academic opinion to Henry's cause by consulting the universities of Europe about the canon law concerning marriage. Oxford and Cambridge sided with the king, along with six other European universities. Predictably the pope was unmoved by Henry's arguments and so the king sought to increase his own hold over the Church in England to put pressure upon the pope.

The clergy in England were in a difficult position: they owed their spiritual allegiance to the pope, but as they were Englishmen they owed their temporal loyalty to the king. Disputes between the papacy and the monarch had occasionally arisen during the Middle Ages, as between King John and Innocent III (see p. 58), but on the whole relations between the pope and monarch had remained amicable. This co-operation resulted in Wolsey gaining the power from both the pope, by his position as papal legate, and from the king (see p. 92). This combination of power in the hands of Wolsey weakened the resistance of the Church to attacks by the crown.

Before Wolsey died (see p. 94) he had been summoned to stand trial for high treason on the grounds that he had exercised the power of the pope in England as papal legate and so weakened the king's influence. Henry now used the same device against the clergy, arguing that they had accepted Wolsey's authority, and so by implication the pope's. The clergy were given the opportunity of buying Henry's favour by offering a large payment of cash. The see of Canterbury alone paid £100,000.

Between November 1529 and May 1532 four sessions of Parliament were held. By the use of statutes and Acts of Parliament the king reduced the clergy's privileges in an attempt to force the pope to grant the divorce. In 1531 the king was acknowledged 'so far as the law of Christ allows, supreme head of the English Church and clergy', thereby threatening the authority of the pope in England. A further important act was the Act of Annates in 1532, which halted certain papal revenues.

Suddenly at the end of 1532 the need for a divorce became urgent for Anne Boleyn was pregnant by Henry. If the child was a boy, and hence a future king, then he must be born in wedlock. In January 1533 Henry and Anne were secretly married – although Henry had still not officially divorced Catherine. Henry's position was made easier by the consecration of a new Archbishop of Canterbury, Thomas Cranmer (1489-1556), who was firmly behind the king. Ironically the pope gave Cranmer full powers, possibly because he knew little of Cranmer and wished to be conciliatory in his appointment, and Parliament gave him more. One of the most important measures passed by Parliament was the Act of Appeals in 1533 by which theological disputes were directed to the Archbishop of Canterbury for judgement rather than to the pope. The split with Rome was widening. Events then moved very fast. Archbishop Cranmer opened proceedings against Catherine on 8 May 1533 in

Henry VIII

Dunstable. On 23 May he pronounced that Henry's marriage to Catherine was null and void, and that Henry's marriage to Anne was valid. On 1 June 1533 Anne Boleyn was crowned queen of England.

When the pope learnt of Henry's marriage with Anne Boleyn, he excommunicated Cranmer and gave Henry a month to repent. Henry refused and was excommunicated in September. Under Henry's direction the Parliament of 1533-34 severed the remaining links with Rome. The pope was to have no part in the appointment of English bishops and all payment of taxes to Rome were forbidden. In 1534 the Act of Supremacy was passed which declared that the king was the Supreme Head of the Church of England. The pope was then officially designated the 'Bishop of Rome'. Papal authority had been irrevocably replaced by royal authority: the Church of England was now independent of Rome.

The speed of the division was breakneck and had been spurred on by the need for a legitimate male heir. Henry and Anne's child was born in September. To Henry's great disappointment it was a girl, who was christened Elizabeth. The question of the succession, which had been at the root of the break with Rome, still needed to be resolved.

CATHOLIC REACTION

Despite these extraordinary events and the denials of the pope's authority in England, there was no large-scale Catholic uprising. Henry had been careful to sanction his actions by the use of Parliament, and he still considered himself Catholic, but without acknowledging the authority of the pope. The principal Catholic martyr was Sir Thomas More (1478–1535). He had been at one time Henry's Lord Chancellor, having taken over from Wolsey, and was the author of *Utopia*. He argued the Catholic case in Parliament, but the mood of the country was against him and he was finally executed for refusing to take an oath that Henry was the Head of the Church of England. Other executions included those of John Fisher (1459–1535), the Bishop of Rochester, and four Carthusian monks. In 1539 Parliament passed The Act of Six Articles which outlined the beliefs of the Church of England, and they contained no trace of radical Protestantism. Just to prove that England had not become Protestant, twenty-two Protestants were burnt at the stake.

Thomas Cromwell

Cromwell (1485–1540) was Wolsey's protegé and had risen in his service. Like Wolsey, Cromwell had risen from a lowly birth – his father was a smith in Putney, London. He had become an MP in 1529 and after Wolsey's downfall he transferred his services to the king. Cromwell first became prominent in 1533 when he became Chancellor of the Exchequer and rose to become Lord Privy Seal in 1536, but his real power came not from office but by acquiring the king's confidence. He had a flair for administration and some historians have seen him as the architect of a revolution in the administrative machinery of government, supervising a shift from informal decisions made by the king, to a reliance upon departments which had their own defined procedures. This is a debatable point, but Cromwell was certainly the architect of the Dissolution of the Monasteries.

THE DISSOLUTION OF THE MONASTERIES

If the initial breach with Rome had been largely the result of the need for a male heir, the subsequent despoliation of the Church occurred because of Henry's desperate need for money – large amounts of which were needed for coastal defences to repel a supposed invasion by France, Charles V and the pope. Quite apart from the monasteries' huge wealth of jewels, church plate and relics, they owned huge tracts of land, variously estimated at between a fifth and a quarter of all the cultivated land of England. At a time when his Treasury was empty and Henry was Supreme Head of the Church of England, such wealth was too tempting to be ignored. In 1535 commissioners were sent out to uncover the 'manifest sin, vicious carnal and abominable living' in the smaller abbeys. They went to work with enthusiasm and, knowing what they were expected to find, they discovered a vast amount of evidence. On the basis of their reports Henry dissolved the monasteries in two phases.

The first phase, in 1536, affected the smaller monasteries with endowments of under £200 pounds a year. In the same year the only uprising concerned with the destruction of the monasteries took place. It became known as the Pilgrimage of Grace, but it was also a reaction against agrarian conditions and Henry's ministers. The rebellion, which was based in the north, was quickly crushed and over the next three years the larger monasteries fell into crown hands. By 1539 Parliament passed the Second Act of Dissolution which stated that the monasteries had 'of their own free will ... without constraint, coercion or compulsion' liquidated themselves and that now monastic property was in the hands of the crown. The medieval dominance of the monasteries had come to an end in three short years.

The End of Medieval England

The end of the medieval era in England is usually considered to be marked by the accession of Henry VII in 1485. A stronger case can be made for the year 1538. In that year the last monasteries were dissolved and Cromwell issued injunctions which stipulated that every parish church should have an English Bible and that shrines should be destroyed. The shrines and reliquaries were smashed, including those of the major saints such as St Thomas Becket at Canterbury, and the jewels and precious metals were sent to the Treasury. It was obvious that the crown had replaced the thousand-year dominance of the pope as the arbitor of religious affairs in England.

The monasteries were physically destroyed. The stone was used to repair buildings and city walls, the lead was stripped from the roofs and the precious metals were carted away to be melted down. The destruction of medieval art, books and architecture was enormous. The resulting 'bare ruined choirs' of the monasteries gave the population visible proof that a major element of medieval life had disappeared.

There was also a less obvious long-term result. The huge monastic estates were sold to augment the king's immediate income. A major chance of the king increasing his long-term revenue, and thereby existing without parliament, had been lost. The new owners of the previously monastic lands were mainly nobles and the wealthy gentry, who further increased their wealth and political power. These landlords now had a vested interest in seeing that the papacy and the monasteries would never return, whatever a future monarch might wish.

Other administrative changes were becoming effective. With the increasing power of the Star Chamber at a national level and the JPs, who were often gentry, at the local level, the great hereditary noble families began to slowly decline in importance. This was a gradual change, but it is indicated by the greater number of men of humble origins who gained high posts in government. To some extent this change was indicated by parliament. In the sixteenth century the House of Lords and the House of Commons became recognisably divided as entities and the first recorded instance of the name 'The House of Lords' first occurs in 1544, a possible reaction to the new gentry who were challenging the Lords' power.

Wales

The medieval era also came to an end in Wales. Even though Edward I had conquered Wales by 1284, the Welsh language, laws and customs had survived in many areas. In 1536 and 1543 the legal Union of England and Wales was accomplished by Parliament. Instead of giving

Wales its own effective government, the country was simply incorporated into England. English laws, county administration, land tenure, customs of tenure and inheritance replaced the Welsh methods. The English saw the process as a step towards civilising the country: the Welsh saw it as crude annexation.

Four More Wives

To Henry's intense relief Catherine died in January 1536. By this time Henry was looking to rid himself of Anne Boleyn. Whilst she had held Henry at arm's length, Anne had proved irresistable, but Henry now began to tire of her. A male heir had still not been born and Henry began to consider other possible wives – this time he was attracted to a maid of honour, Jane Seymour (1509?–37), but before he could marry her Anne had to be removed. In a mock trial Anne was accused of following 'her fickle and carnal appetite' with other courtiers; she was found guilty and beheaded in May 1536.

Contemporary accounts indicate that Henry loved Jane Seymour best of all his wives, and she gave him a son, the future Edward VI. The succession was secure. She died twelve days after the birth on 12 October 1537 and a heart-broken Henry heaped honours upon her family.

The process of finding a wife now fell to Henry's chief minister, Thomas Cromwell (see p. 92). For political reasons Cromwell decided upon Anne of Cleves (1515–57) and arranged for a flattering picture of her to be painted. Henry agreed to the marriage on the basis of the painting. However, when Henry met her in real life his illusions were shattered; she was plain and simple, and he unflatteringly called her 'My Flanders Mare'. The marriage was a farce, never consummated, and quietly forgotten. Anne was content with a yearly income of £500 and two houses. Parliament annulled the marriage, Cromwell was beheaded in 1540 for the Cleves fiasco and other alleged misdemeanours, and Henry began to look for yet another wife.

Cromwell's rivals had pushed forward Catherine Howard (d.1542), daughter of the Catholic Duke of Norfolk, who became Henry's fifth wife. But Catherine had apparently been reckless before her marriage to Henry and was subsequently accused of amorous encounters with courtiers. She was subsequently beheaded at the Tower of London in February 1542.

Henry's sixth and last wife was more fortunate, for the twice widowed Catherine Parr (1512–1548) outlived Henry, gained the respect of his children and later married Jane Seymour's brother Thomas. The succession was in theory, and in practice, secure in the person of Henry's son Edward.

The Last Years

By 1538 Henry was master of all he surveyed. He had established a national church, with himself at the head, and at last he had a son, Prince Edward. Through the sale of the monastic lands he had chosen the short-term financial benefit to the long-term income which the lands offered. Even with the sale of lands, and the debasing of the coinage (lessening the silver content while keeping the face-value the same) Henry's highly expensive wars, with Scotland, between 1542 and 1546 and France between 1543 and 1546, meant that he was permanently in need of money. The Scots were defeated at the Battle of Solway Moss in 1542, after which the Scottish king James V died, reputedly of a broken heart. His heir was his six-year-old daughter, Mary. Despite this victory, and the capture of Boulogne from the French in 1545, the wars achieved little and peace treaties were signed in 1546.

By the end of his life Henry became bad tempered and ill. He had an appalling ulcer, possibily syphilitic, on his leg which left him speechless with pain. The young Renaissance king, cultured and high spirited, had turned into a grim and bitter old man. He became so grossly fat in later life that he could hardly get through a doorway and needed a 'device' to carry him upstairs. Even when he was dying no one had the courage to tell him. He died in the early hours of 28 January 1547, aged fifty-five.

Edward VI, 1547–1553

Even though Edward came to the throne at nine, and died when he was fifteen, a great deal is known about Edward, for his personal journals survive. He recorded seeing 'a bear hunted in the river, and also wildfire cast out of boats and many pretty conceits'. He was certainly an able scholar and well taught: at the age of seven he knew Latin well, had 'made forty or fifty pretty Latin verses' and was about to embark on the reading of Cato; by the age of fourteen he was almost fluent in both French and Greek. His education extended beyond the classics, for he was deeply interested in theology, fortifications and defenses, and in the affairs of state and reform of the currency.

THE PROTECTOR SOMERSET

Henry VIII had decreed in his will that a council of ministers should govern in Edward's name until he came of age. After Henry's death, the scheme quickly collapsed and Edward's uncle, the Duke of Somerset, Edward Seymour (*c.* 1506–52), became the most prominent member of the council, and styled himself the Lord Protector of the realm. What was remarkable about Somerset was his humanity in the face of religious intolerance. Not a single person was burned or tortured for religious belief during his protectorship, and he was a supporter of the poor against the major landowners. Somerset continued to implement Protestant reforms. In 1549 the Act of Uniformity made Cranmer's *Book of Common Prayer* compulsory in all churches and abolished the Latin Mass. This provoked rebellion within Cornwall, and passive resistance from other Catholic areas of the country. The rebels described the new service as 'like a Christmas game'.

LORD PRESIDENT NORTHUMBERLAND

Somerset's downfall came through a lack of political skill. His rival, John Dudley, Duke of Northumberland (1502?–53), plotted ceaselessly against him, and the chance came when a rebellion broke out in Norfolk. Somerset was sympathetic to the protesters' demands, but Northumberland crushed the rebels in battle. By his support for the poor, Somerset lost his power in the council and was sent to the Tower of London where he was executed in 1552. The Protectorate had lasted two years and nine months. At his execution it was alleged that many diped their handkerchiefs into his blood, supposing it to have the virtue of a martyr's.

Northumberland, who styled himself Lord President, had a very different temperament to Somerset: he was intolerant, greedy and ruthless. He actively encouraged the destruction of religious statues and paintings, and aided the return of exiled extreme Protestants from the continent. The Church of England was steered in a decidedly Protestant direction – a new more plainly Protestant prayer book was introduced and the eight medieval and Catholic orders of priesthood were simplified to three: bishops, priests and deacons.

However swiftly the reforms went forward, all depended on Edward staying alive. Unfortunately for Northumberland Edward fell ill in January 1553 and by May he was clearly dying.

LADY JANE GREY: THE NINE DAY QUEEN

Northumberland made desperate plans to keep himself in power by marrying his son, Guildford Dudley, to the great-granddaughter of Henry VII. He talked the Privy Council and Edward into accepting Lady Jane Grey as his successor but she was obviously a puppet, a shy, immature girl, with none of the qualities needed to be a successful queen. The succession was secured for Jane on 21 June 1553. On 6 July Edward died.

The rightful heir, Mary – Henry VIII's only surviving child by Catherine of Aragon – asserted her own claim to the throne. Both she and Northumberland raised armies, but Northumberland's dispersed once Mary reached London. As she rode through the streets, bonfires were lit and banquets were held in celebration. Northumberland, Dudley and Lady Jane were all subsequently executed.

Mary Tudor, 1553–1558

Mary was thirty-seven when she became queen, unmarried and almost beyond middle age by Tudor standards. As a girl she had been vivacious and aged eleven she had dazzled the court with her dancing and the gems that she wore. By the time she became queen her looks had changed. She still had reddish hair and pale eyes, but she had few teeth and her constant bad health sapped her energy. This was exaggerated by living a life of extreme Catholic piety. She rose at daybreak and heard private Masses, never ate before the afternoon, and 'transacted business incessantly until after midnight'.

Her reign ushered in an official return to Catholicism. Catholic bishops were reinstated and the Latin Mass was restored. These mild measures were welcomed by large numbers of people who had yet to embrace Protestantism, but discontent grew over Mary's proposed marriage. She longed for a child and heir to the throne, and when the Emperor Charles V proposed his son, Philip (1527–98), the match seemed perfect to her. Philip was the heir to the Spanish throne, with whose help England could be restored to Catholicism. Mary was delighted and, despite all advice, pressed on with the preparations. It was in reaction to the marriage, and Mary's revival of Catholicism, that the only serious revolt of the reign took place in 1554. A Protestant gentleman named Thomas Wyatt reached London with 3,000 men, but the revolt was quickly defeated. With the opposition crushed, Mary married Philip in a solemn ceremony at Westminster Abbey in 1554.

Mary apparently adored Philip while he saw her as unattractive and lacking 'all sensibility of the flesh'. At first he was outwardly polite, but soon rumours spread of his liaisons with other women at court. Politically the marriage was a fiasco: many English people deeply distrusted Philip, who symbolised both foreign interference and Catholicism, and Parliament declared if Mary should die without an heir Philip would have no claim to the throne. Philip for his part thought that the English were obstinate and isolated from mainland Europe. He left as soon as possible for Spain; everyone rejoiced except Mary.

With Philip absent, Mary turned her mind to imposing Catholicism. Cardinal Pole (1500–58), who had arrived from Rome, advised her that the laws to burn heretics should be revived. In 1555 the Bishops Latimer and Ridley were burned together at the stake in Oxford. As the flames started to rise, Latimer said, 'We shall this day light such a candle as I trust shall never be put out.' The elderly and respected Archbishop Cranmer was also burned; as he was dying he stuck his right hand in the flames as a punishment for signing a document embracing Catholicism. These deaths sent a shock wave of horror across England. In all about 300 people were burnt for heresy; they were mostly ordinary people rather than religious fanatics.

Mary had few friends in court, and those who supported her, such as Cardinal Pole, were generally out of touch with the feelings of the country. A year before she died, Mary was reported to be prematurely aged, wrinkled and anxious, but mentally alert. Philip returned briefly to England and persuaded her to go to war with France. The forced loans needed for the war met great opposition and during the fighting England's last continental possession, the port of Calais, fell to the French in 1558. No effort was made to recapture it. Mary fell into melancholia. Her marriage had brought her loneliness and misery rather than the happiness she craved. After Philip's brief visit to England she believed she was pregnant, but in reality she had a tumour or dropsy. In her last illness she reported that she had seen 'many little children play before angels singing pleasing notes' in her dreams. She died on 17 November 1558.

Elizabeth I, 1558–1603

The day on which Elizabeth came to the throne was treated as a national celebration for two centuries afterwards. Within a month Elizabeth was reported to be incomparably more feared than Mary, a good sign for the strength of the crown and the unity of the kingdom.

As a queen Elizabeth deliberately fostered the idea that her long reign was a golden one, with great battles won, adventurers sailing the high seas, poets writing . . . and herself, regal and commanding, on the throne. 'The Elizabethan Age' is still often seen through such rose-tinted glasses. Behind the glittering reputation was a remarkable woman. She could speak Latin, Greek, French, Italian and Spanish extremely well, could dictate a letter, write one herself and listen to a verbal report all at the same time. Like her grandfather, Henry VII, she often counted every penny – in 1599 she worked out that the king of France owed her £401,734 16s. 5½d. She was also extremely frugal on her own account and in 1553 managed to save £1,500 out of an income of £6,000. Elizabeth also drank, spat and swore 'round mouth-filling oaths' which, whilst not uncommon for great ladies, was hardly part of the myth.

Elizabeth's first task was was to settle the religious issue. She had inherited a country which had veered towards Protestantism under her

Elizabeth I

father and her half-brother, and then lurched towards Catholicism under her half-sister. Elizabeth favoured political stability over religious doctrine, and by making it clear that she would 'not make windows into men's souls' she deliberately chose 'the middle way'. She remained the head of the church (though she was now called 'Governor' to placate both sides) and the Supremacy Bill and the Uniformity Bill, which made the Church of England law, were passed in 1559. There were no burnings or torture on those who did not conform, but rather fines or penalties.

ELIZABETH AND SCOTLAND

As England reverted to a mild Protestantism, the danger existed of joint attack by Scotland and France, both of which were Catholic. This religious threat at England's back door was broken in 1559 when John Knox (1505–72), a fiery Calvinist preacher, set Scotland alight with his Protestant teachings. The Protestant nobles attacked the French-backed government forces and drove the French out of Scotland, much to Elizabeth's delight.

The Queen of Scotland, Mary (1542–87), was married to the French king Francis II until his death in 1560. She then returned to Scotland and proceeded to make every blunder possible. Unlike Elizabeth, she married but with little regard to political expediency. Her three marriages were extraordinary episodes, incorporating jealousy, murder, bombings, scandal and Mary's ability for falling desperately in love with unworthy men, and they did not endear her to the population of Scotland or enhance the Catholic cause. She was deposed in 1567 in favour of her infant son James and she fled to England.

Even though Mary was kept as a prisoner by the queen, she posed a serious problem for Elizabeth. Not only was she a direct and legitimate descendant of Henry VII, but her Catholicism could inspire a reaction amongst the old-guard Catholics. Moreover, Mary endlessly schemed to recover the Scottish throne and to depose Elizabeth. She survived until 1587 when her plotting finally caused her downfall and Elizabeth signed her death warrant. A major challenge to the State's stability disappeared, but another followed promptly when Philip II of Spain sent an armada to dethrone Elizabeth.

THE SPANISH ARMADA

Over the previous fifty years Spain and England, once brought close by the marriage of Henry VIII and Catherine of Aragon, and Mary and Philip, had now become bitter enemies. One reason for this was that England was turning aggressively to the world overseas. England's last gateway into Europe, Calais, had been lost in Mary's reign and this encouraged English merchants and seamen to exploit the New World. On the high seas Francis Drake (1540?–96) and John Hawkins (1532–95) had been plundering Spanish vessels in the New World. In December 1577 Drake, in his ship *Golden Hind*, attacked the Spanish-held coasts of Chile and Peru, and in 1580 returned to England with an estimated £500,000 worth of captured money and jewellery.

A further reason for Philip's hatred of England was that the country remained Protestant. Moreover England actively supported the Protestants in the Netherlands, who were fighting their Spanish overlords. Philip, an ardent Catholic, was determined to act. Under pressure from Spain the pope excommunicated Elizabeth and called on Catholics to dethrone her. Various plots were devised, but Francis Walsingham, who was in charge of an elaborate intelligence network, passed on the information to Elizabeth's most important minister William Cecil (1520–98) who stopped them before they became dangerous. It was obvious to Philip that more drastic measures were needed, and in 1587 he made plans for the invasion of England. Drake responded to the threat by attacking Cadiz and causing damage to the Spanish fleet moored there – he later boasted that he had 'singed the King of Spain's beard'. Despite these and other setbacks, Philip collected an impressive fleet of ships (in Spanish, *armada*), which sailed in 1588 to conquer England. In all the Armada consisted of 130 ships, of which thirty-seven were of serious fighting value and the rest were transport ships for the soldiers from the Netherlands. The English navy was small and had only twenty-one vessels of 200 tons or over, but its number was increased by merchant ships. As the Armada approached England the Spanish hoped that English Catholics would rebel, overthrow the queen and install Philip as monarch.

No Catholic rising took place, and the Spanish Armada was defeated by a combination of skill and luck. The plan was that the Armada was to sail up the Channel, meet up with the Spanish forces in the Netherlands, and protect the troops as they crossed to England. In the crisis Elizabeth was magnificent. The English navy was able to do little damage as the Armada swept up the Channel, but she made a rallying speech to the soldiers ready to repel the invasion: 'I know I have but the body of a weak and feeble woman, but I have the heart and stomach of a king, and of a King of England, too.'

The Armada reached Calais and dropped anchor in tight formation to await the troops from the Netherlands. The English deliberately set fire to eight of their own merchant ships and the wind carried them into the formation. In panic the Spanish ships cut their anchors and were dispersed. A 'Protestant wind' drove them past their rendezvous with the troops and out into the North Sea. The ships of the Armada made their way home round the treacherous coasts of Scotland and Ireland and many ships foundered; the men who successfully returned were weak from lack of food. Philip organised other armadas, in 1596, 1597 and 1599, but they were either diverted or scattered by bad weather.

THE LAST YEARS

After 1588 England was relatively secure from external attack, but within the country religious problems began to grow more acute. In Europe, Catholics were forcefully countering Protestant ideas in a movement known as the Counter-Reformation, and a new Catholic teaching order called the Jesuits had been founded in Belgium. Over 100 Jesuits had been smuggled into England by 1580 and secretly moved around the country reviving and strengthening Catholicism. They were hidden for long periods of time, but if caught faced the death penalty. Over 200 were executed between 1577 and 1603. At the other end of the religious spectrum, radical Protestants, called Puritans, were becoming more extreme and even suggesting that the monarch should not be the head of the church. The most radical Puritans either fled to the Netherlands or faced persecution and death.

Elizabeth's last years were dominated by a revolt in Ireland in 1598 and the rise of an over-mighty subject, the Earl of Essex. In Ireland the Catholics rebelled and Essex, a court favourite of Elizabeth, was given an army of 20,000 to quell the uprising. He failed and came home in disgrace, having disobeyed the queen's instructions. The conduct of the campaign was investigated and in a desperate measure Essex led a band of men to depose her councillors. Despite the queen's affection for him, he was executed for treason in 1601.

ELIZABETH'S REPUTATION

Elizabeth's reign was a long and glorious one lasting almost fifty years. To what can her success be attributed? Firstly, she was a queen who successfully ruled alone. The reigns of the other two queens, Matilda in the twelfth century and Mary, had been associated with bloodshed and conflict. Elizabeth also tried to avoid making any definite decision about complex problems and hoped they would evaporate if she delayed long enough. An example of this hesitation was the extreme reluctance with which she signed Mary Stuart's death warrant, and then told her ministers that they had somehow tricked her into it. As one of her ministers remarked, she would blame them if something went wrong and take the credit when things went right. Elizabeth was also unmarried, the 'Virgin Queen', which gave her a political weapon with suitors; almost every Parliament in her reign raised the question of her marriage, for the succession to the throne was still a crucial and unresolved issue. Elizabeth managed her Parliaments and the nation by a mixture of autocratic power, charm and intelligence. She told her last Parliament: 'And although you have had, and may have, many Princes more mighty and wise, . . . yet you never had, or shall have, any that will be so careful and loving.'

By the end of her life Elizabeth was lonely and desolate. She had no close relations and all her trusted ministers had since died. But rather than the aged and infirm woman of her last years, the enduring image of the reign is of a noble and courageous queen who faced terrible difficulties and survived triumphantly. She died on 24 March 1603. The post horses were already saddled for the long journey up to Scotland where her successor, James VI of Scotland, was waiting to ascend the throne as James I of England. The irony was that he was the son of one of Elizabeth's most dangerous former enemies, Mary, Queen of Scots.

The English Renaissance

From the start of the sixteenth century, classical Greek and Roman culture had become increasingly important to European thought. This reawakening, or 'rebirth' (hence the 'Renaissance'), opened up the writings of the ancient world to English scholars and, with the establishment of grammar schools, to schoolboys as well. When Henry VIII came to the throne he was considered a 'Renaissance Prince', combining martial and sporting skills, including 'royal' tennis, with a deep interest in theology, music and learning. From Henry onwards all the Tudor monarchs were educated in Latin and Greek, but it was during Elizabeth's reign that the English Renaissance flowered.

Elizabeth's reign encompassed new discoveries, victories, such as that over the Armada, and peace and prosperity which encouraged the growth of the arts. The queen herself inspired great poems such as *The Faerie Queene* by Edmund Spenser (1552?–99), and numerous portraits which represented her as a symbol of the nation. Courtiers became patrons of the arts, employing men like Hans Holbein (1497–1543) and Nicholas Hilliard (1547–1619) to paint their portraits. Music was also sponsored, and composers such as William Byrd (1543–1623) and Orlando Gibbons (1583–1625) replaced traditional medieval music with new techniques of composition and performance.

Striking changes were also evident in the architecture of the age as the wealthy courtiers built great houses. In the 1520s Wolsey had started Hampton Court Palace, which was a precursor for the first great house of the Elizabethan age, that of Longleat in Wiltshire. Longleat House included the new style of large windows, which were copied extensively, notably at Hardwick Hall in Derbyshire, built between 1591–7. Many more substantial houses were built in the early 1600s in styles favouring smaller windows and brick rather than stone. Famous examples include Hatfield House in Hertfordshire, extended by Robert Cecil and large enough to accommodate the entire court if necessary.

LITERATURE AND DRAMA

In England literature and drama dominated the domestic cultural scene. New heights of elegance and energy were achieved in poetry, particularly within plays. In 1574 the first actors' company was formed and in 1576 the first theatre was opened in Shoreditch. By the end of the century at least six theatres were in use, including The Globe, opened in September 1599. New plays soon followed, and out of the host of playwrights, who included Christopher Marlowe (1564–93) who wrote *Doctor Faustus* (*c.* 1590), one emerged as the outstanding author of the times: Shakespeare.

WILLIAM SHAKESPEARE, 1564–1616

Though he spent his working life in London, Shakespeare was born in the thriving market town of Stratford-upon-Avon in 1564 and received a first-rate education at Stratford Grammar School. He was first well known as a poet, with such poems as *Venus and Adonis* (1593) and *The Rape of Lucrece* (1594), but by 1591 he had written his first play, *The Comedy of Errors*. Shakespeare eventually owned an acting company which became

William Shakespeare

the best in London and famous throughout Europe. His thirty-eight plays were written between 1591 and 1612. He invented new forms of English history play and romantic comedy, but is particularly renowned for his towering tragedies: *Hamlet* (1600), *Othello* (1603), *King Lear* (1604), *Macbeth* (1605), and *Antony and Cleopatra* (1607). There are few contemporary anecdotes about his life in London and almost all that is known about him comes from legal records or financial dealings. These help to build up a partial picture of his life but throw little light on his personality. After writing his last play, *Henry VIII*, in 1612 in collaboration with John Fletcher, he retired to the best house in Stratford. He died in 1616 and was buried in the parish church there.

Shakespeare's plays and poems remain unmatched in the English language for their vitality and power. They have a universal appeal, for they deal with the everyday life of tavern and peasants as much as with the court and royalty. The plays have many levels: they are entertainments which are exciting or funny, but at the same time they are unsurpassed in their insight into the human condition, and the expressiveness of their verse and prose.

CHAPTER SIX

The Stuarts,
1603–1714

James I, 1603–1625

Elizabeth I had no direct heir to succeed her and so King James VI of Scotland, great-great-grandson of Henry VII, ascended to the English throne as James I. He seemed an excellent successor. He had had twenty years experience as the king of Scotland and, as a moderate Protestant, had dealt with the religious situation well. Unfortunately this experience had been gained in the Scottish system: the English system of government, influenced by Parliament and the Church, was very different.

On a personal level James was scholarly and intelligent, and especially enjoyed detailed theological debates. This interest may have encouraged his hatred and suspicion of witchcraft and bolstered his belief in the divine right of kings, which asserted that the sovereign had a God-given right to the throne and was the source of all laws. James's image was tarnished by his appearance and by his habits. He had thin rickety legs and a tongue which was too large for his mouth, which made him drink 'very uncomely' and slurred his speech. He gave strong indications that he was homosexual (see p. 117) and was paranoid about being assassinated, perhaps unsurprisingly in view of the murder of his father, Lord Darnley, and the execution of his mother, Mary Queen of Scots.

THE BIBLE AND THE GUNPOWDER PLOT

At first James was content with the religious status quo in England, so long as neither the Catholics nor the Puritans threatened his own authority. Both sides hoped for his support and both had their hopes raised: on his journey from Scotland James received a petition from the Puritans and agreed to a conference to discuss the issues; he also allowed greater freedom for Catholic worship.

In January the following year, 1604, James acted as self-appointed mediator between the moderate of the Church of England and the more hard-line Puritans at the two-day Hampton Court conference. The Puritans suggested that the time was right for a new English version of the Bible. James agreed and personally organised the making of the revision, which was completed in 1611. The 'Authorised Version' – though in fact never authorised – became the standard Bible in use. During the conference James took a neutral line until the Puritans used the term 'presbyter' (meaning a church elder, not subject to a bishop) which he associated with the militant puritanism of Scotland. The conference quickly ended. The Puritans left and the king declared: 'I shall make them conform themselves, or I will harry them out of the land.' Groups of Puritan exiles fled to Holland, but they were determined to establish their own communities. In 1620 a number of exiles, and Puritans from England, set sail from Plymouth in *The Mayflower* for the Americas. They were blown off course and landed at a place they named Plymouth Rock. These pilgrim fathers founded the New England colonies.

Whilst the Puritans tended to argue their case or emigrate, the Catholics took direct action. After an initial relaxation James reintroduced the Catholic recusancy laws (penalties for not attending Church of England services), and several attempts were made against his life. The most serious was the Gunpowder Plot in 1605. A group of Catholic conspirators decided to kill the king, peers and MPs as they assembled for the opening of Parliament. However, a veiled warning was given to a nobleman in the Lords, who passed the message to the government. The cellars of the Houses of Parliament were searched and Guy Fawkes was caught red-handed with the explosives. The event is still remembered by bonfires and fireworks on 5 November.

REX PACIFICUS

James's initial attempts at religious conciliation had shown that he was prepared to follow his motto of *Rex pacificus* (the royal peacemaker). In his desire for peace, harmony and unity, he embarked on a plan to unify the laws and constitutions of England and Scotland. He was unsuccessful, but from 1604 onwards he used the title king of Great Britain to signify the union of the kingdoms by one monarch.

James also desired peace in Europe. In 1604 he brought the fifteen-year-old war with Spain to an end and sought to placate both Protestants and Catholics. In February 1613 James's daughter, Princess Elizabeth, married Frederick, the Elector Palatine of the Rhine, and James joined a Protestant union of European princes. However, peace was more important to him than religious war and in 1618 he had Sir Walter Raleigh (1552?–1618), the veteran privateer of Elizabeth's reign, executed to please the Spanish.

The king also sought financial co-operation between Crown and Parliament. James had some legitimate increases in expenditure: he had a family, whereas Elizabeth had none, but he was also lavish in giving gifts. By 1608 the crown's debt had risen to nearly £600,000 and a new, permanent source of income was sought. A solution was the Great Contract: in return for the abolition of various financial rights by the crown, Parliament would grant a yearly income. The scheme soon collapsed and short-term expedients were again used. The order of baronets was established in 1611 to generate money: a baronetcy could be bought for £1,095. By 1622 the honour had been so abused that the price had fallen to £220.

FAVOURITES

In 1612 James's able treasurer and secretary, Robert Cecil, Earl of Salisbury (1563–1612), died. Cecil's death allowed the Howard family to achieve dominance at court. Their time in power saw a decline into scandal and indebtedness, and one historian has said, 'It is difficult to see any benefits whatever from their period of dominance at court.' By 1618 the anti-Howard faction had promoted George Villiers into James's affection, and the Howard family fell from grace.

George Villiers (1592–1628) was the son of a Leicestershire knight, who had few prospects before he arrived in court. James fell in love with the younger man (James was forty-seven, Villiers twenty-two) and Villiers rose rapidly to power. In successive years from 1616 he became viscount, earl, marquess and, in 1623, Duke of Buckingham. From 1617 he and his supporters ruled the country through James. The king's love for him was demonstrated by obvious physical affection and endearments: 'My only sweet and dear child I pray thee haste thee home . . . and so Lord send me comfortable and happy with thee this night.' When he was criticised over his over-close relationship, James replied, 'Christ had His John, I have my George.'

PARLIAMENT, 1604–1610

Relations between James and his first Parliament of 1604–10 were on the whole cordial. Looking back from the end of his reign, and with the problems that were lead to civil war (see p. 124) in mind, it is easy to forget that a huge amount of undisputed legislation was passed: 128 statutes between 1604 and 1606. This collaboration was increasingly under threat from the growing conflict concerning the raising of revenue and the king's powers over Parliament. The Commons were more rebellious than the subservient House of Lords. They forced out James's schemes for the unification of England and Scotland and the Great Contract (p. 117). They also asserted their rights: in 1604 James challenged the right of a suspected outlaw, Francis Goodwin, to become an MP; the Commons forced James to compromise, thus establishing an an important precedent of being able to decide disputed elections.

Apart from one short-lived Parliament in 1614, which achieved nothing and became known as the 'Addled Parliament', no Parliament was summoned between 1610 and 1621.

THE THIRTY YEARS' WAR

Despite James's desire for peace in Europe, England was eventually drawn into conflict. In 1618 James's son-in-law, the Elector Palatine, Frederick, accepted the crown of Bohemia but by 1620 he had been driven out of both the Palatinate and Bohemia by the Spanish; he and James's daughter, Elizabeth, were forced into permanent exile. James was in a dilemma: it was obvious that the only way to recover the Palatinate was by war, yet he wished to build up diplomatic links with Spain through the proposed marriage of Prince Charles and the Spanish Infanta. Charles and Buckingham took the matter into their own hands, and in a mad-cap scheme rode incognito to the Spanish court. The Spanish were shocked by such behaviour and refused the proposed marriage. Charles and Buckingham felt slighted and the pressure to go to war increased.

On their return to England Charles and Buckingham bullied James into reversing his previous foreign polices. In February 1624 Parliament was summoned and its members, encouraged by Buckingham, bayed for war against Spain. £300,000 was raised and a mercenary, called Mansfield, led a disastrous attempt to recover the Palatinate from Spain: the expedition faltered after it had crossed the Channel, and the money had been wasted. (War with Spain was only formally declared after James died.) Furthermore, as part of a marriage treaty between Prince Charles and the French princess Henrietta Maria, England helped the Catholic French attack La Rochelle, a centre of Protestant Huguenot resistance. James died in March 1625, aged fifty-eight.

Charles I, 1625–1649

Until 1612 the hopes of the court and of the nation lay with James's eldest son, Henry, whose gifts promised well for the future; his sudden death at the age of eighteen was believed by many to be calamitous. Charles was next in line and succeeded James in 1625, a year which has been seen as a turning-point in English history. The most obvious reason for this judgement lies in the new king's character. Until Henry's death Charles had lived in his shadow, and in the following year his sister Elizabeth had married the Elector Palatine and left England. As a child Charles was shy and lonely – traits which remained with him all his life and were indicated by a stammer and a cold reserved manner. Within two months of succeeding to the throne, he married Henrietta Maria. There was little love between them and the marriage was at best a dignified and formal affair.

PARLIAMENT

During the 1620s Parliament had been summoned by James in 1621 and 1624, and by Charles in 1625–6 and 1628–9. By 1629 the relations between King and Parliament had deteriorated to such an extent that the Speaker was forcibly held down in the chair by two MPs – in order to stop Charles dissolving Parliament before financial and religious resolutions had been passed. In the 1630s no Parliaments were called at all. The reasons for the breakdown in co-operation between Parliament and the king were numerous, but centred upon the raising of taxation and parliamentary rights.

The Parliament of 1621 started well. After the eleven-year break the members were not initially rebellious, but disputes soon occurred. Three parliamentary leaders were arrested and the liberties of Parliament appeared threatened. The Commons responded with a protestation, which claimed that their privileges were 'the ancient and undoubted birthright and inheritance of the subjects of England'. Although the last Parliament of James's reign in 1624 was less acrimonious, MPs were still very wary of the crown's power.

Charles's marriage to the Catholic Henrietta Maria had not endeared

Charles I

him to an overwhelmingly Protestant Parliament. When he ascended the throne in 1625 the Commons voted him a meagre £140,000, and angered him when they granted customs duties (called tunnage and poundage) for only one year instead of for life. War was declared against France and Spain, but Parliament refused financial support until the favourite, Buckingham, was dismissed. To improve his standing, Buckingham organised military expeditions to Cadiz and La Rochelle, both of which ended in humiliating failure. The Commons attempted to bring Buckingham to trial, in a process called impeachment, at which point Charles dissolved Parliament to save his friend.

Between mid-1626 and 1628 Charles used the crown's emergency powers to finance the wars. £240,000 worth of forced loans were collected, and those who did not pay were imprisoned. Eventually the expense of war meant that in 1628 Parliament had to be recalled. It was alarmed by the forced loans (for if taxes could be raised without Parliament, an absolute monarchy could be established). The House of Commons drew up a Petition of Right which emphasised the ancient rights of the people, and asserted that no man could be imprisoned without trial. With great reluctance Charles accepted it. Once again Parliament attempted to impeach Buckingham but he was assassinated at Portsmouth. Charles was heart broken; his subjects were delighted.

RULE WITHOUT PARLIAMENT, 1629–1640

Charles, resentful at the Petition of Right and the rejoicing at Buckingham's death, was determined to rule without Parliament. He did so for the next eleven years. This period has been assessed in two contrasting ways. Amongst the historians who have seen an attempt to impose royal absolutism these years have been called the 'eleven years' tyranny'. The alternative label, 'the personal rule', stresses the part that Charles himself played, and claims that his policies were no more than an exploitation of existing laws rather than an attempt to establish tyranny.

The most obvious element of change in the eleven years was the increasing influence of 'Arminianism' within the Church of England. Arminian clergy, who included the Archbishop of Canterbury, William Laud (1573–1645), and several notable bishops, stressed the role of the sacramental and ceremonial aspects of the church service rather than the sermon and the scriptures. Laud's policies reached every parish in England and seemed to be 'a plain device to usher in the Mass'. The general fear of Catholicism was reinforced by the activities of Catholics associated with the queen. Puritans, however, were harassed for being too Protestant; Laud urged bishops to inspect their bishoprics and punish anyone who did not conform. Many Puritans fled, thus increasing the numbers in the New England colonies.

The crown's financial position dramatically improved in the eleven years. By 1635 various financial devices had reduced the yearly debt to £18,000: a major expense had been the wars with France and Spain, which were halted in 1629 and 1630 respectively. Spending by various departments was reduced, and fines, customs and taxes were assiduously collected or extended. Ship money had previously been collected in coastal areas for the navy, but now it became a permanent land tax throughout England. Long-forgotten fines were also imposed: for instance, a medieval fine was reinstated for encroachment upon royal forests, and the limits of a Nottingham forest were extended from six to sixty miles. The most substantial improvement in the crown's finances came from increasing customs duties, from £300,000 before 1634–5, and thereafter £500,000 following the introduction of new customs rates. These measures allowed Charles to 'live of his own', so long as war did not break out.

IRELAND

From 1610 onwards an official policy of introducing Protestant 'plantations' into Ireland had been adopted. Land in the north of Ireland was divided up among wealthy City of London companies, and the new settlers, about 13,000 by 1622, were English or Scottish Protestants. Private plantations were also started in the Ulster region, and the proximity of the region to Scotland meant that many Scottish Presbyterians settled there. The area of English political domination, called the Pale, centred around Dublin. Elsewhere Catholics still predominated.

In 1633 Thomas Wentworth (1593–1641), who became the Earl of Strafford, arrived in Ireland as Lord Deputy. He was highly successful and, like Laud, was intimately involved with Charles's 'personal rule': he forced several prominent nobles to return lands to the Church and to the crown, obtained three grants from the Irish Parliament in 1634, and transformed Ireland's finances to the extent that permanent financial support for the monarchy seemed possible. His ecclesiastical reforms, which imposed the Arminian ideas of Archbishop Laud, were particularly disliked.

THE MAKING OF THE CIVIL WAR

The reasons for the English Civil War have been debated by historians for centuries. Looking back from the 1630s the prospects for war seemed unlikely. Apart from the abortive attempt on the throne by the Earl of Essex in 1599, the period between 1569 and 1642 was the longest period of internal peace that England had known – indeed England was probably the most peaceful country in Europe. The few riots that occurred were usually in response to grain shortages or enclosures and rarely resulted in death.

Historians have given many long-term reasons for war: the crown's disputes with Parliament, starting in Elizabeth's reign and escalating in James's and Charles's; the tensions between Puritans and the Church of England; the locally organised resistance to the financial, religious and political policies of the crown; and the increasing, capitalist prosperity of the gentry and merchants who challenged the privileges of the established nobility. Immediately after the Civil War, however, contemporaries looked no further than the beginnings of Charles's reign to see the causes of the conflict. The irony is that in 1637 the king was apparently at the height of his powers, yet eight years later he had lost the Civil War. In 1637 Charles seemed financially secure, there was no organised opposition, and he was served by an efficient administration; it is possible that he could have continued to reign without Parliament for many years. The position suddenly changed as a result of the attempt by Charles and Archbishop Laud to impose religious uniformity upon Scotland. This proved to be an act of monumental folly.

SCOTLAND

In 1637 Charles and Laud introduced the English Prayer Book into

Scotland. All protests from the Scots were ignored and riots ensued when the Prayer Book was actually introduced into Scottish churches: in St Giles's in Edinburgh a woman threw a stool at the dean's head and the church had to be cleared by the town guard. As a counter-measure the Scottish Presbyterians signed a National Covenant to 'recover the purity of the Gospel'. When the Glasgow Assembly met in 1638 it abolished bishops: a direct and powerful attack on the King's powers.

The Scots quickly collected an efficient army; Charles responded by sending a poorly organised army to Berwick-upon-Tweed. The two sides were so unevenly matched that Charles signed a peace treaty without a battle being fought. In 1639 he recalled Parliament to vote him more money, but it refused until its grievances had been discussed; after a couple of weeks the 'Short Parliament' was dissolved. The cycle was repeated: the king tried to defeat the Scots and failed. The Scots army invaded England and occupied Northumberland and Durham. A treaty was signed which paid the Scots £850 per day for the trouble of invading England.

THE LONG PARLIAMENT

Charles was now in serious financial difficulties. Parliament was recalled once again in 1640, but the 'Long Parliament' – as it came to be known – resulted in two distinct sides forming. At first the Commons acted together, and Strafford was tried and executed in 1641. Charles had previously promised that 'not a hair of his head should be touched', but pressure from the London mob and the pleas of the queen had changed his mind; Strafford bitterly commented, 'Put not your trust in Princes.' Parliament also greatly increased its own power by making laws stating that it should not be dissolved without its own consent, that it should meet every three years, and that illegal taxes, such as the ship money and forest laws, should be abolished.

Yet as the Commons became more powerful, various of its members began to side with the king, thinking that Parliament had gone too far. The first sign of division came with the Root and Branch Petition of 1640, which attempted to get rid of bishops and bring the Church under control of Parliament. Its Puritan supporters included John Pym and Oliver Cromwell but a moderate party opposed the bill. Two sides began to form, and in 1641 there was a terrible massacre of Irish Protestants in Ulster which split the Commons even more. If the king were to raise an army to crush the revolt of the Irish Catholics, would he then use it against his English opponents? The Puritans argued that the only safe course was to strip Charles of his powers. A long list of grievances was drawn up, called the Grand Remonstrance, and after passionate debate it was passed by only eleven votes in 1641.

Charles not unnaturally rejected the Remonstrance, whereupon Pym suggested that Parliament, and not the king, should control the army. Charles's reaction was foolhardy, for he had won the support of the moderates. Instead of winning over public opinion, he marched into the Commons with a number of troops and tried to arrest his five principal opponents. They escaped just in time; as he entered the Commons a deadly silence ensued and his armed troops allowed no one to leave. Not seeing his opponents, Charles commented, 'I see the birds have flown.' London treated the five MPs as heroes, and Charles, baffled by the disloyalty of his subjects, retreated to Hampton Court Palace.

After eight months the negotiations between the two sides broke down. Charles raised his standard at Nottingham on 22 August 1642 and Parliament recruited an army to 'preserve the religion, laws, liberty and peace of the kingdom'.

The Civil War

At the beginning of the Civil War the support for each side split the country geographically. In broad terms the north, Midlands, Wales and the south-west supported the king, while the south, East Anglia and London supported Parliament. London contained a tenth of the entire population and had a large associated revenue with which to back Parliament. There were some notable exceptions to this broad division: Oxford and Cambridge supported the king, Bristol, Hull and Plymouth supported Parliament. Catholics, supporters of the Church of England, the aristocracy and their tenants tended to follow the king; Puritans, yeoman farmers and merchants tended to follow Parliament. Yet as soon as the position is looked at in detail the divisions become confused: soldiers fought for whoever conscripted them or paid them most, people

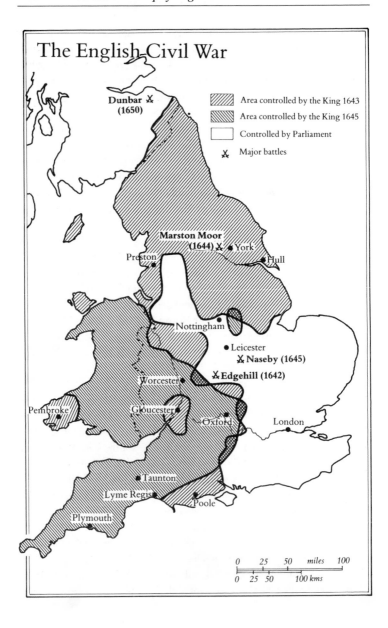

The English Civil War

	Area controlled by the King 1643
	Area controlled by the King 1645
	Controlled by Parliament
✗	Major battles

Dunbar ✗
(1650)

Marston Moor ✗ ● York
(1644)

Preston ● ● Hull

Nottingham ●

● Leicester

✗ Naseby (1645)

Worcester ● ✗ Edgehill (1642)

Pembroke ● Gloucester ●

● Oxford London ●

● Taunton

Lyme Regis ● ● Poole

Plymouth ●

0   25   50   miles   100

0   25   50   100 kms

occasionally changed their allegiances, and in some cases members of the same family fought on different sides. The armies, too, had different characteristics. The Royalist army had a flamboyant image and excellent cavalry, hence their name 'Cavaliers'. The Parliamentarian army had an image of religious zeal, dour temperament and the belief that God was on their side; they supposedly got their name of 'Roundheads' from their short-cropped hair.

As wars go, the Civil War was humane and there were never the excesses of, say, the Thirty Years' War in Europe. Defeated troops were not massacred and there was little wanton destruction of property. Although it is the major battles that are most easily remembered, most of the fighting took place between small local groups who formed and disbanded quickly. In some areas neutral groups were formed to ward off attacks from either King or Parliament. The first major confrontation took place in October 1642 at Edgehill in Warwickshire where the Parliamentarians attempted to stop Charles marching on London. The battle was indecisive: Prince Rupert, the son of the Elector Palatine and so the nephew of Charles, and his Cavaliers defeated the Roundhead cavalry, but chased them for miles across the open countryside; when they returned the Parliamentarian foot soldiers had defeated the Royalist infantry. The king pushed onwards, made a half-hearted attempt upon London, then set up his headquarters at Oxford.

The following year, 1643, Charles seemed to have a coherent military strategy, planning that his northern and western armies should join him in a three-pronged attack on London. The scheme failed because of the necessity to protect supply lines from the north and west, as well as the reluctance of the troops to leave their local areas. Even so, the Royalist side was still on the offensive. In 1644 an alliance was agreed between Parliament and the Scots, which meant that the king was now fighting on two fronts. In the same year a joint Scottish and Roundhead force crushed the Royalists at the battle of Marston Moor (near York), by attacking the Royalist side before they were fully prepared. The king had lost the north.

In 1645 the New Model Army was used in battle for the first time at the battle of Naseby. Largely the creation of Oliver Cromwell, it was a precursor of modern armies as it efficiently welded together a large number of troops. Professionalism was the key: discipline was strict – no swearing or gambling was allowed, training was thoroughly and the men could be trusted to obey orders in a crisis. Perhaps more importantly the soldiers were regularly paid – in the later stages of the war the unpaid Royalist troops deserted in large numbers. Soon the New Model Army became more than a match for the Royalist soldiers. When Cromwell saw the king's army at Naseby he 'could not but smile . . . in assurance of victory'.

After some hard fighting the Parliamentarian forces won the day, and the king's cause was all but lost. In 1646 Charles surrendered to the Scottish army in Nottinghamshire and, on payment of £400,000, he was returned to the Parliamentarian side.

THE ARMY, POLITICS AND THE LEVELLERS

However, the New Model Army was becoming increasingly radical and from the spring of 1647 many of the rank and file began to establish links with the radical movement in London. During the 1640s London had been a centre of ideological and religious ferment, and three pamphleteers – John Lilburne (1616–57), William Walwyn (1600–80) and Richard Overton (?–1653?) – emerged as the leading propagandists for the Levellers. The Levellers demanded a whole series of religious and secular reforms: the abolition of the monarchy and the House of Lords, as well as religious toleration, law reform and an extension of the franchise. By May 1647 they had obtained significant influence within the army – at a time when the divisions between the army and Parliament were becoming increasingly obvious.

In May Parliament decided to disband the increasingly costly and ideologically suspect New Model infantry regiments. In response General Fairfax ordered the army to assemble at Newmarket and on 2 June a troop of cavalry seized the king from his Parliamentary guards. Perhaps uniquely in the sixteenth and seventeenth centuries the army now became politicised. It was common enough for soldiers to mutiny over poor wages or conditions, but in June 1647 the leaders of the New Model Army, under pressure from radicals in the lower ranks, wrote *A Representation of the Army*. The *Representation* announced that the army was 'not a mere mercenary Army' but had a political programme, which included a purge of Parliament. To force the Commons to agree to its proposals the army marched slowly to London. Discipline was maintained and the army's appearance of moderation was enhanced when several nobles and fifty-eight MPs joined it. On 6 August 1647 the army occupied Westminster, without resistance, and effectively controlled Parliament.

THE PUTNEY DEBATES

Levellers were still highly influential in the army and they set out their own proposals for a new constitution in *The Agreement of the People. The Agreement* was debated between the Levellers and the more conservative senior officers in the famous Putney debates (28, 29 October and 1 November). The discussions centred upon the extent of the franchise. The senior officers were horrified that the Levellers wished to extend the vote to all 'free Englishmen' (which did not include women or servants) and strongly argued against the proposals.

Ten days after the last debate Charles fled from his captivity at Hampton Court. It is debatable whether the leaders of the army engineered his escape, but it served their purpose well. The army closed ranks against the possible threat from Charles, and abandoned the Leveller *Agreement*. The power of the Levellers began to wane. A series of small Leveller-inspired mutinies took place, as at Ware, Hertfordshire, in November 1647 and later in 1649 in Burford and Oxford, but all were easily crushed. The leading Levellers were imprisoned and their pamphlets censored or banned. By 1650 the Levellers had lost their political significance.

THE EXECUTION OF CHARLES I

After Charles escaped from Hampton Court in 1647 he took refuge at Carisbrook Castle on the Isle of Wight. Although he was a prisoner – Oliver Cromwell's cousin was the governor there – the king still schemed and plotted. He gained the backing of the Scots, and in 1648 the so-called 'Second Civil War' took place when risings within various provinces, with some Royalist support, took place all over England. These were unco-ordinated and the army defeated them one at a time.

However, the risings persuaded the leaders of the army that there could be no peace whilst the king was alive. Ironically Parliament was hesitant to impose the death sentence. To get a compliant Commons 110 MPs were refused entry and a further 160 MPs voluntarily withdrew. This left a small 'Rump' Parliament to continue.

Parliament's difficulties were still not over, for half the judges refused to try Charles on the basis that 'No court can try the King'. Charles made no defence: he simply denied that the court had any validity. Finally the king was sentenced to death, and on 30 January 1649 he was executed in Whitehall. It was the first and only time that an English king had been tried by a court representing the people, found guilty and executed. Contemporaries reported that, at the execution, the huge crowd gave a great groan when Charles's head was held up for all to see.

To many Puritans the Civil War and the execution of the king indicated that a perfect society was not only possible, but was imminent. It was believed that King Jesus would replace the old monarchy and a 'godly reformation' would transform society. Some foresaw that God would 'sooner or later shake all the Monarchies of the Earth', and others saw 'the kingdom of Jesus Christ begin to flourish, while the wicked . . . do now perish and fade like a blowne–off–blossom'. This enthusiasm was not, of course, universal as many people were horrified by the execution of Charles and were fearful for their land and property. A balance was now needed between radical reforms and the stability required for local law and order.

The Commonwealth, 1649–1653

OLIVER CROMWELL

Oliver Cromwell (1599–1658) was a country gentleman from Huntingdonshire who had been converted to puritanism at about the age of thirty. He became an MP and had supported the 'Root and Branch Bill' of 1641 (see p. 124). During the Civil War Cromwell had commanded men from the eastern counties, known as the Eastern Association, had instigated the creation of the New Model Army, and had risen to be a lieutenant-general, second only in command to General Fairfax. He then became a general and, after Fairfax's resignation in

Oliver Cromwell

1650, the leader of the army: an all-powerful post.

Cromwell's character is remarkably difficult to assess. Some historians have seen him as an evil genius, whilst others emphasise his belief in democracy, 'godly rule' and toleration. At times he could be enlightened and a revolutionary idealist (usually when there was not a great deal of political pressure on him), and at others a pragmatist, carefully building up political alliances and weighing various factions. He was also caught between conflicting pressures: he attempted to rule through Parliament, but had gained his power from his leadership of the army, which included many radical Puritans. In the end the demands of Parliament and of the army radicals were incompatible. As a historian has remarked, 'In the last resort he was sitting on bayonets and nothing else.'

THE REVOLUTION CONTINUES

The Rump Parliament continued in power after the king's execution and in February 1649 the House of Lords and the monarchy were formally abolished, along with the Anglican Church. The exchequer and the admiralty were also replaced by a council of state and sub-committees. Revolutionary as these measures were, the Rump Parliament appeared to be rather conservative in nature. The abolitions were not made effective until several months later, which indicated a reluctance to implement them, and other sweeping reforms were dropped. Much was talked about; little happened. In 1653 Cromwell dissolved Parliament; the reason for this decision is unclear, but the radical army leaders probably exerted pressure upon him. In July 1653 a nominated assembly met – formally the Assembly of Saints, popularly called the Barebones Parliament, after one of its members, named Praise God Barebones. In December its more moderate members despaired of making progress and handed power back to Cromwell.

IRELAND AND SCOTLAND

In 1649 Cromwell led an army across to Ireland to campaign against the Catholic Irish and to stop Charles's son, the future Charles II, gaining a foothold there. He 'like a lightning passed through the land', in the process of which he inflicted two terrible massacres on the towns of Drogheda and Wexford. Cromwell was not usually cruel, but even by the standards of those times his brutality shocked people. The massacres are still remembered.

Scotland was the next flash-point. Charles II landed there in 1650 to claim his inheritance. To gain allies he allowed himself to be crowned by the more powerful Presbyterian faction. His apparent religious 'conversion' was seemingly a political move to gain support and in later life he favoured Catholicism (see p. 136). Two campaigns were mounted by Charles; the first was defeated by Cromwell in Scotland at Dunbar in 1650. The second attempt in 1651 was more successful for Charles and a Scottish army marched rapidly south into England. Cromwell and the army followed; they caught up with the Charles at Worcester and crushed the Royalist forces. Charles was forced to flee and escaped to France, from where he bided his time and waited to return.

The Protectorate, 1653–1658

On 12 December 1653 the Instrument of Government was passed which gave Cromwell the official title of Lord Protector. He had refused an offer of the crown, but signed documents as 'Oliver P' in supposedly mock contrast to the royal form of 'Charles R' meaning 'Charles Rex'. After the failure of the Barebones Parliament the question had arisen as to how the country should best be governed. The framework of government, established in 1653, meant that Cromwell was restrained by a council and a small Parliament. The Lord Protector wanted government by consent, but as he said, 'Where will you find it?'

Cromwell instigated various reforms and his religious toleration was notable. Jews were allowed back into the country for the first time since the reign of Edward I, and new sects flourished, such as the Society of Friends (also known as Quakers) under the leadership of George Fox (1624–91). In the parishes the Anglican Book of Common Prayer was replaced by the Directory of Worship, which allowed congregations to choose their own form of worship. There was no state harassment concerning religion and, as one dissenter believed, England was becoming 'a land of saints and a pattern of holiness to all the world'.

Perhaps Cromwell's greatest achievement was in strengthening England's position abroad. A Royalist historian said of him, 'His greatness at home was but a shadow of his glory abroad.' Under the command of Admiral Blake, the Dutch navy was defeated in the First Dutch War (1652–4), Dunkirk was occupied, a Spanish treasure ship containing £600,000 of silver was captured, and at the battle of Tenerife he sailed into the harbour, silenced the shore garrison and sank sixteen ships without losing any of his own. Within Britain Cromwell integrated English, Scottish and Irish MPs into a truly British Parliament. At various times Royalist supporters had risen in revolt and after one such attempt in 1655 Cromwell appointed a small number of major-generals, one to each regional district, to take control of the country. Some were strict Puritans and banned such 'ungodly' behaviour as drinking, swearing, gambling and even going for a walk on the Sabbath. However, the image of the joyless oppression instigated by some of the major-generals has too often coloured the tone of the Protectorate as a whole. By 1657 they had had become so unpopular that Cromwell agreed to Parliament's request that their rule should be ended.

In 1657 Parliament nominated Cromwell's son, Richard Cromwell

(1626–1712), as his successor; the following year, on 3 September, the Lord Protector died. Within two years Charles was invited back to England as king. Richard Cromwell quickly realised that he had not his father's genius and retired to his farm. Confusion between political factions and the army was the result. After a year of generally indecisive government General Monck marched his army down from Scotland and assembled a Parliament. Charles was invited to become king and the Commonwealth and Protectorate came to an end.

Charles II, 1660–1685

Charles II arrived back in England in 1660 and was met by cheering crowds as he made his way to London, causing him to wonder wryly why he had stayed away so long. He was crowned on 23 April 1661 and was married to Catherine of Braganza, the daughter of the king of Portugal, in the same year. It is debatable whether he loved his convent-bred wife, and his mistresses and liaisons with other women were, and still are, legendary. Two mistresses were especially notable. The first was Louise de Keroualle, later Duchess of Portsmouth, who was Catholic and probably the most influential. Her complement, rather than rival, was the Protestant orange-seller, and later actress, Eleanor 'Nell' Gwynn. In all Charles fathered at least fourteen illegitimate children, but produced no legitimate heir.

Charles was essentially a cynic and pragmatist who was willing to change his beliefs for political advantage (see p. 132). He was also a man of wit, intelligence and charm, but he has been described as congenitally lazy and self-indulgent.

THE RESTORATION

The most obvious point of the Restoration was that the monarchy was re-established, although it was still limited by laws passed in previous reigns. The crown could not enforce unparliamentary taxation, such as forced loans, nor could it arbitrarily arrest MPs. Parliament was also restored on the old basis of two Houses, the Commons and the Lords. The third restoration was of the Church of England and the bishoprics.

Even though Charles was now king, both he and Parliament were aware that he had been *invited* back to rule and that the Parliament still contained people who had fought against Charles I. The vengeance upon Charles's enemies was limited but effective: the 'regicides' who had signed Charles I's death warrant were executed, but other prominent supporters of the Commonwealth, including the poet John Milton, escaped punishment. Parliament, however, was still suspicious of Charles and set about limiting his power. The king's income was set at £1.2 million per year, which was not enough to run the government effectively and pay off his debts. Charles tried various schemes to rid himself of having to rely financially upon Parliament, but none of them worked. His treasurers, such as Danby between 1674 and 1678, were often very successful at increasing royal revenue, but the king was equally adept at spending lavishly, not least upon his mistresses and his personal pleasures.

The most dramatic change came about with the restoration of the supremacy of the Anglican Church. After a strongly Royalist Parliament was elected in 1661, action was taken against those who were Protestant but not Anglican. These people, grouped together under the term 'nonconformists', included Baptists, Congregationalists and Quakers. The measures, known as the Clarendon Code, had the dual role of retaliation and of limiting the potential influence of the nonconformists; they were silenced by laws requiring them to agree with every word of the Book of Common Prayer and forbidding them to hold a government office or go to university. Between one and two thousand church ministers were forced out of their posts.

THREE GREAT DISASTERS: PLAGUE, FIRE AND WAR

In three consecutive years the country experienced three major disasters. Fortunately one of the greatest of English diarists, Samuel Pepys (1633–1703), recorded the events in graphic detail. His diaries make compelling reading and give a wonderful insight into the times. The first disaster was the return of the bubonic plague in 1665. It was the last great outbreak and hit London especially hard; the city was brought to a standstill and tens of thousands died. Carts carrying the dead were wheeled through the dark, insanitary streets and crosses were painted on the doors of the houses where people had died.

In 1666, as the plague was diminishing, a fire started in a baker's shop in Pudding Lane and rapidly spread through London's closely-packed wooden buildings. The fire raged for three days; in some places the ground was too hot to walk upon for two weeks afterwards. Rebuilding started quickly, with an order from the king that buildings should be built of brick. Christopher Wren (1632–1723) rose to prominence as a surveyor and architect: his masterpiece, the new St Paul's Cathedral, rose phoenix-like from the ashes and was a marvel of its age with its high-spirited and dramatic classical style.

In 1665 the Second Dutch War had started, and by 1667 the king's finances were so depleted that he ordered the English fleet to be laid up in the Medway at the mouth of the Thames. The Dutch saw their chance, burnt several of the vessels and towed away the warship *The Royal Charles*. The English sailors, who were unpaid and mutinous, stood and watched.

ANTI-CATHOLICISM AND CATHOLICISM

Between 1668 and 1681 religion was often at the forefront of politics. Charles antagonised many Anglicans and Protestants by his support of Catholicism and by treaties with the French king Louis XIV. In 1670, in a secret clause in the Anglo-French Treaty of Dover, Charles agreed to 'reconcile himself with the Church of Rome as soon as his country's affairs permit', whereupon Louis would pay £150,000 and provide 6,000 troops to support Charles's, and England's, return to Catholicism. This clause remained secret, but there were other signs of the king's support for Catholics and collaboration with the French. Louis gave him a subsidy of £375,000 in 1670; in 1672 Charles issued a Declaration of Indulgence which allowed religious freedom for Catholics and nonconformists. Two days later England and France declared war against the Protestant Dutch.

To protect themselves the Dutch, under the leadership of William of Orange, broke the dykes, flooded the land and survived the campaign against them. This caused serious problems for Charles, who again ran out of money and was forced to call Parliament. Parliament was by now in angry mood and, fearful of the power of France and Catholicism, in 1673 passed the Test Act which compelled holders of public office to take the sacraments of the Church of England. Charles's brother and heir, James, Duke of York, was a Catholic and had to give up his position as Lord High Admiral.

Five years later, in 1678, another wave of anti-Catholic mania hit the country. A Protestant clergyman Titus Oates had heard a rumour of the possible forced conversion to Catholicism of England by French troops and, embellishing the facts, whipped public feeling to new heights with tales of plots to kill Charles and burn down Parliament. He was generally believed and several Catholics were hunted out and killed. Parliament agreed with the mood of the people and set about the radical step of excluding the rightful heir, James, Duke of York, from the throne because he was Catholic.

The 'Exclusion Crisis' over James's right to succeed to the throne focused attention upon two groups of MPs. Those who supported James tended to be Anglicans and were nicknamed 'Tories' after Catholic outlaws in Ireland. In opposition were the 'Whigs', so called after the Whiggamores who were fiercely Protestant Scottish drovers. The Whigs supported the claim of Charles's illegitimate son, the Protestant Duke of Monmouth. At times civil war seemed a possibility, but by 1681 the tide of anti-Catholicism was dying down and Charles decided to call a Parliament at Oxford, away from the Protestant mobs of London. Even so the Whigs were confident that Charles would have to give way because of his need for money; to their despair the king simply dissolved Parliament. Once again he had been in secret talks with Louis XIV, who had agreed to pay a subsidy so long as no more Protestant Parliaments were called.

After Parliament was dissolved Charles set about increasing his own power. In 1683 a plot was discovered by which the Whigs hoped to kill Charles and James at a lonely farm in Hertfordshire called Rye House. This gave Charles the excuse he needed and he executed his principal opponents. Popular opinion had changed so much that James was brought back to London and once again made Lord High Admiral. The succession was clear, and for the last years of his life Charles lived quietly, going to the races at Newmarket, walking in the parks with his dogs, called King Charles' spaniels, which he had brought over from Holland. He died on 2 February 1685 after a heart attack.

THE ARTS AND SCIENCE

In the arts the trend under the Stuarts was towards the secular and rational, with considerable influence from classicism. The great architect and theatre designer, Inigo Jones (1573–1652), and the inspired architect of many London buildings after the Great Fire in 1666, Sir Christopher Wren, both drew on fresh classical Roman sources, as did the painters Rubens (1577–1640) and van Dyck (1599–1641).

Drama declined from the heights of Shakespearean tragedy, through the bloodier and more secular Jacobean revenge plays of John Webster (*c.*1580–*c.*1634), Thomas Middleton (*c.*1580-1627) and Cyril Tourneur (*c.*1575–1626), to virtually nothing in mid-century. At the Restoration, the return of drama was largely to triviality and bombast. The poet and playwright Ben Jonson (1572–1637) and the poet Andrew Marvell (1621–78) both had an incisive clarity: the works of the Restoration composer Henry Purcell (1659–95) had a simple profundity.

The greatest literature was religious: John Donne's (*c.*1572–1631) meditations led to the great lyrics of George Herbert (1593–1633) and Henry Vaughan (1621–95) in mid-century. Slightly later, John Bunyan (1628–88) spoke for the very powerful forces of radical puritanism and the socially underprivileged in his writing, most notably *The Pilgrim's Progress*. After the Restoration John Dryden (1631–1700) consolidated English verse satire. The greatest literary figure of the century is the creator of the one true English language epic, and of some of the most powerful religious poetry outside the Bible, John Milton (1608–74). His *Paradise Lost* (1667) towers above everything else with its dramatic retelling of man's fall and its aim 'to justify the ways of God to man'.

One of the most lasting influences came from secular thought. Francis Bacon's (1561–1626) emphasis upon experimental science inspired the foundation of the Royal Society in 1662. The Society became the focus for scientific debate and attracted a wide range of scientists, including the chemist Robert Boyle (1627–91) and later the astronomer Edmund Halley (1656–1742). King Charles himself took a keen interest in the Society and founded the Royal Observatory at Greenwich in 1675: Wren designed the building. The second half of the century was dominated by two giants of the intellect, both of whom had powerful secularising effects: John Locke (1632–1704), whose theories of the mind laid the foundation for 'modern' thought, and Isaac Newton (1642–1727), whose mathematical explanation of physics founded the modern understanding and exploration of the universe.

James II, 1685–1688

On his accession James II's position was probably stronger than that of any previous Stuart, for in his last years Charles had milked Royalist feeling and destroyed the political power of the opposition. Yet James only lasted on the throne for three years. The reasons were twofold: his character and his religion. Like Charles II, he could be obstinate, but whereas Charles could modify his beliefs to fit in with the political climate, James was more high-principled: especially about religion. He summed up his attitude, stating that if he had 'agreed to live quietly and treat his religion as a private matter . . . he could have been one of the most powerful kings ever to reign in England . . . but he would think of nothing but the propagation of the Catholic religion'. It cost him his crown.

At first all went well: Parliament voted him £2 million, James recognised the Church of England as the established church, and a rebellion led by the Duke of Monmouth was defeated. Monmouth, the eldest illegitimate son of Charles II, landed at Lyme Regis in June 1685 and proclaimed himself king. It was a futile attempt and his forces were destroyed at the battle of Sedgemoor in Somerset in July. Monmouth was captured and executed, the executioner taking seven blows to behead him. A reign of terror by Judge Jeffreys in the south-west resulted in the execution of over 300 men and the transportation overseas of many more.

With the crown more secure than ever, James started to implement policies which favoured religious toleration for nonconformists and Catholics, but especially for Catholics. He launched a campaign to strengthen Catholics in high places: they replaced Protestants in the army, as heads of Oxford colleges, and in the most important offices of state. Protestants became fearful for the future. To any plea for concessions the king would say: 'I will make no concessions, my father made concessions and he was beheaded.' He continued the pressure for

Catholic equality and in 1687 issued a Declaration of Indulgence which aimed at complete religious toleration. Anglican opposition became vocal. In 1688 the Archbishop of Canterbury and six bishops wrote a letter pleading with James to reconsider. They were tried for 'seditious libel', but were then acquitted; they walked free through cheering crowds, amongst whom were strict nonconformists. Forty years before nonconformists and Anglicans had been on opposite sides in the Civil War; now they were united against Catholicism.

However, only intervention from outside England could cause James to change or reverse his policies. On the same day as the acquittal, the Bishop of London and six laymen – later called the Immortal Seven – invited William of Orange, the husband of Mary, James's daughter, to England to protect English Protestantism.

The Glorious Revolution

William had kept a close eye on the political situation in England through a network of agents who had spread propaganda and built up contacts. In 1688 a son was born to James II which meant that Mary was no longer next in line to the throne. William decided to accept the invitation from the Immortal Seven, knowing that powerful groups of supporters could be mobilised on his behalf in England.

William's tactics were twofold: to state that he wanted to protect Protestant rights – rather than bidding directly for the crown – and to avoid a civil war by not provoking full-scale battles. He evaded the English navy, which was expecting him to land on the east coast, and sailed to Torbay in Devon where he landed on 5 November 1688. He then marched slowly towards London, the Royalist forces retreating before him. James was no match for the situation, and, after his daughter Anne had deserted him, he fled. To William's embarrassment James was captured, but was allowed to escape again. (He arrived at the French court, where the verdict on him was: 'When you listen to him you realise why he is here.') William had defeated James without a battle.

Before leaving the country, James had tried to create a political vacuum by cancelling parliamentary writs, disbanding the army and throwing the Great Seal, which was needed to authorise major state decisions, into the Thames. The fear of anarchy meant that William was welcomed as a monarch who could restore law and order and preserve the Protestant succession, but there were still major problems to overcome, not least the question of who was to become monarch: William or Mary? Uniquely in English history Parliament agreed to recognise them as joint sovereigns – Mary was technically sovereign, but William refused to rule as only regent or consort. In return the new monarchs had to accept a Bill of Rights, which established the supremacy of Parliament over the monarchy. Under it the monarch could not suspend laws at will, as James had done, and made illegal a standing army in peacetime without parliamentary consent. Parliament also declared that the subject of its debates could not be questioned by the crown. The monarch still had considerable influence over government by making appointments to office, but the centre of political power was now located much more clearly in Parliament.

The results of the Glorious Revolution and the resulting Bill of Rights have been much debated. In 1688 Parliament's position in the constitution was relatively weak: by 1714 it had become the dominant part. One view is that the Bill of Rights was effectively a bargain agreed between the crown and Parliament which preserved and developed the English constitution. An alternative theory suggests that William's revolution was to link England closely with European wars and diplomacy; this in turn created the need for a greatly increased income from taxes and revenue to finance the higher expenditure. All of this revolutionised public finance and necessitated the calling of Parliament more frequently, thus enhancing parliamentary power.

William and Mary, 1689–1702

Although the reign was technically joint in nature, Mary handed over responsibility to William, believing in the biblical tenet, 'Wives, be obedient to your husbands in all things'. Mary died in 1694; behind his stern exterior William suffered greatly from his loss.

KING WILLIAM'S WAR, 1688–1697

William had held power in Holland as *Stadholder* and had successfully defeated the French invasion in 1672 by breaking the dykes and flooding the countryside (see p. 136). On becoming king of England his primary aims were to make the throne secure and to limit the power of the Sun King, Louis XIV of France. As a result England became involved in the European theatre of war, with William a prime instigator: he made all the major decisions himself, including preparing the Flanders campaigns, arranging subsidies, negotiating with the allies and concluding peace treaties. In February 1689 the Dutch declared war upon France; a Grand Alliance between Holland, England, Spain and many of the German states soon followed. France was now militarily and politically isolated and William's ambition of a coalition became a reality. However, he faced a serious threat in Ireland.

IRELAND

In 1689 James II left France for Ireland, in an attempt to use the country as a first step to regaining power in England. Ireland was already under the control of the Catholic Earl of Tyrconnel and James's arrival heightened Catholic fervour and support still further. The Parliament in Dublin passed a stream of anti-English legislation. The Protestant areas in the north became concerned and took refuge behind the city walls of such towns as Londonderry and Enniskillen. Even before James's arrival thirteen apprentice boys in 1688 had slammed the gates of Londonderry in the faces of Catholic troops – an event which is still celebrated to this day by the Protestants of Northern Ireland.

On 19 April 1689 the siege of Londonderry began. At its height the inhabitants were forced to eat dogs, rats and even candles and leather. English ships made several half-hearted attempts to relieve the city and finally succeeded on 30 July. An English army was sent to Ireland and won a major victory at the battle of the Boyne in 1690 when William himself took charge and inflicted a crushing defeat on the Catholic forces. Afterwards the war degenerated into skirmishes and lasted until 1691. More men lost their lives through illness than in battle.

By October 1692 the Irish Parliament was dominated by Protestants and William used the narrow band of Anglo-Irish landed nobility and gentry to keep the country subservient to English rule.

EUROPE

The war in Europe went generally in William's favour. There was no overall strategy in Flanders and two indecisive battles took place, at Steenkirk (1692) and Neerwinden (1693). The French captured several garrisons along the Meuse and William's major success was the recapture of Namur in 1695. At sea in 1690 a combined Anglo-Dutch fleet was beaten off Beachy Head but won a victory in the Bay of La Hogue. Eventually war weariness and lack of money meant that peace was concluded by the Treaty of Ryswick in 1697. Various territorial concessions were made by Louis XIV, but William's greatest gains were formal recognition as king of England, and a promise by Louis not to aid William's enemies, including James II.

POLITICS

The political identities of individual MPs were blurred and confusing, as members of such groups as the 'Whigs', 'Tories', 'Court', 'Country', 'Church', 'Patriots', 'Jacobites', 'Trimmers', 'Republicans' and 'Commonwealthmen' merged and split apart; the two most important groupings were the Whigs and the Tories. Broadly the Tories were less sure of the legality of William's claim to the throne and many still supported James II. They fervently supported the Anglican Church, but also wished to have a less expensive maritime war and to avoid the high costs of a land war. The Whigs supported the Protestant succession of William, tended to tolerate Protestant dissenters, and favoured a war against France even if this meant an expensive conflict in Europe. The general political pattern, therefore, was that the Whigs came to power in times of war and the Tories in times of peace. The Whigs, many of whom were city financiers, had the power and the means to be able to raise large amounts of money for the war effort. A major innovation was the Bank of England, founded in 1694, which persuaded people to invest with safety and thereby help the war effort. An important side effect of this development was that investors wanted internal stability and became unwilling to back efforts to overthrow the government by violent means.

From 1694–98 a Whig government, known as the Junto, had been in power, but with the peace they had fallen from grace. In 1701 Louis XIV once again attacked the Netherlands, and also placed an embargo upon English trade with France and Spain. The mood of the nation and Parliament swung towards war as Louis's expansionist policies became unacceptable. William began to prepare a land campaign against Louis, led by John Churchill (1650–1722), the Earl of Marlborough. Before the campaign could be launched, however, William was thrown from his horse, suffered a broken collar-bone and died from the resulting complications on 8 March 1702. As he and Mary were childless, the crown passed to her sister Anne, James II's second daughter, who was also a Protestant.

Queen Anne, 1702–1714

Queen Anne's character has been summed up as 'ordinary'. Apart from being queen there was nothing notable about her, and less so about her husband, Prince George of Denmark, whom one historian described as 'a kindly, negligible mortal'. George was not a clever man, ate and drank vastly, but was devoted to Anne as she was to him. The dominant themes of the reign were the foreign war, which only ended a year before her death, and the struggle for political supremacy between various factions.

MARLBOROUGH AND THE EUROPEAN WAR

Until 1707 Anne had a special and intense relationship with Sarah Churchill, whose husband had been made captain-general of the Grand Alliance against France, and in 1702 was created Duke of Marlborough. He was desperate to attack the French but was hindered by the Dutch who feared an invasion by France. In 1704 he collected his troops as if to give battle against the French on the Moselle; to the horror of the Dutch, he rapidly marched his troops past the appointed spot, through Germany and ended up facing the French army at Blenheim. His entire strategy depended on outright victory, for the Dutch border was left undefended and in England opposition to the expense of the war was growing. The resulting victory was one of the greatest in English history: the French army was routed with 14,000 casualties and 11,000 prisoners, including several French generals.

The battle of Blenheim was the start of a string of successes: Gibraltar was captured in 1704, and Marlborough defeated the French at Ramillies, Oudenarde and Malplaquet over the next five years. After the victory at Ramillies in 1704 he was promised a sumptuous palace at Woodstock, near Oxford, which was built at the expense of a grateful nation and named Blenheim. In 1707 Louis XIV sued for peace, but this was rejected and the war continued, ironically allowing the French to gain the upper hand. Only in 1713 was the Treaty of Utrecht signed between France and England, giving England some new possessions in Nova Scotia, Newfoundland, Gibraltar and Minorca, and the sole right to supply slaves to Spanish colonies. To many Europeans the treaty indicated that England now had a commercial and colonial supremacy, especially in the Americas.

POLITICS

The politics of the time followed the pattern established under William and Mary: in times of war the Whigs came to power (1705–10), in times of peace the Tories (1702–5, 1710–14). The reign also saw each party gaining increasingly separate identities and competition at both a national and local level became intense. In London different coffee-houses became centres of support, and nationally the growing numbers of newspapers were divided between the parties, which were now perceived as being so different that contemporary commentators thought that any co-operation between them would be like 'mixing Oyl and Vinegar' or like the 'lamb [lying] down with the leopard'.

THE UNION OF ENGLAND AND SCOTLAND

The most important measure to be passed by Parliament during Anne's reign was the political union of England and Scotland. James I had unified the crowns of the two countries but no more. The Scots and the English each had their own Parliaments and state religions, and as a result of the conflicts of the seventeenth century tensions had increased rather than diminished. The difficulty of having one king ruling two countries became apparent when a Scottish attempt to start a trading settlement on the coast of Panama ended in failure in 1698. King William had been displeased with the venture and refused to help the hundreds of

Scottish investors who had lost money. Union was made all the more urgent because many Scots supported James II, and France's traditional influence within Scotland might provoke rebellion.

William had proposed a union of the two countries, but he died before it could be implemented. Although Anne inherited the plans, it took another crisis before it was agreed. In 1704 the Scots declared that they would choose their own king on the death of Anne and support the choice by force; England threatened trade sanctions. War seemed likely for a time, but a compromise was reached whereby Scotland kept its own church and law courts but would be represented in the London Parliament and have equal trading rights with England. In 1707 the last Scottish Parliament assembled and on 1 May 1707 the 'United Kingdom of Great Britain' came into existence.

POLITICS AND ANNE'S LAST YEARS

By 1707 Anne had tired of her favourite, Sarah Churchill, Duchess of Marlborough, and replaced her with a Tory supporter, Abigail Masham. Following a libel case brought by the Whig government upon a Tory clergyman, the Tory party rallied in 1710 and gained such strength that the queen was able to dismiss the Whig government and replace it by Tory ministers. Marlborough was also dismissed on a charge of corruption, and he sought refuge abroad.

With Europe at peace, attention became focused on the issue of the succession. The Act of Settlement of 1701 had stipulated that the throne should pass to James I's granddaughter Sophia, Electress of Hanover, and her Protestant descendants. The heir-presumptive was therefore George of Hanover, but many Tories supported James II's son, James. By 1714 it was clear that Anne was dying. After vehement arguments between the two Tory leaders, Viscount Bolingbroke and the Earl of Oxford, she rejected them both and in the political vacuum the moderate and Whiggish Earl of Shrewsbury came to power. On 1 August 1714 Anne died widowed, friendless and almost forgotten, as Shrewsbury hurriedly secured the succession for George, Elector of Hanover.

CHAPTER SEVEN

Order and Disorder,
1714–1837

The political history of eighteenth-century England is dominated by five men: King George II (reigned 1727–60); his grandson George III (1760–1811); and in Parliament the prime ministers Robert Walpole (1720–42) and the father/son combination of William Pitt the Elder (1757–66) and William Pitt the Younger (1784–1806). At the same time industrial, commercial and religious forces were changing the face of England for ever.

THE HANOVERIAN SUCCESSION AND THE ROLE OF PARLIAMENT

Despite Anne's numerous children, none survived her. The strongest hereditary claim to the crown was that of James Stuart, the son of James II; to his supporters he was known as James III; his opponents called him 'the Pretender'. He was barred from the throne because he was Catholic, and the 1701 Act of Settlement had declared that the crown should pass to James I's Protestant granddaughter, Sophia, Electress of Hanover. Both Queen Anne and Sophia died in 1714 and so Sophia's son, George, became king of England at the age of fifty-four. It was a notable achievement for fifty-eight people could claim closer kinship to Queen Anne than George. Parliament had used its powers to dictate the succession and bypassed the hereditary right of a contender for the throne.

George I, 1714–1727

King George travelled from Hanover in 1714 and arrived in London in thick fog. It was an ominous portent, for he cared much more for his beloved Hanover than for England, knew nothing about the English Constitution, and spoke very little English. Even before he arrived his reputation had been somewhat tarnished, as he had locked up his errant wife in a tower for having an affair with a Swedish colonel; she was not even allowed to see her children again. This did not stop George having his own mistress, who was so thin that she was nicknamed the Maypole. His half-sister also had a huge influence upon him, and she was so fat that she was called the Elephant. The influence of these two and his two Turkish servants, and his pleasure in activities such as cutting out paper patterns, meant that soon jokes about him abounded. These jibes were used and augmented by the Jacobites, the supporters of James Stuart. On the day of George's coronation, 20 October, there were Jacobite riots in Birmingham, Bristol, Norwich and Reading, and later in Oxford, a strong centre of Jacobite support.

THE 1715 UPRISING

At the French court James Stuart waited to lead an invasion. Three uprisings were planned in 1715; the English government was most concerned about one in the south, but by a series of arrests and the garrisoning of troops in strategic towns such as Oxford, the threat was dispelled. The most serious uprisings took place in Scotland and the north of England, where the Jacobites rose in force. On 6 September 1715 James was proclaimed King James III at Braemar by the Earl of Mar (James himself was still in Paris); eighteen Scottish lords enthusiastically joined Mar and he soon had over 5,000 troops. At first the Jacobites were successful: Perth was captured and an expedition was sent south into Lancashire, where it occupied Preston on 10 November. This success was short-lived, for the English army forced them to surrender four days later. In Scotland on the previous day a battle between the English and Jacobites at Sheriffmuir was indecisive, but the morale of the rebels evaporated and many went home.

In December 1715 James Stuart arrived in Scotland, though without the hoped-for French army. His six-week stay was one of continual disappointment, and his depressing face and uninspiring speeches did nothing to help. James left Scotland in February 1716 and eventually settled in Rome, where he lived on a pittance from his supporters. The Jacobite uprising faded away and a potential crisis had come and gone – although a much more serious one occurred later when James's son, 'Bonnie Prince Charlie', led the rebellion of 1745.

THE SOUTH SEA BUBBLE

The second crisis of the reign was equally serious, though very different. The South Sea Company had been founded in 1711; in 1713 it had acquired a monopoly in the Spanish slave trade and trade opportunities in South America. When the government agreed that the company should finance the National Debt the share prices rose dramatically; many people were gripped by share fever. At the beginning of 1720 £100 worth of stock in the South Sea Company was valued at £128; by June it had reached £745 and by July £1,000. A swarm of companies buzzed into life: the more dubious included schemes for importing jackasses from Spain, or for producing radish oil. By September the bubble had burst and the valuation of stock tumbled. By 1 October the price was down to £290. Those who sold out in time made a fortune, but large numbers of people were financially ruined.

The South Sea fiasco had political implications as well. Those who had lost money were outraged, especially as several government ministers had been implicated. If the government was defeated, an election would be called and Jacobite supporters might be returned. Several government ministers were ruined, both financially and politically, but the crisis was the making of Robert Walpole (1676–1745), who was now looked to as someone who could sort out the financial chaos.

ROBERT WALPOLE: THE FIRST PRIME MINISTER

Despite the outcry over the South Sea Bubble affair, Walpole defended the implicated ministers and the crown. He was derisively called 'the Screen' for his protection, but his actions were rewarded in 1721 when the king promoted him to be Chancellor of the Exchequer. Walpole proceeded to lead the House of Commons for the next twenty years. He belonged to a well-established Norfolk family and had the appearance of a typical country gentleman; he had a red face, a hearty laugh and was described as a 'coarse, noisy fellow'; he boasted that 'he always talked bawdy, because in that all could join'. Politically Walpole was a Whig, and two of his principal beliefs were in the power of Parliament and in the benefits of keeping the country at peace. He actively encouraged trade by the removal of certain export duties, and his love of peace meant that money and manpower were not wasted on warfare. In 1733 he proudly told the queen, '50,000 men [are] slain this year in Europe, and not one Englishman'.

His political position was further strengthened by the new dynasty. In the 1701 Act of Settlement Parliament had insisted that there should be a Privy Council of eighty members. This arrangement proved to be unwieldy and George I reduced it to thirty, from which a smaller group formed the cabinet, and a smaller group still of about six formed the inner cabinet. It was here that important decisions were made. Whether George I's lack of English was the main reason why he did not attend the cabinet meetings is debatable, but he was often abroad and as a result the cabinet acquired an increased element of power. The idea of a first minister among equals, called the prime minister, had developed, but this position was always occupied by a peer, who could not exercise direct control over the House of Commons. Walpole refused to be made a lord, so that he could influence the lower house; thus he is often regarded as the first prime minister. He flourished in this role and used it to increase his power, much to the annoyance of his political enemies. When George I suddenly died of a heart attack in 1727 whilst travelling to Hanover, Walpole's opponents were delighted as they foresaw his downfall.

George II, 1727–1760

In his early life one of George II's passions was hatred of his father; the dislike was mutual. The prince had been so determined to see his mother, imprisoned in Hanover, that he had swum across the moat. George I distrusted his son and in 1717 had first placed him under virtual house arrest, and then banished him from court, whereupon the prince and his companions became the centre of the opposition.

Prince George succeeded to the throne at the age of forty-four. Like his father he was not the most intelligent of men, and he could be strong-willed; unlike his father he was influenced and at times subtly dominated by his wife, the intelligent Caroline of Anspach. She and Walpole got on famously (or as many saw it at the time infamously – for there were rumours of an affair). The queen's influence helped Walpole to keep his position as prime minister in the new reign. His enemies continued to accuse him of corruption and of putting relatives into government posts. In 1737 George II and Walpole each received a severe blow with the death of Queen Caroline. From then onwards Walpole found it harder to maintain his supremacy, and was subjected to considerable pressure to commit the nation to war.

THE WAR OF THE AUSTRIAN SUCCESSION, 1741–1748

Since the Treaty of Utrecht in 1713 the British had a limited trading right with the Spanish colonies, but a thriving illicit trade had grown up. The Spanish disrupted this trade by a growing number of coastguards: between 1713 and 1731 they boarded 180 British ships. After a lull in coastguard activity in the mid-1730s, the Spanish resumed their patrols. The opposition in Parliament was outraged, especially when a Captain Jenkins presented his ear (which had been torn off by the Spanish in 1731 and was now pickled in a bottle) and used the incident as an excuse for war. After failing to find a compromise Walpole was forced into war with Spain in 1739.

War had also broken out in Europe. A coalition of Central European rulers, with French support, had formed to despoil the new Archduchess of Austria, Maria Theresa, of her lands in Austria, Bohemia and Hungary. England became involved because of George II's concern about the security of his Hanoverian homelands; in 1741 he received a subsidy of £300,000 from Parliament and went to Hanover to organise the war against France. Eventually his fear of a French invasion of the electorate led to a treaty being signed in 1741; it was seen as a humiliating sign of weakness. Many MPs held Walpole responsible, and after a succession of defeats in the Commons, he resigned in February 1742. It was a move of constitutional importance: the king had requested him to stay, but Walpole had fallen because he had lost the support of the Commons. It was now not enough solely to have the backing of the monarch. Walpole was promoted to the House of Lords, with the title Earl of Orford, and died three years later in 1745.

George II tried to maintain the neutrality of the electorate in the European wars, but occasionally he was forced to fight. In 1743 he commanded the Hanoverian forces and won a great victory over the French at Dettingen. (This was the last time a British monarch commanded an army and led it into battle.) Despite the victory George's desire for neutrality continued and he was criticised for not following it up by an attack upon France. There were other successes, and France and Spain were pushed onto the defensive. France saw England as the cause of her European troubles and so declared war in 1744: the European war was no longer about protecting a distant country but the security of England itself. As most English troops were protecting Hanover, the country was vulnerable to invasion. The French prepared a large fleet, but the transport ships were wrecked by a storm the night before their departure for England and the invasion was cancelled.

The following year a more successful attempt to overthrow the Hanoverians was made, this time by the Jacobites led by 'Bonnie' Prince Charles.

THE YOUNG PRETENDER

In 1745 Charles Edward Stuart (1720–88), son of James Stuart and grandson of James II, set out for Scotland. He was in his early twenties and seems to have been the young dashing hero of legend, having distinguished himself at the battle of Dettingen against George II. He was convinced that Scotland and England would rally to his support.

The campaign did not get off to a good start. On 23 July Prince Charles landed on the Isle of Eriskay in the Outer Hebrides on a 44-gun frigate with only seven men. The first man he met advised him to go home, to which the prince replied, 'I am come home'. French support and troops were needed to ensure the success of the invasion, but France waited to see the outcome of Charles's plans and his success. He had to rely on the power of his personality and his illustrious name to raise supplies and troops, but within weeks he had an army of 1,500 and captured Falkirk, followed by the great prize of Edinburgh on 17 September. Four days later the English forces were routed at Preston-pans and Scotland was now in his control.

By the end of October Charles had an army of some 6,000 men and the decision was taken, on the rumour of widespread Jacobite support in Lancashire, to advance into England. As the army moved south it became more depleted as people returned to the Highlands, but the Jacobites entered Carlisle, marched to Manchester, and then on 4 December captured Derby. Panic broke out in London and people withdrew money from the banks as fast as they could – it was alleged that withdrawals were only slowed down by paying out in sixpences or by heating the coins to make them too hot to handle. (The great popularity of what became the British national anthem, 'God Save the King', dates from this time.) English reinforcements were rapidly brought over from Flanders.

The expected flood of followers to the Jacobite cause in Lancashire had not materialised and at Derby Prince Charles reluctantly agreed to return to Scotland. The long retreat began. The French invasion force, which had collected at Dunkirk and could have saved the rebellion, was unable to leave because of the English ships patrolling the Channel. The Jacobites retreated northwards, with an occasional success, as at Falkirk in 1746, but they were constantly harried by the English army. The final decisive battle took place on 16 April 1746 at Culloden, near Inverness. The Jacobites gained some new recruits in Scotland but the Duke of Cumberland's English forces outnumbered the 5,000 or so Jacobites. The terrain favoured the English, who set about destroying the Jacobite ranks with their eighteen heavy field-guns: when the Jacobites charged they were cut down mercilessly. The battle was over in forty minutes and afterwards Cumberland told his troops not to spare the wounded. He then ordered that suspects should be shot, crops burnt and cottages destroyed, for which he earned the nickname 'Butcher Cumberland'. These actions were perhaps unnecessarily harsh, but indicated the English fear of the claims of Prince Charles and the threat posed by the Scots. After all, the 'Young Pretender' had successfully kept an army in the field for over a year, had advanced as far as Derby, and had shown how ill-prepared the English forces were.

Charles fled and hid in the Highlands. He was not betrayed, despite the huge £30,000 price on his head; with the help of such supporters as Flora MacDonald he escaped to France. On the continent he roamed from one country to another and although he married he produced no heir. He died in 1788 at Rome, one hundred years after his grandfather, James II, had lost his throne. The Jacobite cause finally died with him.

WILLIAM PITT AND THE SEVEN YEARS' WAR, 1756–1763

With the political downfall of Walpole in 1742, a new star emerged in Parliament, that of William Pitt (later known as the Elder Pitt). Unlike Walpole, who favoured peace, Pitt believed that the strength of the British economy depended on defending trade and overseas expansion: 'When trade is at stake, you must defend it or perish.' After the Treaty of Aix-la-Chapelle, which ended the war of the Austrian Succession in 1748, war again broke out in 1756. Once more Britain was at war with France, mainly over colonies and commerce. The main areas of conflict were in the Americas and India. Britain's ally, Prussia, fought against France and Austria in Europe. In Britain Pitt was seen as the only viable prime minister for the war, although his overwhelming self-confidence and such statements as 'I know I can save the country and I alone can' did not endear him to many in Parliament.

The first few years of the war were disastrous. In North America Fort Oswego was lost to the French and an attack on Fort Niagara was abandoned. In Europe the French occupied the Hanoverian homelands in 1757; a national scapegoat was found in Admiral Byng, who was blamed for the loss of Minorca to the French when he called off a naval engagement in 1757. The patriotic uproar was so great that he was executed – 'to encourage the others', as Voltaire wryly remarked.

From 1758 the combination of Pitt's organisational skills and firm objectives led to a succession of British victories. In that year Britain captured the French Fort Duquesne in America, which was renamed Fort Pitt and later became known as Pittsburgh, Guadeloupe in the West Indies, and Senegal, the West African centre of the French slave trade. French fleets in the Channel and the Mediterranean were also destroyed. A further success in 1758, the capture of Louisburg at the mouth of the St Lawrence river, had enhanced the reputation of General Wolfe. His unorthodox military methods were disliked by his seniors and they hinted that he was insane. In which case, George II commented, he hoped Wolfe 'would bite some of his other generals'. The king's confidence in Wolfe was fully repaid in 1759 when he brilliantly captured the French Canadian fortress of Quebec. Five thousand men were rowed with muffled oars past the French positions and climbed a tiny trackway up to the plains overlooking the city. After a fierce day's fighting Quebec was taken on 13 September 1759, although Wolfe was mortally wounded. In 1760 France formally surrendered Canada to Britain. At the height of these military successes, George II died aged seventy-eight.

George III, 1760–1820

George II's son, Frederick, Prince of Wales, had died in 1751 and he was succeeded by his 22-year-old grandson. As the new king, George III had several advantages over his grandfather and his great-grandfather: he was the first monarch since Queen Anne to be born and educated in England and to speak English without a foreign accent. He was described as 'tall and full of dignity', and he had a strong sense of religion. This led him to issue proclamations to encourage piety and virtue at court, which he thought had become morally disreputable in the previous reign. As a young man he had had several short-lived love affairs and was persuaded out of them by his mentor, the Earl of Bute. George eventually married Charlotte of Mecklenburg-Strelitz. She was considered plain in looks and dull in character but George, ever mindful of his duty, remained loyal and the marriage produced fifteen legitimate children.

There are various ways of interpreting George III's policies. One, which was widely publicised by his opponents, was that he was intent on restoring Stuart despotism. He appointed four different men to lead the government in the 1760s: the Earl of Bute (1762–3), George Grenville (1763–5), the Marquess of Rockingham (1765–6), and then the Elder Pitt (1766–7), now Earl of Chatham, enabling his critics to claim that he wanted to control policy through puppet prime ministers. The Wilkes' affair and the assertion of royal control over the American colonies encouraged the view that the king was essentially a tyrant.

Yet these criticisms were not compatible with George's character or the way in which he saw his own constitutional role. The king agreed with his mother's opinion that his grandfather, George II, had been a puppet at the hands of Parliament, and he was determined to redress the balance. But a *balance* it was, and he was determined to defend the rights of Parliament, the rights of the monarchy, and the power and might of the empire at whatever the cost. These were the fundamental concepts behind his policies, but his fatal flaw was his insecurity. A strong minister might have relieved George of some of his burdens, but he chose loyal, rather than able, politicians. The best example of this trait can be found in the friendship between George III and his prime minister Lord North (1770–82). In many ways George III ruled Lord North, and both were tarred with the same brush over the loss of the thirteen American colonies.

PEACE, WILKES AND LIBERTY

The war against France and Spain continued to be a success for Britain. Several West Indian islands were captured from the French as well as Spain's Cuban naval base of Havana. British successes forced the French and Spanish to submit and in 1763 George III signed the treaty ending the Seven Years' War. Many powerful people were horrified at the cessation of such a successful war, especially as newly acquired possessions such as the lucrative island of Guadeloupe and the fishing rights off Newfoundland were returned to the French. Pitt was incensed, and though he was ill he made a three and a half-hour speech in the Commons, in which he asserted that France 'is chiefly if not solely to be dreaded by us in the light of a maritime and commercial power . . . and we have given her the means of recovering her prodigious losses and becoming once more formidable to us at sea.'

There were other critics of the treaty, notably John Wilkes (1727–97), a journalist and MP. Attacks upon the government had been increasing in the newly emerging newspapers, and in the *The North Briton* Wilkes fiercely criticised the crown and the establishment. In issue 45, published on 23 April 1763, he went too far and attacked the king himself. Wilkes was put in prison, but was released because he was an MP and won his case for compensation. 'Wilkes and Liberty' became the rallying call for those people anxious to limit the power of the crown. The cry even reached the disaffected elements in the American colonies. After various escapades, such as a duel which got him thrown out of the Commons and amorous adventures on the continent, Wilkes returned and once again stood for Parliament. To the crown's horror he was elected; expelled from Parliament, he was re-elected, re-expelled and re-elected again – but this time Parliament declared his opponent the winner. Wilkes challenged this decision and eventually took his seat. He later became Lord Mayor of London and allowed a printer to publish parliamentary debates, thereby setting a precedent which continues to this day. By his actions Wilkes had highlighted many people's fear of arbitrary government: Pitt himself had insisted that the liberties of all Englishmen would be in jeopardy if the government's pressure upon Wilkes was successful.

JOHN WESLEY AND METHODISM

The early decades of the eighteenth century in England were marked by a lack of religious zeal. As the country grew in prosperity, people looked back with distaste on the religious turmoil of the previous century; in religion, as in politics, it was thought that the head should rule the heart. Many people preferred good humour and good manners to religious fanaticism. The order of society was maintained and, with many of the Anglican clergy coming from the local gentry, it was not surprising they had a conservative outlook.

Into this tranquil religious atmosphere stepped John Wesley (1703–91). In 1729 he and George Whitefield set up a society which was devoted to a method of Christianity based on prayer, self-sacrifice and charitable deeds. They were criticised as being 'Bible Moths' or 'Methodists'. For nine years Wesley was unsure of the exact nature of his faith, until 'a quarter before nine' on 24 May 1738, when his heart felt 'strangely warmed', 'I felt a trust in Christ, Christ alone for my salvation'. From then on he treated 'the world as his parish' and devoted himself to preaching. In the next fifty-three years he travelled 224,000 miles and preached over 40,000 sermons – an average of over two a day. His aim was to stir religious feelings and to make his audiences choose between sin and salvation.

Early Methodists were largely drawn from the poorer classes, such as the tin miners of Cornwall and the urban poor whom the Church of England had ignored. Wesley wanted to work within the established church, but Anglicans and aristocrats treated the Methodist movement with deep suspicion; the aristocratic reaction was summed up by the Duchess of Buckingham, who said, 'It is monstrous to be told that you have a heart as sinful as the common wretches that crawl upon the earth.' Inevitably Wesley was forced to create his own organisation, which irrevocably split from the Anglican Church in 1784, by which time 356 Methodist chapels existed. This break away greatly strengthened the dissenting religious tradition inherited from the age of the great Puritan rebellion against King and Church in the seventeenth century.

THE ARTS

In the first half of the eighteenth century the dominating element in philosophy and the arts was 'reasonableness', a concept based on the assumption of what was 'generally true'. Its inspiration came from classical Roman sources, so much so that the poets and translators were collectively known as 'Augustans', a term which referred to the heyday of classical writing in the reign of the Emperor Augustus. It was a great age for translations – Alexander Pope (1688–1744) made a fortune out of his Homer – but the best that the English Augustans in classical forms could achieve was mock-epic, a type of brilliant satire never surpassed. Pope's two masterpieces, the *Rape of the Lock* and *The Dunciad*, had serious intent – the latter attacked Walpole for what was seen as political corruption. For four decades the energy of all the satirical endeavour came from a group of writers, dominated by Pope, Jonathan Swift (1667–1745) and John Gay (1685–1732), calling themselves the Scriblerus Club.

In painting, too, satire was used to great effect, reaching its peak in the work of William Hogarth (1697–1764). Generally, however, painting celebrated the newly acquired wealth and social standing of individuals with brilliant full-length portraits set in ordered landscapes, as in those by Thomas Gainsborough (1727–88) and Joshua Reynolds (1723–92). Lavishly designed formal landscapes and parks also formed the settings for the great new country houses of Blenheim, Chatsworth and Castle Howard; Italian influences were strong in these displays. They were strong too in music, especially in the early work of the German G. F. Handel, who arrived in England in 1710. He was closely involved with the court and his *Dettingen Te Deum* celebrates the 1743 victory; his *Music for the Royal Fireworks* was to celebrate the Peace of Aix-la-Chapelle. His later operas and oratorios, especially the *Messiah* of 1742, were powerfully conceived and widely performed.

The court was based in London; so were nearly all the people who were thought to matter. At the start of the century, the loose fictions of Daniel Defoe (1660–1731) ranged widely, though focused on the middle-classes (even his hero Robinson Crusoe acts like a local tradesman, alone on the desert island). It is generally agreed that the birth of the novel as a proper form was in the 1740s with *Pamela*, followed by *Clarissa*, written by Samuel Richardson (1689–1761); Henry Fielding (1707–54) with *Joseph Andrews* and his masterpiece *Tom Jones*. A form of controlled anarchy was expressed in the extraordinary and influential *Tristram Shandy*, by Laurence Sterne (1713–68). The towering literary figure of the last half of the century was Samuel Johnson (1709–84), whose penetrating understanding of so much of what he experienced was accurately recorded in the first biography in English, *The Life of Samuel Johnson* by James Boswell (1740–95). Johnson's appeal to what was 'common sense', may sum up the century; his influence was great, even to Jane Austen (1775–1817), whose six fine novels still bring lasting pleasure and admiration.

The American War of Independence

North America had been explored and first settled in the sixteenth century. A series of separate settlements and areas had developed along the narrow coastal strip of the Atlantic seaboard, and their names indicated the British connection: New England, New York, Virginia (after the virgin Queen Elizabeth), and the landing point of the Pilgrim Fathers, Plymouth Rock. The settlements were primarily commercial enterprises set up by individuals or companies, or havens from religious persecution, but the fierce conflict of the Seven Years' War (see p. 154) indicated how valuable a prize North America had become. The expense of the Seven Years' War in the Americas led the British government, entirely reasonably in its view, to impose certain taxes upon the colonists to pay for their own defence; the most controversial of these were the 1764 sugar tax and the 1765 stamp duty. There was resistance to the enforcement of these taxes and the colonists began to insist that their own assemblies had exclusive control over internal policies and the raising of revenue. Whilst all but the extremists emphasised that they were loyal British subjects, the cry of 'No Taxation without Representation' was gaining strength as a rallying cry – although it was essentially propagandist as few American colonists wanted to be represented in the British Parliament.

Gradually the situation got worse. In 1770 a local confrontation led to five Bostonians being killed and the colonial press had a field day describing the 'Boston Massacre'. In 1773 Boston was again the centre of events when, as a gesture against continuing taxation, £10,000 worth of tea was flung into Boston Harbour, an event which became the 'Boston Tea Party' of folklore. The harbour was closed as a reprisal and many colonists became more determined to resist what they saw as British aggression. In September 1774 the first Continental Congress of twelve colonies met at Philadelphia. The divisions between Crown and colonists widened, especially in the next couple of years when a succession of battles (Lexington, Concord, Bunker's Hill) demonstrated that open war had erupted between the colonists and Britain. In 1776 Thomas Jefferson produced the Declaration of Independence. It is a remarkable document, not only for the then revolutionary assertion that 'all men are created equal', but also because there was a major shift in political emphasis: previously the revolutionaries had sought to protect their traditional British rights against Parliament; now they stated they were protecting their *natural* rights against a supposedly tyrannical George III.

A turning-point came in 1777, with a surprise surrender of the British army at Saratoga in October and the missed opportunity over the winter to eliminate the American army led by George Washington (1732–99) at Valley Forge. Other European powers now became involved, with the French, Spanish and Dutch all declaring war on Britain. Britain was thus fighting a land battle in America and a maritime war against other European naval powers. Elsewhere the rest of the British Empire was vulnerable: Gibraltar was attacked, Minorca was lost and the West Indies threatened. The American war effectively ended in 1781 when the British General Cornwallis was forced to surrender at Yorktown. The

Treaty of Versailles in 1783 recognised the independence of the American colonies. The first British Empire had come to an end, and the words of a French statesman seemed all too true: 'Colonies are like fruit which drops from the tree when ripe.'

William Pitt 'the Younger'

The loss of the American colonies led to rapid changes in British politics. Britain had suffered a terrible military blow and Lord North resigned in 1782. The combination of the loss of the American colonies and the resignation of North, whom George III had so steadfastly supported, caused the king to consider abdication. He remained, however, and within a year he had a new and powerful ally in Parliament, William Pitt 'the Younger'.

William Pitt (1759–1806), the son of William Pitt 'the Elder', showed academic brilliance and political insight from an early age. At fourteen he went to Cambridge, where he was noted as a mathematician, poet and historian. By twenty he was an MP and in 1783, at the age of twenty-four, he accepted the office of prime minister. As a personality he was considered isolated, with none of the geniality of his principal rival Charles James Fox (1749–1806), but he was a brilliant speaker and dominated the House of Commons. His time in office can be separated into two parts, the years of peace (1783–93) and the years of war against the French (1793–1806).

The American War of Independence had resulted in a national debt of £243 million, unstable political groupings and depression. Pitt set about reinvigorating the country's financial position. Customs duties were reorganised, which made imports cheaper and smuggling less profitable, and taxes were increased – the best known amongst these is the 'Window Tax', which was implemented if a house had more than seven windows. Trade was encouraged and a commercial treaty was signed with France in 1786. When opposition was raised against the treaty Pitt pointed out that while France had gained a new market of eight million people for their goods; Britain had gained a market of twenty-four million French citizens.

The Growth of Empire

AUSTRALIA

One result of the loss of the American colonies was that the legal system had lost an area to which convicted criminals could be transported. Other places were now sought, for the conviction rate was high – there were over 160 offences for which a criminal could be transported – and the jails were overcrowded. The coasts of Africa and South Africa were both considered, but the final solution was to send convicts to Botany Bay in Australia. In 1788 the first shipload of 750 convicts arrived; for the next half-century the Australian colonists received thousands of convicted felons as well as far greater numbers of free settlers.

The claiming of Australia for Britain had been the work of Captain James Cook (1728–79) in 1769–70. He had previously been a key figure in charting the St Lawrence river before Wolfe's attack on Quebec (see p. 154), and he used his mapping skills to great effect around the coasts of Australia and New Zealand. It was Cook who discovered that New Zealand was, in fact, two islands. Whilst still at the height of his powers he was killed by native warriors in Hawaii.

INDIA

In 1600 the East India Company had been formed. At first it established a few small trading centres, depending for their existence upon the tolerance of local rulers. Goods from India became fashionable in England as the growing population bought more tea, silks, sugar and cotton. Between 1709 and 1749 England's trade with India doubled from £1 million to £2 million. As business increased, so the commercial and political power of the East India Company grew.

Britain was not alone in establishing herself in India, and by 1744 the principal enemy was France. During the war of the Austrian Succession (see p. 151) the small French and British forces attacked one another. By 1748 the French governor, Dupleix, had the upper hand and controlled many of the local princes. Only a desperate remedy could save the British from being forced out of India altogether. In this situation Robert Clive (1725–74) of the East India Company won an unexpected victory in 1751 which proved to be the turning-point of the war. He attacked the pro-French town of Arcot with 800 men and sent 5,000 fleeing in panic. The French East India Company, worried by the financial implications of its involvement in India, withdrew Dupleix and so left the way clear for the growth of British influence.

The British forces still had to contend with local princes, such as the Nawab of Bengal. In 1756 the infamous incident of the 'Black Hole of Calcutta' occurred when 146 British prisoners were kept overnight by the Nawab in a room 18 feet by 14 feet; in the morning only twenty-three remained alive. Revenge came the following year when Clive defeated the Nawab at the battle of Plassey. He was appointed governor of Bengal and amassed a great fortune, though as he said later, 'I stand amazed at my own moderation'. The company's influence in India continually grew as it gained control of appointments, finances, land and power.

By 1772 corruption among company officials and traders was rife, a terrible famine had killed a third of the population of Bengal, and, as Clive said, 'the Augean stable there is to be cleared'. The government decided to intervene and in that year increased its supervisory role over the company. Warren Hastings was sent out as governor-general and he proved to be one of the greatest figures in the history of British India. He set about reforming the legal and financial systems, though he was often impeded by the members of his own council. Eventually his opponents got the upper hand and Hastings was ordered back to England and impeached by Parliament in 1788. His trial for corruption and cruelty took seven years; the cost of his defence used up his personal fortune and, though he was acquitted, he was impoverished until the East India Company gave him a large pension. His reforms and defence of British interests meant that the company's position in India was secure. The basic pattern of government there was not changed again until 1858.

The French Revolution and The Napoleonic Wars

As the trial of Hastings progressed, the public's attention shifted towards France. When the Bastille fell in July 1789 opinions quickly became divided. In Parliament the opposition leader Charles James Fox declared it was the 'greatest event that has happened in the world' and the poet William Wordsworth found it 'bliss to be alive'. All over the country 'Correspondence clubs' were set up urging support for the Revolution and to further its aims in Britain. Theoretical backing was given by Thomas Paine (1737–1809) in his famous book *The Rights of Man*.

Unsurprisingly a reaction set in. The chief defender of the State and of the status quo was Edmund Burke (1729–97); his most famous work, *Reflections on the Revolution in France*, attacked the French Revolution. Soon the situation on the continent began to look more threatening. France occupied Belgium and increased its influence across Europe. To counter the threat, in 1793 Britain declared war. British forces were ineffectual and in 1797 the navy mutinied twice, which sent shock waves through the financial markets. The war took a new turn when Napoleon Bonaparte became a general of the Republican armies; in 1798 France invaded Rome, imprisoned the pope, captured Malta and proceeded to Egypt.

Napoleon's triumphs were thwarted by the Royal Navy and Horatio Nelson (1758–1805). Nelson had risen rapidly through the ranks of the navy and his early exploits included killing a bear single-handed in the Arctic and making daring attacks on Spanish ships. His first victory as a commander came in 1798 when he annihilated the French fleet amidst the sand-banks of the Nile. Whilst Napoleon dominated Europe through military success and diplomacy, the British controlled the seas; Napoleon commented: 'Whenever there is water to float a ship, we are sure to find you in the way.' In 1801 a deadlock in the war produced the temporary Peace of Amiens. Meanwhile Pitt had resigned because of the situation in Ireland.

IRELAND

Since the Middle Ages Ireland had had its own Parliament, which enjoyed limited power. In an attempt to win greater independence, and inspired by the American revolutionary example, a separate Irish 'Volunteer' force was created. This display of strength enabled the Irish leader, Henry Grattan, to extract a Declaration of Independence from the British government in 1782. Further pressure was exerted in 1791 when the Society of United Irishmen was founded, based on republican ideas from France. When the war between Britain and France broke out the French sent a fleet of thirty-five ships to Bantry Bay in southern Ireland to help the Irish win freedom: the planned invasion only failed because of a gale.

A sequence of rebellions and merciless reprisals convinced Pitt that the two nations should be united and that the Parliament in Dublin should be incorporated into that in London. An Act of Union became law on 1 January 1801 and the nation became known as the 'United Kingdom of Great Britain and Ireland'. Pitt had also promised concessions for Catholics, but when George III refused – because he believed it would be breaking his coronation oath to defend the Protestant religion – Pitt resigned.

NAPOLEON, NELSON AND WELLINGTON

After Pitt's resignation and the Peace of Amiens, the new prime minister, Henry Addington, initially set about disarming to save money. British tourists flocked to France to see the new bridges, buildings and roads being constructed. The peace was short-lived: the tourists remaining when war was resumed were interned.

Napoleon, who had styled himself Emperor of the French in 1805, was determined to conquer Britain either by invasion or blockade. By 1805 his army was encamped along the French coast, but an invasion was impossible whilst the British navy patrolled the Channel. Britain rapidly built seventy-three military forts along the coast, called Martello Towers. Volunteers were armed; even Pitt, who replaced Addington as wartime prime minister, received a uniform and gun.

Everything depended upon sea power. In 1805 a French fleet attacked the British possessions in the West Indies and returned home with Nelson hard on their heels; ahead of them lay further British naval forces, so the French commander-in-chief, Villeneuve, took refuge at Cadiz. On 21 October the two fleets met near the Straits of Gibraltar, at Trafalgar. Before the battle Nelson hoisted from his flagship *Victory* the message 'England expects that every man shall do his duty'. The French and Spanish fleets were overwhelmed; towards the end of the battle Nelson died from a sniper's bullet. As a memorial Trafalgar Square was laid out in London: standing in the middle is Nelson's

Column, with a statue of England's greatest admiral on top.

Though the possibility of invasion passed, the war still had many years to run. Napoleon closed all the European ports under his power to British trade, and this, combined with grain shortages, led to hunger and poverty for many. The war had reached an impasse: Britain could not be attacked, but had no strong foothold on the continent. In 1807 Napoleon invaded Spain and Portugal. The resulting nationalist uprisings against him allowed British forces to gain a foothold in the Iberian Peninsula. In 1809 a successful campaign in the peninsula was led by Arthur Wellesley, later the Duke of Wellington (1769–1852). It has been suggested that he acted as the role model for Victorian schoolboys (and hence the British character), for Wellington kept his emotions under control and stuck doggedly to his task. He was helped by Spanish guerrillas, who were tenacious fighters; their combined efforts slowly pushed back the French, whose reserves were now being used for the invasion of Russia. Napoleon's Russian campaign was a disaster; his European enemies

The Duke of Wellington

united against him, Paris was taken, and with Wellington in Toulouse Napoleon was forced to come to terms. In 1814 he was banished to Elba, off the coast of Italy, with a large pension.

The following year Napoleon escaped from the island and landed in France; supporters flocked to him. Only two armies had remained in the field, the British under the command of Wellington, and the Prussian under Blücher. Napoleon moved swiftly to avoid the armies uniting, defeated the Prussians, and forced Wellington to retreat to Waterloo in Belgium. On Sunday 18 June 1815 Wellington and Napoleon met in battle for the only time. The waves of French attack were resisted and in the late afternoon Blücher's regrouped Prussian troops attacked the unguarded flank of the French, who broke and fled. Napoleon's dreams of maintaining a great French Empire vanished and he was sent into exile on the island of St Helena, where he died in 1821.

THE AGRICULTURAL REVOLUTION

When George III came to the throne in 1760, agriculture and agricultural techniques were changing. There had been several innovations by individuals earlier in the century, but these tended to take many years before they were accepted by the farming community. In 1700 Jethro Tull invented a seed drill which buried the seeds at a uniform depth instead of throwing them onto the ground; he was rewarded by a bumper crop the following year. In the 1730s Walpole's brother-in-law, Viscount Townshend, developed a system for rotating crops on the same field all the year round. Later in the eighteenth century new methods of animal breeding by Bakewell and Coke led to increased production of meat, cheese and milk. For the successful farmer there were huge profits to be made, helped by the increased demand of the growing population.

The attraction of high profits led landlords to 'enclose' fields, by fencing off land into large units, rather than maintain the small individual strips used since medieval times. For the poor, enclosure was often disastrous: they were forced from their homes and lost their jobs and livelihoods. After 1760 the pace of enclosure quickened, and by 1801 six million acres had been enclosed in England. The Napoleonic Wars produced price rises of food and land which increased enclosures still further.

THE INDUSTRIAL REVOLUTION

Historians have placed the start of the Industrial Revolution anywhere between 1650 and 1800, but most would agree that a real take-off in manufacturing output started in the 1740s and continued well into the nineteenth century. It is futile to look for a single cause, for the economic picture then, as now, was a tangled web of interlocking systems. Population increase meant a greater market, war acted both as a hindrance, because of disrupted supplies, but also created military demand, and new scientific ideas fed back into industry. As early as 1709 Abraham Darby had discovered a method for using coal to smelt iron, but he kept the process a family secret for forty years. When the process became widely known, the third Abraham Darby and John Wilkinson (1728–1808) built the world's first iron bridge in 1789, at Ironbridge. Wilkinson also developed a steam blast-furnace, an improved steam engine with James Watt (1736–1819), and new techniques for making cannon. By the end of the century he had become the greatest ironmaster in the world. The development of the metal industry stimulated coal production and coal exports doubled between 1760 and 1800.

Industrialisation caused a change in working practices. Previously, industrial work had largely depended on the 'putting out' system, where workers collected the raw materials, worked on them at home and then sold them back to the supplier; the work was often sweated labour and the pay pitiful. New textile inventions such as the spinning jenny (1764) and looms which could use steam power meant that the machinery became too expensive to be dispersed. The 'putting out' system was gradually replaced by factories and industry became concentrated in one locality or building. As the enclosures forced many off the land and the factories offered jobs, new industrial towns such as Birmingham and Manchester began to expand rapidly.

If there was one product associated with the Industrial Revolution more than any other it was cotton cloth: before 1700 there was little production in England; by 1800 it dominated the industrial scene. In 1760 £227,000 worth was produced; by 1800 output had risen to almost £16 million in value – a staggering 7,000 per cent increase. This rise took place mostly in the north, in counties such as Lancashire and Yorkshire and showed that the manufacturing wealth of the nation was moving steadily northwards from the south and south-east of the country.

TRADE, COMMERCE AND TRANSPORT

As certain individuals became more prosperous during the Agricultural and Industrial revolutions, they sought to increase their profits by overseas trade. Liverpool particularly benefited from the 'Golden Triangle': cotton was sent to West Africa where it was sold in return for slaves; the slaves were taken to the southern colonies of America and sold for raw cotton which was brought back to Liverpool to be processed. Between 1690 and 1725 Liverpool doubled in size as a result of this trade. Trade with the New World enabled the west coast ports of Bristol and Liverpool to expand rapidly, but London still outpaced them both. It probably had the greatest concentration of shipping in the world, and imports included wine, sugar, coffee, textiles and tea. The huge amount of tea imported, or smuggled, meant that commentators became concerned about the nation's health: one wrote that the 'injurious effects of tea' were comparable to that of gin. Banking boomed as a result of this enormous expansion of trade. In 1800 there were over 400 small banks around the country; two of these, Lloyds and Barclays, were to grow into today's high street giants. Stocks and shares also became more popular with dealers, who first met in coffee-houses, and after 1773 in the Stock Exchange.

The transport revolution affected England powerfully as well. Early in the century travelling from London to Edinburgh by coach had taken nearly two weeks: the mud roads were often in an appalling condition, deeply rutted, and the much publicised highwaymen were a threat. Despite the glamorous image, highwaymen were often ruthless and cruel. The most famous was Dick Turpin (1705–1739); his escapades have been romanticised and embellished (his ride on Black Bess from London to York is completely fictitious and was made up in the nineteenth century), but his vicious treatment of his victims was a disgrace. By the middle of the century private individuals had grouped together to form Turnpike Trusts which employed a new breed of road builder, including John McAdam who invented the first satisfactory road surfaces since the days of the Romans.

Whilst roads were slowly improving, canals rapidly came to prominence at the end of the century after a scheme of the Duke of Bridgewater caught the public imagination. The great canals carved out routes all over England, linking the major rivers and towns and allowing the easy transportation of heavy loads – if only at the pace of a walking horse. The Grand Junction Canal, finished in 1805, linked London and Birmingham and enabled Birmingham to emerge as one of the great industrial centres.

THE MONARCHY

Although George III had taken an interest in agriculture, to the extent that he was known as 'farmer George', he was increasingly oblivious to the wars and innovations of the last years of his reign. From 1788 the king had been showing signs of madness. Historians have debated whether it was caused by the strains of office or whether he suffered from a rare disease called porphyria, the symptoms of which fit well with the known medical facts of the case. He became a lonely figure, ambling around in a violet dressing-gown, talking to himself: a blind old man, with long white hair and only the star of the Order of the Garter pinned to his breast to indicate who he was. Public sympathy for him grew, and after his death in 1820 he was generally remembered as a kindly and basically well-intentioned king.

The Prince Regent: George IV, 1820–30

From 1812 to 1820 the Prince of Wales exercised all the powers of the monarch as Prince Regent, before he reigned from 1820–30 as George IV. Perhaps the most memorable things about him as an individual were his disastrous marriage and his fine artistic taste. Early in his life he was charming and outstandingly handsome, but his love of gargantuan meals soon made him fat and repellent. He had huge debts and, unlike his frugal father, continued to spend lavishly: by 1796 he had unpaid debts of £600,000. His relationships with women were equally complicated. In 1785 he had secretly married a Catholic widow, Mrs Fitzherbert; the marriage was declared legally null and void under the terms of the 1772 Royal Marriages Act and proved to be a lasting embarrassment. He lived with her for ten years, before another match was proposed, this time with his cousin Caroline of Brunswick. When he first met her, he said: 'I am not well, pray get me a glass of brandy.' Caroline was dirty (she hardly ever changed or washed) and used foul language. The Prince of Wales only managed to get through the wedding in 1795 by being drunk. As the two became increasingly estranged Caroline acted as a focus of political opposition. George was relieved of the burden of the marriage when she died in 1821.

George IV was as a man of style and good taste: he did not follow fashions, he set them. English kings in the eighteenth century had lived in old-fashioned buildings which were often sparsely furnished. George was determined to change this and extensively renovated and extended Windsor Castle and Buckingham Palace. His favourite architect was John Nash (1752–1835), who laid out St James's Park and Regent's Park, both in London. Perhaps Nash's most unusual and bizarre building was

The Brighton Pavilion

the Royal Pavilion in Brighton. Here the whims of George had full rein: the results were the exterior domes and minarets and the interior richness of decoration and dragon chandeliers.

THE SUCCESSION

When George IV died in 1830 the succession was in doubt. His only child, a daughter, had died in 1817, and his childless second brother died in 1827. Next in line was his third brother, William, Duke of Clarence, who became king in 1830. He had lived contentedly for many years with an actress, Mrs Jordan, but when it seemed likely that he would succeed to the throne he married Princess Adelaide of Saxe-Meiningen in 1818. She was an admirable wife, but both of their daughters died in infancy, thus opening the way for the ultimate succession of Queen Victoria.

William IV, 1830–1837

Whereas George IV had been extravagent, William had much plainer and cheaper tastes. He had served in the navy and so was called 'Sailor Billy', and because of his eccentricities he was also known as 'Silly Billy'. He surprised many friends by having a coronation ceremony which cost only one tenth that of George IV's. His modest spending was popular with the nation and his pleasure at becoming king was evident: he travelled through London in an open-topped carriage, bowing to anyone who seemed vaguely interested.

UNREST AND REFORM, 1815–1832

Much of the population lived in poverty during these years. For those in work in the factory towns wages rose more slowly than the cost of living and corn prices fluctuated wildly; many of the soldiers and sailors who had defeated Napoleon were now unemployed. While some people enjoyed the leisured ease of Regency England, others suffered. In some parts of the country workers joined together to protect their interests. One such group, known as Luddites after their leader Ned Ludd, went into factories and smashed the new machinery which was pushing down their wages. Mass rallies were also held to protest against the lack of government reforms and the general distress. In 1819 a huge crowd gathered at St Peter's Fields in Manchester; the local magistrates became scared at the size of the crowd and sent in the cavalry. They hacked through the crowd to get to the speaker; six people died and over 400 were injured. In sombre contrast to the glorious victory at Waterloo, this ugly incident was called 'The Peterloo Massacre'.

In Parliament the Tory party, from 1812 until 1827 led by the Earl of Liverpool, was dominant. In 1821 Robert Peel became the Home Office minister and he reformed the criminal code: the death penalty was abolished for over a hundred offences and the appalling conditions of some prisons were improved. Peel was also concerned to prevent crime: he created a police force for two parishes of London, although he had originally planned the force to cover the entire country. The police force was seen at first as another weapon in the hands of the Tory government, and so the 'Bobbies' or 'Peelers' faced hostility from the general public. One leaflet read: 'Join your brother Londoners in one heart, one hand, for the abolition of the new police!' By 1835 the suspicion of the police had subsided and it became a requirement for boroughs outside London to organise their own forces.

IRELAND

The Irish Union with England in 1801 had not solved Ireland's problems: Catholics could still not legally hold office or be elected to Parliament. In 1823 an Irish Catholic lawyer, Daniel O'Connell (1775–1847), founded the Catholic Association to further the aims of the Catholic majority. In 1826 the Association had its first political success with the election of an MP; in 1828 O'Connell himself was elected for Clare but could not enter Parliament because he was a Catholic.

The situation in Ireland convinced the Duke of Wellington, who became leader of the Tory party in 1828, that the law had to be changed. The Emancipation Bill, favoured by the duke and Peel, caused bitter controversy: George IV threatened to abdicate and the bill was deeply unpopular in England amongst Protestants, who resented any increase in Catholic power. However, the possibility of civil unrest increased in Ireland to such an extent that the king reluctantly agreed to the bill and it was passed in 1829. The outcome was that up to sixty Irish MPs could enter the House of Commons.

THE REFORM BILL, 1832

Catholic emancipation had divided the Tory party, for many of its supporters were anti-Catholic churchmen or Protestants who owned land in Ireland. The 1830 election following George IV's death coincided with a period of agricultural unrest as farm workers protested against taxes and destroyed the machines which had replaced their traditional jobs. Like the Luddites there seems to have been no central organisation, and they too followed an apparently mythical leader, Captain Swing. As polling took place it became known that a revolution had taken place in France; although the news seems to have had little influence on the voters, it added to the tense atmosphere. The Duke of Wellington's administration remained in office after the election, but his dismissal of parliamentary reform meant that the new king, William IV, turned to the Whig, Earl Grey, to form the next government. Grey reluctantly accepted, but only on condition that a Reform Bill should be passed as he feared a revolution if the situation continued as it was.

The electoral system was corrupt and out of date. Small 'rotten' boroughs sent one or two MPs to Parliament whilst the huge new manufacturing towns were under-represented. The worst 'rotten borough' was at Old Sarum, near Salisbury, where two MPs were sent from 'a green mound and a wall with two arches in it'. The Reform Bill, when it was presented to Parliament, provoked outrage in many, for 107 seats were redistributed and the number of voters would be doubled. The Tory opposition bitterly opposed the bill and the House of Lords stopped it from proceeding. Lord Grey was determined to get it through and called another election – at such short notice that many people, including the king, were unprepared. William's advisers argued that the necessary preparations could not be made in time but he brushed the objections aside, walked into the House of Lords, his crown crooked, and read out the speech ending the session of Parliament.

The result of the election was a bigger Whig majority, but again the House of Lords halted the bill's progress. In October 1831 various disturbances broke out, notably at Nottingham, Derby and Bristol; violent revolution seemed close. After much political bargaining and the threat of the creation of fifty new peers, the Lords backed down and the

Reform Bill was passed. The consequences of the reforms were not as great as either side had hoped or feared. However, Parliament's capacity to accept the reform helped to maintain the nation's confidence in the democratic process and was probably an important factor in averting a continental-style revolution.

THE ROMANTICS

Partly inspired by the political revolutions at the end of the eighteenth century, a new artistic movement emerged. The extraordinary visions of William Blake (1757–1827) highlighted the creative powers of the mind and nature. What is properly called the Romantic Revolution came principally from the poets and painters: the increasing attention paid to a more realistic nature led to a remarkable release of the imagination. In 1798 the young William Wordsworth (1770–1850) and Samuel Taylor Coleridge (1772–1834) published anonymously the first edition of *Lyrical Ballads*. Despite initial criticism, it established in English poetry an enhanced freedom of form and of subject. Coleridge's astonishing *Rime of the Ancient Mariner*, with its dream-like capacity to report, apparently directly from the unconscious, first appeared in it. The liberation of the senses, linked with the release of imaginative powers, found a brief expression in the tragically short lives of John Keats (1795–1821) and Percy Bysshe Shelley (1792–1822). The lyric poetry of Lord Byron (1788–1824) broke the same moulds, but his unbridled imagination allowed him to produce high-spirited satire. English poetry had, by 1830, changed for ever. In painting, John Constable (1776–1837), and above all J.M.W. Turner (1775–1851), initiated a very similar development in their individual response to the light, colour and movement of the natural world.

CHAPTER EIGHT

Victoria and Empire,
1837–1910

THE SUCCESSION

Queen Victoria was born on 24 May 1819 and christened Alexandrina Victoria. Her father, the Duke of Kent, King William IV's brother, died in 1820 when she was eight months old. From then on Victoria was supervised by her mother and her mother's confidant, Sir John Conroy. They protected her to such an extent that Victoria was not allowed to go out unaccompanied or go to court, which her mother portrayed as a hotbed of vice.

William IV intensely disliked the Duchess of Kent, believing that she had aspirations to become regent if he died before Victoria came of age at eighteen: he had the great satisfaction of seeing her reach that age, even though he was to die one month later. The young queen now ruled in her own right, without the 'protection' of her mother.

The Victorian Era, 1837–1901

Like the reign of Elizabeth, the Victorian era is often portrayed as a golden period of English history. Commerce flourished, industrial productivity and exports soared, great manufacturing cities grew, and the British Empire expanded across the world.

Of all the innumerable changes one was particularly significant – a marked population movement from the countryside to the towns. In 1801 the census had shown that 30 per cent of the population lived in towns; by 1851 this figure had risen to over 50 per cent, and by 1901 80 per cent lived in urban or suburban areas. This shift in population provided a ready labour force for industry, but also produced problems. At first governments were unwilling to tackle the urban squalor and poverty that such a shift in the population and the growth of industry created. However, few employers actively cared for their workforces, and slowly successive governments realised that only laws could change conditions. Each new law had to be enforced, and the greater municipal and state control of living and working conditions meant that successive governments intervened more in the lives of individuals. This was evident from the number of civil servants: in 1832 there were just over 21,000, by 1880 50,000, and by 1914 over 280,000 people were employed by the government.

Victoria: Queen and Wife

Through the many changes of the age, Queen Victoria was a symbol of security and stability. Even when she was young she had great forcefulness of character, as shown by her refusal to sign documents when she was weak with typhoid in 1835. When she became queen her natural dignity was remarked upon; within her first year a commentator remarked, 'She never ceases to be Queen, but is always the most obliging, unaffected Queen in the world.' However, others saw Victoria as essentially limited, stubborn and immature.

A year after her coronation in 1838, the queen fell in love with her handsome cousin, Prince Albert of Saxe-Coburg-Gotha. They were married in the following year and from that time Victoria relied heavily on Albert, who was clearly her intellectual superior, for advice. His influence was noticeable at once: before her marriage Victoria had regularly got up late, but the morning after her marriage the couple were seen walking together in the early morning mist. A gloomy diarist noted: 'That's not the way to provide us with a Prince of Wales.'

It was essentially a happy marriage, even though there were stormy moments, and the differences over how to relate to the children. They had nine: Victoria in 1840, who later married the Emperor of Germany, and in 1841 Edward, Prince of Wales, who was the future Edward VII; three boys and four girls followed. Prince Albert stressed the importance

Queen Victoria

of home life, paying meticulous importance to the education of the children, and their family life set an example for the rest of the nation. In the previous century royalty had been renowned for gambling, heavy drinking and sexual licence; Victoria and Albert strongly disapproved of all three, although their eldest son was to indulge in the pleasures of life with little restraint. The three establishments they inherited, Buckingham Palace, Windsor Castle and Brighton Pavilion, were either too big or not secluded enough for the couple, so they bought two additional homes, Osborne House on the Isle of Wight, and Balmoral Castle in Scotland. Here they found the privacy they wanted, and Victoria wrote, with obvious satisfaction, 'We can walk about anywhere by ourselves without being followed or mobbed.'

Internal Unrest and Recovery, 1837–1851

THE HUNGRY FORTIES: CHARTISTS, CORN AND POTATOES

Victoria had been crowned amid traditional pomp and splendour, but in the country at large an industrial and agricultural depression had begun. The next decade became known as 'The Hungry Forties', and in response to the need for political and economic reform it saw the rise of two independent and powerful pressure groups: the Chartists and the Anti-Corn Law League.

THE CHARTISTS, 1838–1848

The Chartists owed their name to the support of a six-point 'Charter' which demanded secret ballots, universal male suffrage, equal electoral districts, the payment of MPs, that MPs should not have to own property, and the introduction of annual elections. The Chartist movement was predominantly a mass working-class organisation: though well organised and capable of drawing huge crowds, it was a movement which flourished in times of hunger and desperation. By 1838 there were over a hundred Chartist organisations around the country. They complained that they were 'bowed down under a load of taxes, and our workmen are starving. Capital brings no profit, labour no reward, the workhouse is full and the factory deserted.' What was remarkable about the movement was that it sought to influence Parliament through a series of petitions, first in 1839 with 1.5 million signatures, then 1842 with 3.25 million, and finally in 1848 with a reputed 6 million signatures. All were rejected decisively by Parliament. Yet the petitions emphasised that the majority of Chartists wanted to work within the law, though a minority wanted violent revolution. Unsurprisingly the English establishment was deeply suspicious of the Chartists, moderate and extremist alike, and such militant statements as 'We are to be free, though we wade through streams of blood . . .' did nothing to calm the authorities' nerves.

Trouble flared briefly after each petition was rejected. In 1839 the north was tense but the only rising occurred in Wales, in Newport, where twenty miners died during an unsuccessful revolt. After the 1842 petition several policemen were killed in Manchester, workers forced factories to close and rioters looted food shops. A general strike seemed imminent, but Robert Peel's government rushed troops to the worst areas and the situation was brought under control. When the 1848 petition was delivered to Parliament, militant Chartists planned to storm it, but a combination of a large number of troops and very heavy rain dampened their spirits and the petition was delivered peacefully. From this time on, the Chartist movement disintegrated. On the continent in 1848 violent revolutions took place in France, Austria, the German and Italian states and Hungary, but in England the rule of law prevailed.

Although the charter had not been granted, the Chartists' campaign had dramatically highlighted the plight of the poor. Largely as a consequence, during the 1840s Robert Peel's government implemented important reforms, including the Mines Act in 1842, the Factory Act in 1844, and the setting up of the Commission on Public Health in Towns, which led to the 1848 Public Health Act. Nevertheless, it took a hundred years to implement five of the Chartists' six points – fixed annual elections were never introduced.

THE ANTI-CORN LAW LEAGUE

The second major movement of the 1840s was the Anti-Corn Law League. Unlike the Chartists, the organisation was fundamentally middle-class and drew much support from nonconformists in large industrial cities, such as Manchester, who resented the power of the Anglican landowners. The Corn Laws of 1815 had forbidden corn to be imported into Britain until its price had risen above 80 shillings per quarter. The league believed that this kept prices artificially high and caused the poor great hardship. Against the league were the vested interests of the landowners who foresaw bankruptcy and ruin. Like the Chartists, the league organised on a regional basis (this allowed for effective fund raising: in 1844 over £100,000 was collected) and sent petitions to Parliament – which were again rejected.

A particularly successful tactic of the Anti-Corn Law League was to elect MPs to Parliament: by this method a single message 'reaches all over the kingdom'. By 1845 there were twelve Abolitionist MPs and their forceful speeches began to influence Parliament. The terrible Irish famine increased the pressure, and despite fierce opposition by the landlords the Repeal Bill went through in 1846. The Anti-Corn Law League had been successful; food prices were stabilised and the threat of a mass uprising faded away.

THE IRISH FAMINE, 1845–1848

The 1841 Irish census had recorded a population of nearly nine million in Ireland, about half of whom lived in 'windowless mud cabins of a single room'. Many rented small areas of land from absentee English landlords, surviving on a staple diet of potatoes – an acre of which could feed far more people than an acre of wheat. In 1845 and 1846 a fungus attacked the Irish potato crop and left the population starving and destitute. Those who could not pay their rent were evicted, and the hated landlords used the army or police to quell any protests. With the famine came typhoid and cholera, and by the 1851 census over one million Irish people had died and two million had emigrated, mainly to the United States of America.

The famine had been one reason for the repeal of the Corn Laws, but ironically there was no shortage of corn in Ireland. Instead, the corn was harvested and then shipped to England for the English markets: no effort was made to distribute it amongst the Irish. The English landowners profited whilst the Irish starved. It was hardly surprising that the Irish who emigrated took with them a deep resentment of England and of English rule in Ireland.

THE GREAT EXHIBITION OF 1851

By the early 1850s the economy had begun to improve in the aftermath of the 'Hungry Forties'. To mark the revival properly, and Britain's overwhelming industrial strength, Prince Albert promoted the Great Exhibition of 1851. It was held in a vast glass 'Crystal Palace' in south London which covered over twenty-one acres, was a third of a mile long and, as it incorporated trees within it, had to be over a hundred feet high. The exhibition was opened on 1 May 1851 by Queen Victoria with Prince Albert at her side.

Hundreds of thousands of people flocked to see the huge range of exhibits from Britain and across the world, which included many marvels of engineering. The Great Exhibition proved to be an immense success. *The Times* commented that Britain's might was such that 'the power and domination [of] empires of old were but as provinces'. Charles Dickens, who was conscious of the desperate needs of the poor, also complained that there was far too much to see. The exhibition made a profit of over £180,000; this money was used to buy land in South Kensington for the establishment of new museums, which were to include the Science Museum and, appropriately, the Victoria and Albert Museum.

'The Workshop of the World'

From the early 1850s until the 1870s Victorian England prospered as never before. An expanding population and little competition from abroad ensured a worldwide market for the manufactured goods being produced by the new machinery and a steady flow of inventions. The demand for raw materials rose dramatically: between 1850 and 1875 annual iron output rose from two million to six million tons; between 1856 and 1870 coal production rose from 65 million to 110 million tons; and between 1845 and 1875 cotton textile output rose from 978 million to 3,573 million yards.

The transportation of the goods and raw materials was revolutionised by the development of railways. The first railway had opened in 1825; by 1850 there were 5,000 miles of track, but by 1875 the network had mushroomed to over 14,500 miles. Railways linked the major cities and the ports, thus increasing the flow of exports. In some cases urban areas developed substantially as 'railway towns', notably Crewe and Swindon, whilst others benefited from the food brought in to feed an ever-expanding population. London received fish from as far away as Lancashire and Wales, and coal from Yorkshire and the Midlands. One unforeseen result of the nationwide network was that time-keeping in each region had to be standardised so that accurate train timetables could be drawn up.

By the 1870s the vast expansion of industrialism began to slacken as foreign competition from Germany and America made inroads into

British trade. Britain was still the world's leading industrial power but the gap was closing fast.

Literature and Art

An impressive number of fine authors flourished in mid-nineteenth-century England. Charles Dickens (1812–70) was an outstandingly popular novelist, who established a huge following with his first novel *The Pickwick Papers* (1836–7). His larger-than-life characters, his humour, sentiment and his increasingly critical observations of social wrongs, as well as his incessant journalism and lecturing, gave him an immense readership in Britain and the United States. His semi-autobiographical novel *David Copperfield* (1849–50) portrays the conditions in which he had been made to work as a child. Perhaps nowadays most people associate him with the short ghost story, but one with a social message, *A Christmas Carol* (1843). His attacks on corruption in England in, for example, *Bleak House* (1852–3), *Nicholas Nickleby* (1838–9) and *Oliver Twist* (1837–9) established him as a novelist of genius and compassion.

Other great contemporary male novelists included William Makepiece Thackeray (1811–63) who wrote *Vanity Fair* (1848), Anthony Trollope (1815–82) who created the engaging 'Barchester' Chronicles (1855–67), and Charles Kingsley (1819–75). There were also a number of outstanding female novelists. Mrs Gaskell (1810–65) described the politics and the poverty of Manchester. In the isolation of the bleak Yorkshire parsonage at Haworth, the three Brontë sisters, Charlotte (1816–55), Emily (1818–48) and Anne (1820–49) were all writing substantial novels. Of these the most celebrated was Charlotte's *Jane Eyre* (1847), although possibly the greatest is Emily's only novel *Wuthering Heights* (1847). The Brontës had to use male pseudonyms to get their early works published. Arguably the finest writer of the age, Mary Ann Evans (1819–80), called herself George Eliot; her novel *Middlemarch* (1871–2) is a work of towering importance.

Among English poets Robert Browning (1812–89) and his wife Elizabeth Barrett Browning (1806–61), Alfred, Lord Tennyson (1809–92) and Matthew Arnold (1822–88) dominate the second half of the century. Only slightly less important but much less publicly acclaimed, though all in their way revolutionary, were John Clare (1793–1864), Arthur Hugh Clough (1819–61) and Gerard Manley Hopkins (1844–89).

The most important movement in the visual arts was that of the Pre-Raphaelite Brotherhood, led by Holman Hunt (1827–1910), John Everett Millais (1829–96) and Dante Gabriel Rossetti (1828–82), and of William Morris (1834–96). The group simply bypassed the industrialisation of England and instead returned to the artistic conventions before Raphael. One result of this was to paint nature in a realistic manner. They also painted with photographic precision, using bright colour and concentrating on detail: the exact opposite of the 'impressionist' movement in France. The desire for accuracy in their paintings was often taken to extremes, and the girl who modelled for Millais's painting 'Ophelia' nearly died from hypothermia because she had lain for so long in a bath full of cold water.

Politics, 1851–1868

Between 1851 and 1868 the internal political situation was complex as groups of MPs merged and then split apart. There were five main groups: the Whigs, the radicals, the Liberals, the Peelites (the followers of Sir Robert Peel) and the Tories. The first four groups tended to merge, form a government, and then after a while split apart. The Tories would then take over for a short time, before another anti-Tory grouping was arranged. The main figure to emerge within Parliament was Viscount Palmerston; he was foreign secretary from 1830–41 and 1846–51 and was then prime minister from 1855–65.

Britannia, Rule the Waves': Trade and Empire, 1851–1868

Palmerston's chief concern was to uphold British interests and prestige abroad. In 1850 he defended his foreign policy with a four and a half-hour speech, ending with the declaration: '. . . a British subject, in whatever land he may be, shall feel confident that the watchful and strong arm of England will protect him against injustice and wrong.' This summed up his policy, that British interests always came first, whether the cause was just or not. His uninhibited patriotism ensured him widespread popularity.

As foreign secretary Palmerston had been highly effective in promoting British interests and influence around the world. Under his pressure Belgium, which had been demanding self-determination from Holland, was granted independence; a treaty was signed in 1839 in which Britain guaranteed Belgian neutrality (it was this treaty which was formally to involve Britain in World War I seventy-five years later). Other diplomatic triumphs included an intervention in Portugal in 1833, whereby Britain and Portugal became firm allies, and the apparent settlement of the 'Turkish question' in 1841, as a result of which British routes to India were safeguarded and Russian expansion checked.

HONG KONG AND THE OPIUM WAR OF 1839

The settlement of the Turkish question was regarded at the time as Palmerston's greatest triumph, but his most lasting legacy followed the war in 1839 between Britain and China. British merchants had built up a highly profitable trade in exporting opium from India to China. The growth of the trade caused the Chinese authorities serious concern over its effects on the health of the population. In 1839 the Chinese banned the opium trade and poured over £1 million worth into the sea. Palmerston sent a British naval and military force to China and forced the Chinese to make important treaty concessions: the country, with its population of 350 million, was opened to foreign trade; the Chinese paid £6 million compensation; and the island of Hong Kong was leased to Britain for 150 years (the lease ends in 1997, and it is a matter of speculation today about how smoothly the transfer from British to Chinese rule will be).

Palmerston's successes continued, but a deep dislike had grown up between Queen Victoria and himself. Palmerston frequently supported the revolutionaries around Europe (though *not* in Britain) who wanted greater democracy. The queen was sometimes related to the monarchs against whom the revolutionaries were fighting, so it is not surprising that a difference of opinion between them existed. Albert and Victoria also found Palmerston's raffish private life objectionable: in 1851 the queen demanded Palmerston's resignation after he had unwisely congratulated Louis Napoleon of France on his overthrow of French

The Expansion of the British Empire
'1815–1914

n Is
sh until 1863)

Cyprus

GYPT
r occ 1882)

Wei Hai Wei

BURMA

Hong Kong

Aden

Laccadives

LO-
PTIAN   BR.
AN   SOMALILAND   Ceylon   FED.
MALAY
Maldives   STATES - Singapore
Seychelles

NDA

Zanzibar   Chagos   Cocos Is

HODESIA
ECHUANA
AND   · Mauritius

ON OF
TH AFRICA

INDIA

BR. BORNEO   Gilbert Is

Solomon Is
Ellice Is

NEW
GUINEA

AUSTRALIA   Fiji Is   Tonga

Norfolk I.

NEW
SOUTH
WALES

Tasmania   NEW
ZEALAND

Extent by 1815

Additions to 1914

king, Louis-Philippe. The question of who controlled foreign policy hung in the balance. Finally Palmerston agreed to resign, but his successors were to be equally determined to prevent Albert and Victoria interfering in British foreign policy.

Crimea and the 'Valley of Death', 1854–1856

The Crimean War erupted, while Palmerston was out of office, as an attempt by Britain, France and Turkey to limit Russian power in the Eastern Mediterranean and the Middle East. A joint Anglo–French force was sent to the Crimea to capture the Russian naval fortress of Sebastopol. It was a war of mud and disease, with more men dying of illness than in battle, and for the first time war conditions were vividly described to the British public by frequent reports in *The Times*. The war is popularly remembered for a heroine and a military folly. The heroine was Florence Nightingale (1820–1910) who, with a small team of nurses, set about transforming the hospital conditions for the injured men. Although she became known as 'The Lady with the Lamp' because of her routine of visiting the wards each night, she was also a tough and implacable campaigner whose 'masculine' qualities were rather more in evidence than her feminine ones in her confrontations with the authorities.

During the war heroic deeds were matched by blunders and stupidity – as demonstrated by the Charge of the Light Brigade on 25 October 1854. A crucial message was misunderstood and 600 cavalrymen attempted to capture some Russian cannons; they rode straight towards the guns, which were firing continuously upon them. Over one-third of the brigade were killed or injured. Tennyson, in his poem 'The Charge of the Light Brigade' caught the mood:

> Their's not to reason why,
> Their's but to do and die:
> Into the valley of Death
> Rode the six hundred.

The French General Saint Arnaud commented, '*C'est magnifique, mais ce n'est pas la guerre*' (It is magnificent, but it is not war). As if to prove the point, the commander of the Light Brigade, Lord Cardigan, calmly returned to his yacht, had a bath, dined, drank a bottle of champagne and went to bed. Despite such military blunders Sebastopol eventually fell and the war ended in 1856. Russia had for the moment been contained and the moribund Turkish Empire propped up for another sixty years.

PALMERSTON RETURNS

Early British failures during the war had led to Palmerston's return as prime minister in 1855. Apart from a short interlude in 1858 he remained in office until his death in 1865. Foreign affairs continued to dominate the headlines, and his successes for Britain included a second war with China (1857–60) and his support allowed the newly unified state of Italy to survive. But despite this the heyday of Palmerston's foreign policies was nearing its end.

The Indian Mutiny, 1857–1858

Of all British possessions, India was the most valuable and the most highly prized. It was the 'jewel in the crown' of the British Empire, a vast subcontinent, over two-thirds of which was now ruled by the East India Company. Over 150 years the territory under British control had steadily increased. East India Company troops overthrew Indian princes to protect British interests, Christian missionaries converted Indians, landowners were dispossessed, cheap British goods forced countless Indians out of work, and European reforms outlawed some unacceptable traditional customs like thuggee (sacrificial murders) and suttee (where Hindu widows were burned with their dead husbands).

In 1857 a simmering discontent, mainly in north and central India, flared into the Indian Mutiny when sections of the army of Bengal attacked British troops and civilians. The cities of Delhi, Cawnpore and Lucknow all suffered during the fighting; there were some Indian atrocities and several bloody reprisals by the British. The mutiny spread further than the army and included many Indian landowners and some of the peasantry; most of British India, however, remained loyal and the last remnants of the mutiny were finally crushed in November 1858. One result was to increase British suspicion of the Indians. The British government also took over the administration of India from the East India Company and increased the number of Europeans in the army. The British governor-general became known as the viceroy (meaning 'in place of the king') to show that the crown and government, instead of the East India Company, were now in control.

In Europe further setbacks occurred as Palmerston was outmanoeuvred both by the tsar in 1863 and, more humiliatingly, by the German chancellor, Bismarck, in 1863–4. Another dispute arose between the queen and Palmerston concerning foreign policy, and Prince Albert had to leave his sick-bed to tone down a letter from Palmerston to the Northern side of the American Civil War – had he not done so, it is highly likely that Britain and the United States would have gone to war.

Queen Victoria and the Death of Prince Albert

That Queen Victoria adored and idolised Albert is evident from the comments in her *Journals* and letters. She described him as 'my beloved and perfect one', who raised the monarchy 'to the *highest* pinacle of *respect*', and wrote, 'I only feel . . . quite happy when Albert is with me'. In such circumstances his death from typhoid, on 14 December 1861 at Windsor Castle, was a devastating blow to her, and she mourned for him for the rest of her life. The queen continued to work and to see government ministers, but for many years her public appearances were rare and she became known as 'The Widow of Windsor'. Gradually, however, her grief over 'her misfortune', as she termed Albert's death, receded and she became more actively involved in the issues of the age. From the late 1860s onwards she was once again in the public eye over her relations with two of her greatest prime ministers, Gladstone and Disraeli.

GLADSTONE AND DISRAELI

After Palmerston's death in 1865, much attention was focused on the political battles between the two leaders of the main political parties: Disraeli for the Conservatives, and Gladstone for the Liberals. They were flamboyant figures, both passionate about their politics and each apparently loathing the other. William Ewart Gladstone (1809–98) was staunchly Anglican in his religious beliefs, and sometimes seemed to believe that he was putting God's will into practice. Queen Victoria disliked his high-mindedness and was once reported as complaining, 'He speaks to Me as if I was a public meeting.' It was also alleged that once, when Gladstone arrived late for a meeting with the queen, he apologised, explaining that he had three hands. When Victoria asked him to explain, he replied that he had 'a right hand, a left hand, and a little behind hand'. Victoria's response was 'We are not amused'. Of course, the main reason why Gladstone irritated the queen was that he was increasingly associated with radical policies which she found unpalatable.

Benjamin Disraeli (1804–81) came from a Jewish business background, was the author of several novels, and became a favourite of the queen. He realised that Victoria was easily flattered and remarked, 'Everyone likes flattery, and when you come to royalty you should lay it on with a trowel.' In 1876 the queen was delighted to receive the title 'Empress of India' from Disraeli, who was then prime minister. In the same year she created him Earl of Beaconsfield.

REFORMS

Undoubtedly Britain, as the 'workshop of the world', was becoming more prosperous, yet the boom in trade masked the human misery of those who worked long hours in dangerous conditions for little pay. Employers often favoured the employment of children, as they were small, agile and worked for pitiful wages. Various Acts of Parliament had been passed to improve conditions of child labour but as late as 1874 over 67,000 children under the age of thirteen were still working in the cotton mills. In 1871 Lord Shaftesbury had made a speech about conditions in the brickfields, where little children were 'three parts naked, tottering under the weight of wet clay'.

Successive governments passed measures designed to improve conditions of work, education and the standard of living; Gladstone and Disraeli continued the momentum of reform. Gladstone first became prime minister between 1868 and 1874 and his government introduced reforms concerning education and university entrance, the civil service, and the army – making it a more effective and modernised force. His most unpopular reform was a licensing act in 1872 which limited the sale of alcohol to specific hours, and he attributed the Liberals' loss of the 1874 general election to 'a torrent of beer and gin'. When he returned to power (1880–5, 1886) other reforms were passed, including the Married Women's Property Act (1882) which allowed married women to keep financial control of their own property, and a secret ballot act.

During Disraeli's term of office (1874–80) acts were passed to improve public health, factory work and the safety of shipping, and legal recognition was given to trades unions. A minor act, but one that literally improved the atmosphere in Parliament, made it illegal to dump poisonous or solid industrial waste into rivers. Previously during hot summers the stench from the Thames had become so unbearable in Westminster that the river was known as The Great Stink.

Despite all these improvements it is arguable that the most important reforms concerned voting rights. In 1867 the second Reform Act was passed by the Conservatives and doubled the size of the electorate from 1.36 million people to 2.46 million. In 1884 the Liberals passed a third Act which increased the electorate, mainly in the rural areas, to 5.7 million. These extensions of the franchise, coupled with introduction of secret ballots (1872) and an attack upon corruption at elections (1883), increasingly meant that political parties had to appeal to a wide range of voters.

SOCIAL THEORIES

Important social theories were also developed, most notably by Karl Marx (1818–83) and Friedrich Engels (1820–95). Marx and Engels, both of whom lived in England for a time, collaborated in writing the *Communist Manifesto*, which was published in 1848. Engels had been interested in Chartism (see p. 179), but he and Marx took little active interest in British politics. It was in the next century that Communism, and Marx's great work of economic, political and social analysis, *Das Kapital*, became the inspiration of communist regimes throughout the world.

Of more immediate impact in Britain was the theory of evolution, as proposed by Charles Darwin (1809–82) in his book *The Origin of Species*, published in 1859. His theory angered many religious people for it seemed to suggest that the scriptures were in error and that man had evolved from apes, rather than being created in the image of God. Scientists for the most part welcomed the concept, and the theory soon began to be seen in wider terms than those of natural history. The idea spread that societies and cultures could also evolve and develop, and that the fittest would survive and dominate. The advanced democratic and economic state of Britain was taken by some to indicate superiority in evolutionary terms over supposedly backward peoples and lands elsewhere.

The Expansion of Empire

Throughout the nineteenth century the British Empire continued to expand. During the last twenty years of the century over 3.5 million square miles of new territory were added. The empire could be roughly divided into three: the white-settled self-governing colonies, including Australia, Canada, New Zealand; the Indian Empire; and a host of dependent territories in Africa, the Caribbean, South-East Asia and the world's oceans. The causes of this expansion were complex. Generally merchants and traders could count on military backing from the government to increase and consolidate their markets. Elsewhere, a combination of local factors, economic and political motives brought varied territories under the flag. In Africa explorers and missionaries opened up new territories for commercial penetration. In the last resort, the desire to increase and protect trading connections was paramount.

The British public were enthralled by the adventures of explorers, the most famous of whom were Dr David Livingstone (1813–73), who preached and set up mission stations across Africa, and a young Welsh-born American journalist, H. M. Stanley (1841–1904). He was sent by his newspaper into darkest Africa to 'find' Livingstone – which he did, at the meeting uttering the famous words 'Dr Livingstone I presume?' Some cynics have argued that Livingstone was not 'lost' at all. Other British explorers included Richard Burton and John Hanning Speke, who reached Lake Tanganyika and discovered one of the sources of the Nile in 1858.

British attitudes towards empire were mixed. Empire meant trade and profit, but the other side of the coin was the conviction that Britain had a duty to bring British ideas of democracy and law to 'primitive' peoples. Kipling described it as 'The White Man's Burden' and Joseph Chamberlain (1836–1914), the colonial secretary from 1895–1903, wanted to expand the empire for the benefit of all: 'We are landowners of a great estate; it is the duty of a landlord to develop his estate.' The enthusiasm to extend both the empire and 'civilisation' had a brutal and ugly side, as numerous wars of imperial expansion demonstrated.

Gladstone and Disraeli had apparently markedly differing views concerning the empire. When Disraeli came to office in 1874 he actively sought to expand it. In 1875 his government bought the ruler of Egypt's shares in the Suez Canal for £4 million, thus ensuring that Britain had a firm financial stake in the quick route of communication to India, Australia and the Far Eastern colonies. He also backed military action to protect and extend British interests, as in the occupation of the Transvaal in 1877, in the Zulu War of 1879, and in the attempt to support the king of Afghanistan against the Russians in 1878. Gladstone professed distaste for these actions, which he saw as morally wrong, but his attitude was far from straightforwardly anti-imperial, even though in speeches he highlighted the 'villages burned, and women and children driven forth to perish', and urged his listeners to 'remember the rights of the savage'. When he returned to power in 1880 he withdrew British forces from Afghanistan, but only gave the Boers of the Transvaal their independence after they had defeated British forces in a short war. In 1882 the Liberal government sanctioned the occupation of Egypt, a move that was to lead to further embarrassment in the Sudan.

EGYPT AND THE SUDAN

In 1878, under pressure from Britain and France, the ruler of Egypt had resigned and handed over the finances of the country to Britain and France. Anti-European riots in Egypt had forced Gladstone to send in British troops to restore order in 1882. This was achieved, but Gladstone was reluctant to send troops to the Egyptian dependency of the Sudan, where a Moslem religious leader, the Mahdi, was preaching a holy war. After some hesitation he reluctantly sent in General Gordon to withdraw the Egyptian army and some British officials from there.

Unfortunately Gordon was a man who believed that God was on his side, and once in Khartoum he set about single-handedly saving the Sudan. The Dervishes, led by the Mahdi, besieged Khartoum but for several months Gladstone delayed sending reinforcements, despite great pressure at home. An army was eventually sent from Britain, but two days before it arrived Khartoum fell and Gordon was killed. Gladstone's reputation was temporarily damaged, but not sufficiently to stop the Liberals winning the 1885 general election.

IRELAND

Throughout the century the Irish question had repeatedly come to the fore, with the potato famine of 1845–9 dramatically highlighting the poverty and desperation of the people. In 1858 an organisation known as the Fenian Brotherhood was founded in the United States and soon became prominent in Ireland. Its aims were to 'renounce all allegiance to the Queen of England, and to take arms and fight at a moment's warning to make Ireland an Independent Democratic Republic'. By 1865 the Fenian leader, James Stephens, claimed that he had 85,000 men ready to take up the armed struggle, but the British authorities learnt of the planned raids through an informer. Before one raid in 1867 Fenians gathered to attack Chester Castle but learnt of their betrayal just in time; the police had to be satisfied with a haul of hastily discarded revolvers. The most dramatic incident came in September 1867 when two Fenians were rescued from police custody; one policeman was shot and died. Three men who were present were charged with the murder though they did not fire the gun; they were hanged and became known as the 'Manchester Martyrs'.

Gladstone was well aware of the problems, and when he came to office in 1868 he declared that it was his mission to 'pacify' Ireland. He was not particularly successful, for each time action was taken it seemed to be both too little and too late. At first a policy of moderation and tolerance was followed. In 1869 the Irish Church Act allowed greater freedom to the Catholic Church, to which the majority of Irish people belonged, and stated that the Protestant Church of Ireland was no longer the established church. A further bid to implement change came in the first Irish Land Act of 1870 which attempted to give peasants some measure of protection against landlords and prohibited 'exorbitant' rents. The act was a failure – not least because the amount deemed to be 'exorbitant' was never defined. The resulting violence caused Gladstone to pass a Coercion Act in 1871 to repress the unrest in the countryside; it gave the police extra powers of arrest and led to the sending over of more troops. There were now more troops stationed in Ireland than in India.

The problem of Ireland continued to exercise a profound influence on British politics. The complexity of the issues was shown by the fact that four of the six governments between 1880 and 1895 were brought down directly by Irish affairs. A crucial factor was the power of the block vote of the eighty or so Irish Nationalist MPs in Parliament, led by Charles Parnell. They became convinced that a measure of home rule for Ireland was the only solution; they would switch sides according to which English party they believed could offer them more. In 1885 they forced out Gladstone's Liberal government, then both Salisbury's Conservative government and Gladstone's Liberal government fell in 1886.

The Irish Home Rule crisis of 1886 split the Liberals and led to a group of Liberal Unionist MPs keeping the Conservative government under the Marquess of Salisbury (and subsequently Balfour) in power between 1886–92 and 1895–1905. These 'Unionist' governments implemented strict measures to improve law and order in Ireland, although a Land Purchase Act of 1891 helped farmers to buy land. An additional bonus for the English government was the disgrace of Charles Parnell in 1891 when it became public knowledge that he had been living with a divorced woman for nine years.

Gladstone's final attempt to introduce a Home Rule Bill for Ireland came in 1893, but although it was passed by the House of Commons, the Lords decisively rejected it. Gladstone finally resigned in 1894 and in the ensuing general election in 1895 the Conservatives with their Liberal Unionist allies came back to power. Gladstone's attempts to solve the Irish problem had failed, and the Liberals seemed to have split beyond repair.

THE SCRAMBLE FOR AFRICA

During the last two decades of the century much of tropical Africa was occupied by the leading European imperial powers: Britain, France, Germany and Belgium. One of the key British figures in the expansion of the empire in Southern Africa was Cecil Rhodes (1853–1902). Rhodes believed it was essential to extend the British Empire in Africa and one of his grand schemes was to build a railway from the Cape to Cairo, running entirely through British territory. This dream was obstructed by the Afrikaners, or Boers, of South Africa, who had no intention of becoming part of the British Empire. The Boers controlled the key areas of the Transvaal and the Orange Free State as independent republics. Rhodes and the other British imperialists wished to incorporate these republics within the empire. Rhodes used his great wealth (he was a self-made diamond and gold millionaire with an income of over £1 million a year) to establish white-settled British colonies to the north of the Boer states. Northern and Southern Rhodesia were named after their founder and granted charters by a grateful British government.

The drive to annex the Boer republics was reinforced by the discovery in 1886 of large gold deposits in the Transvaal. Outsiders, or 'uitlanders' (mainly British), flocked to the mines and soon threatened to outnumber the Afrikaners in their homelands. To protect themselves, the Boers taxed the uitlanders excessively and passed laws which made it difficult for any foreign-born person to vote or to hold political office. Cecil Rhodes, in collusion with the British government, organised an invasion of the Transvaal to coincide with an uprising of the uitlanders, the aim being to overthrow the Boer government. The Jameson Raid, as it became known, was a disaster as the raiding party was easily disarmed and the uitlander rebellion was half-hearted. As a result the prestige of Paul Kruger, the Transvaal president, was greatly increased. Joseph Chamberlain, Britain's colonial secretary, tried to force Kruger to accept British supremacy but he refused. In October 1899 British diplomatic pressure and a military build-up on the border of the Transvaal precipitated the outbreak of war.

THE BOER WAR, 1899–1902

The war was between the British Empire on the one side and the two sparsely populated Afrikaner republics of the Transvaal and the Orange Free State on the other. The Boers had three victories in one 'Black

Week' for the British in December 1899, and besieged the strategically important towns of Mafeking, Ladysmith and Kimberley. The British forces slowly fought back, and when Mafeking was relieved on 18 May 1900 the excessive celebrations in Britain indicated how threatened and humiliated many had felt by the Boer successes early in the war. British forces continued to be reinforced and to push forward, so that by June 1900 the Transvaal's capital, Pretoria, was captured and to all intents and purposes the independent Boer republic ceased to exist.

The war was over, or so the British thought. The Boers, however, intensified their guerrilla campaign using small groups of men, known as 'commandos', who attacked outposts and railway lines and then melted back into the countryside. To overcome these 'hit and run' tactics, Lord Kitchener, the new commander-in-chief in South Africa, invented concentration camps – to 'concentrate' people living in isolated farms into one small area. This policy, together with farm burning, deprived the Boers of assistance and shelter and eventually forced them to come to terms in 1902. Its price was high for by the end of the war over 20,000 Boers had died in the camps through overcrowding and disease. A military victory had been won though the moral battle had been lost. The concentration camps, and other unsavoury tactics, were severely criticised in Parliament and the Liberal leader, Sir Henry Campbell-Bannerman, denounced the war as being fought by 'methods of barbarism'. Eventually £3 million was granted for rebuilding the farms destroyed by Kitchener's forces. The Boer republics were annexed, though the British authorities were at pains to stress that British rule did not imply practical equalities between blacks and whites. Plans were now made to establish a prosperous, united, European-dominated South Africa within the British Empire.

TRADE UNIONS: 'IT IS YOU WHO WILL LOSE OR WIN'

Throughout the century attempts had been made by groups of workers in Britain to improve their working conditions and to increase their political power. In 1834 widespread publicity and sympathy had been gained for six West Country agricultural workers who had been transported to Australia for forming a union – the public outcry was so great that the 'Tolpuddle Martyrs', as the six were called, were eventually released. During the 1840s the activities of the Chartists and the Anti-Corn Law League had dominated the headlines, but in the 1850s unions re-emerged specifically for skilled workers. These 'New Model' unions aimed at securing better wages and conditions for their members rather than at changing society. Particularly successful was the Amalgamated Society of Carpenters, which by 1870 had over 10,000 members and 230 branches. Trade union officials were anxious to stress the non-revolutionary nature of the unions, and in 1871 unions were legally recognised.

In 1868 the first meeting of the Trades Union Congress (TUC) was held in Manchester in order to 'bring trades into closer alliance, and to take action in all parliamentary matters pertaining to the working classes'. The unions represented in 1868 had been predominantly of skilled workers, but during the 1870s and 1880s a new type of union for unskilled workers had evolved. By the turn of the century the unions were giving increasing support to the Independent Labour party, which had been formed in 1889 by the Scottish socialist Keir Hardie (1856–1915). In 1892 he became the first Labour party MP; he arrived at the House of Commons 'in a toil-stained working suit with a cloth-cap on his head and accompanied by a noisy brass band'. It was a sign of the changing social and political order in England. After the 1906 election Labour had twenty-nine MPs.

The End of an Era

In 1897 Victoria celebrated her diamond jubilee to mark the sixtieth year of her reign. The nation rejoiced in style and patriotism ran high. *The Times* asserted that 'No State or no Monarch known to history has ever rejoiced in such homage as our colonies will pay to our Queen'. Yet Victoria reigned over a nation which had become increasingly diverse. The old rural pattern of small villages, with a squire and vicar, survived in some areas, but the towns and cities with their associated industries came to dominate the economy of England. In politics, groups of MPs continued to split and realign: at different times between 1880 and 1914 there were parties or groupings that called themselves Liberals, Conservatives, Whigs, Tories, Liberal Radicals, Liberal Unionists, Tory

Democrats, Unionists, Labour, Liberal-Labour, Independent Labour and Irish Nationalists.

Victoria died on 22 January 1901 at Osborne House. It is a measure of the length of her reign – the longest in English history – that no one under seventy could remember living under another monarch, and that none of the court officials had any experience in dealing with the death of a monarch. The old queen's death had a profound effect on the national psyche and seemed to mark the end of an era. Some commentators felt that an age of optimism and prosperity had died with her and that the future was uncertain and dangerous.

The Edwardian Era

The popular image of the Edwardian era is one of long hot summers where the profits of the empire and industry were enjoyed to the full. The Henley Regatta, for example, apparently symbolised the elegance and ease of the middle- and upper-classes; there women in long flowing dresses and elegant hats would be punted up the Thames by young men in straw hats, blazers and white flannel trousers. In fact the Edwardian era presented England with a series of extremely difficult political, social and economic choices. It was also an era full of conflict.

King Edward VII, 1901–1910

Edward was fifty-nine when he became king, and the country was not at all sure what to make of him. He was a jovial, large, pleasure-seeking prince, fond of racing, shooting, gambling and women. He was involved in several scandals, and in 1890 he was brought to court for playing the illegal card-game of baccarat. One newspaper described the nation as 'profoundly shocked'. Yet Edward was both concerned to glorify the monarchy and to demonstrate his humanity at the same time. He was concerned to reinstate the pomp and ceremony attached to the British monarchy – which had virtually lapsed since Prince Albert's death in 1861: when Parliament opened less than a month after his mother's death, he rode there in a magnificent procession the like of which had not been seen in forty years. His joviality was also evident to all those who knew him: after a trip to Italy in 1903 an Italian journalist summed up his character as 'spreading genial light and warmth all round'. There was, however, another side to his personality: he was greedy, self-indulgent, easily bored and not particularly intelligent or well educated.

Politically, Edward's influence was most noticeable in foreign affairs. He spoke German fluently and had an excellent knowledge of French, Spanish and Italian; these he used to good diplomatic effect, and when he visited France in 1903 the warmth of his character and the fluency of his French did much to improve relations between the two countries and helped to cement the Entente Cordiale – an Anglo–French agreement signed in the following year. Other successful foreign trips took place to Greece, Sweden and Russia. Edward's travels and affability won him the title 'Edward the Peacemaker' in Britain, but German propaganda accused him, not unreasonably, of helping to organise an anti-German system of European alliances.

The king took little less interest in domestic politics until the last year of his life, when the Liberal government and the Conservative-dominated House of Lords battled for power (see p. 205). At the height of the crisis, after a short two-day illness, the king died on 6 May 1910 at the age of sixty-eight, leaving the constitutional problem to his successor, King George V.

LITERATURE

By the turn of the century, under European and American influences, particularly Henry James (1843–1916), the English novel was changing. Joseph Conrad (1857–1924) and Ford Madox Ford (1873–1939) experimented productively and Arnold Bennett (1867–1931) was influenced by French novelists. Rudyard Kipling (1865–1936) was Britain's most famous writer of the times, producing poetry and such books as *Kim* (1901), a story about a boy in India involved in the 'great game' of imperial espionage against Russia. His best known work now is *The Jungle Book* (1894). By contrast, Thomas Hardy (1840–1928) wrote about how fate acted against individuals in the rural, and only seemingly idyllic, setting of the Dorset countryside. Of very different temperament and reputation was the Irishman Oscar Wilde (1854–1900) who wrote, among others, the classic comedy play *The Importance of Being*

Earnest (1895) and a novel about appearances *The Picture of Dorian Gray* (1890).

The category of 'English men of letters' includes other Irishmen, particularly the iconclastic George Bernard Shaw (1856–1950). As well as being Irish, Shaw was a socialist and was sharply aware of the flaws in British institutions: in many plays like *Arms and the Man* (1894) and *The Doctor's Dilemma* (1906) he attacked professions and institutions. His most famous play, *Pygmalion* (1913), was later adapted into the musical *My Fair Lady*.

There was also a strong element both of popular escapism and more profound enquiry into contemporary problems in the works of G.K. Chesterton (1874–1936) and above all H.G. Wells (1866–1946), whose scientific, historical and social interests reached an immense popular readership. Arthur Conan Doyle (1859–1930) created Sherlock Holmes and his companion Dr Watson, who solved crimes in the fog-filled streets of London and beyond; perhaps his best known work, *The Hound of the Baskervilles*, was published in 1902.

Children's Literature

The decades between the 1880s and 1914 were a remarkable period for children's literature in England. Lewis Carroll, a pseudonym for Charles Dodgson (1832–98), wrote the two world-famous *Alice* adventures. Kenneth Grahame's (1859–1932) *The Wind in the Willows*, Edith Nesbit's (1858–1924) *The Railway Children* and many other charming stories, which reached their height later with A.A. Milne's (1882–1956) *Winnie the Pooh* stories, replaced the more overtly moralist and socially descriptive stories of previous years, characterised by Charles Kingsley's (1819–75) *The Water Babies* and the fairy stories of George MacDonald (1824–1905).

SPORT

One of the most enduring British exports during the nineteenth century was sport. Football, rugby, tennis, cricket, squash and snooker became organised in Britain and spread rapidly around the world. Football and rugby quickly became popular in schools, universities and workplaces as they embodied the contemporary and imperialist ideals of health, vigour, sportsmanship, teamwork and individual skill. Clubs and teams in many sports acquired areas of land and headquarters which, today, have become equated with the sports themselves – Wimbledon for tennis and Lord's for cricket, for example.

ARCHITECTURE

Within the cities the Victorian sense of 'mission' and 'progress' was often reflected in English architecture. Old slums in the major cities were torn down to make way for elegant and imposing town halls and streets, as in Birmingham, Manchester, Leeds and London. The prevailing style of the Victorian era was Gothic, which looked back to the Middle Ages for its inspiration. Using Gothic designs, Charles Barry won the contract for the rebuilding of the Houses of Parliament, which had been burned down in 1834.

As well as the grandiose schemes, very large numbers of houses were built, often as back-to-back terraces, for the workers to live in. The more prosperous classes could live away from these areas as the growth

The Houses of Parliament

of the railway network allowed people to travel to and from work, arriving at stations such as St Pancras, Paddington, Waterloo and Liverpool Street. These stations were originally sited on the outskirts of the city, though they were rapidly surrounded by further Victorian development. They are now considered to be in the heart of London.

CHAPTER NINE

Peace and War,
1910–1945

George V, 1910–1936

George V was the second son of Edward VII and Queen Alexandra, but he became heir when his elder brother, Prince Albert Victor, died in 1892. In 1893, at the suggestion of Queen Victoria, he married his dead brother's former fiancée, Princess Mary of Teck. They had six children: Edward (later Edward VIII), Albert George (later George VI), Mary, Henry, George and John. George V gained the affection and respect of the vast majority of his subjects; he and Queen Mary helped to raise public morale during World War I by visiting hospitals and factories. Also during the war this quintessential English monarch changed the family name from the Germanic Saxe-Coburg-Gotha to the British name of Windsor. He loved sailing and had trained for a career in the navy before his elder brother's death changed his status. In 1932 he initiated the Christmas Day radio broadcasts by which he spoke to the nation and the empire, a tradition which has continued to this day. When their silver jubilee was celebrated in 1935, George was surprised by the warmth of public feeling expressed for himself and Queen Mary. They were perceived as kindly and stabilising figures in an increasingly turbulent world; the king was a particularly reassuring figurehead – a bluff, straightforward monarch who spoke to his people over 'the wonderful wireless' in the unadorned accent of a prosperous farmer or a caring family doctor.

The Liberals in Power: Crisis and Reform, 1905–1914

By 1905 the Conservative and Unionist Party had become divided over the question of tariff reform, which meant the abandonment of free trade. One group of tariff reform or protectionist MPs, led by Joseph Chamberlain, favoured putting a tariff on certain imported items, and then allowing the colonies preferential treatment. Tariff reform was meant to protect British industries and boost inter-imperial trade and co-operation. The opposing group of 'Free Trade' Unionist MPs rejected the arguments for tariffs, mainly because they feared the social and political consequences of the dearer food prices that tariff reform implied. Some politicians argued about whether tariff reform would mean that the public would get 'a smaller loaf' of bread. In December the Conservative prime minister Arthur Balfour (1848–1930) resigned having completed a reform of Britain's defence and foreign policies and helping to expose the divisions between the right and left of the Liberal party.

The Liberals formed a government, united under the leadership of Campbell-Bannerman, and called for a general election. In the election of January 1906 the Liberals won a landslide victory, benefiting from the split in the Unionist coalition and from the electorate's desire for change, including social reform. Asquith succeeded Campbell-Bannerman in 1908, and the Liberals remained in power until the wartime coalition government was formed, also under Asquith's leadership, in 1915.

SOCIAL REFORMS

In the first two years a virtual stalemate was reached between the House of Commons, with its huge Liberal majority, and the House of Lords, controlled by the Conservative opposition. Some minor reforms were introduced, such as the provision of school meals in 1906, but otherwise the Lords constantly blocked the reforming legislation sent to it from the Commons. The crisis came in 1909. The fiery, radical, Liberal Chancellor of the Exchequer, David Lloyd George (1863–1945), pushed through a 'People's Budget'; this proposed a tax on the very rich in order to pay for reforms and the building of the Dreadnought class of battleships to meet the German naval threat. It had previously been a parliamentary convention that the House of Lords would not interfere with financial bills, but they were so incensed by the socialistic and confiscatory nature of the budget that they completely rejected it.

To resolve the deadlock two general elections were held in 1910. At the first in January the Liberals lost so many seats that henceforth they had to rely on the support of the Irish Nationalists and the Labour party. In April the budget was approved by both the Commons and the Lords, but the Conservative-dominated House of Lords still retained the power to reject financial bills passed by the Commons, so a second election was held. Once again the Liberals were able to form a government with the support of their parliamentary allies. In May 1911 the House of Commons approved a bill, called the Parliament Bill, to limit, in particular, the delaying power of the House of Lords, and against great opposition from the upper house it eventually became law in the same year. Under its terms the Lords could no longer reject bills outright, and there was to be a general election every five years instead of every seven.

The two most important social reforms implemented by the Liberal government were the introduction of old age pensions (1908) to people over seventy who qualified and the National Insurance Act (1911). In the latter bill the worker, the employer and the government all contributed to a general fund which provided free medical treatment, sick pay, disablement and maternity benefits to sick workers; for some special trades, such as building, unemployment benefits were also given for up to fifteen weeks in any one year. These two major reforms, along with the introduction of school meals and of medical inspections for schoolchildren, were the first steps towards a welfare state, and provided a financial safety net, albeit minimal, against the misfortunes and disasters of life. They indicated that the State had officially accepted a responsibility to assist certain groups of people in need. This was a significant shift from the conventional Victorian belief that state support would lessen people's motivation to find work, to improve their social status, or to 'stand on their own two feet'.

Unquiet Times, 1910–1914

The long-running constitutional stalemate and political wrangling were often overshadowed in the press by the burgeoning suffragette movement. A minority of people had been arguing for women's votes since the 1860's, but the cause was given greater prominence in 1903 when the

Women's Social and Political Union, led by Mrs Emmeline Pankhurst and her daughters Christabel and Sylvia, was formed. The militant suffragette movement grew rapidly and became headline news as women tied themselves to railings, heckled MPs and held massive rallies. In 1913 a bill accepting the right of women to vote was thrown out of Parliament and the suffragettes responded by burning buildings and attacking politicians. The worst incident occurred when Emily Davison threw herself under the king's horse in the 1913 Derby and was killed. When war came the vast majority of suffragettes immediately stopped their action, though a few were outspoken pacifists.

Additional upheaval during the period was caused by the nationwide strikes of dock-workers, railwaymen and miners. The basic grievance was that wages had not kept pace with inflation, but some union leaders, who supported revolution, believed that the 'direct action' of strikes was a way of bringing down the government and gaining political power. Strikes brought various cities and ports to a standstill in 1911: Southampton, Hull, Liverpool, and especially London, which was virtually ruled by a strike committee between 8 and 11 August; troops were often used to quell disturbances, as at Tonypandy in Wales in 1910, and at Liverpool in 1911 where two strikers died. In 1911 the national railway strike caused massive disruption, and the following year, in the largest strike, 850,000 miners stopped working. That was the worst year for strikes, with over 38 million working days lost through industrial disputes.

TWO NATIONAL TRAGEDIES

Edwardian England was giving way to something new. The Lords had had their power reduced; some women were openly campaigning and using violence to win equal voting rights, in contradiction to the Victorian image of women being demure and confined to the home, and the unions, once powerless groups of men, could now organise nationwide strikes. As if to signal the collapse of old values, two disasters shocked the nation in 1912. The first, early in the year but not reported for many months, was the death of Captain Scott and his fellow explorers. They had raced the Norwegian Roald Amundsen to be first to the South Pole, but to their bitter disappointment the Norwegian had arrived a few days before them. Disheartened and ill Scott and his party started on the long walk home across the hostile polar ice and snow: they died of cold. The expedition was noted for its old-style Empire heroism, especially that of Captain Oates; he realised that he was slowing the other members of the team down and so, with the words 'I am just going out, I may be some time', left the tent and walked to his death in a snowstorm.

The second disaster happened on 14 April and was swiftly reported by radio. The passenger liner *Titanic* had been pronounced 'unsinkable', but on her maiden voyage across the Atlantic she struck an iceberg and sank. The heroism of the crew was widely noted; it was said that the band played the hymn 'Nearer, my God, to thee' as the icy waters came over them. Out of over two thousand passengers and crew only about seven hundred people survived. Critics later noted that a particularly high proportion of wealthier ticket-holders were rescued.

Foreign Policy from 1900

Since the turn of the century European political alliances had shifted and strained under the pressures of international hostilities and the associated arms race. In 1894 France and Russia had formed an alliance; ten years later France and Britain signed a treaty, known as the Entente Cordiale. These agreements alarmed the Germans, who felt surrounded on land and threatened by British sea-power, and they responded by forming an alliance with Austria–Hungary and building up the country's military strength. The British foreign secretary, Lord Grey, tried hard to improve relations with Germany and had to some extent succeeded by 1914, but when the war began it was propelled by its own momentum and proved to be irreversible.

The pre-set military plans of the various alliances meant that countries were drawn into the war with great rapidity. The crisis began with the assassination of the the Austrian Archduke Ferdinand on 28 June 1914 by Gavrilo Princip, a Serbian nationalist student. In the ensuing uproar Austria claimed excessive compensation from Serbia, which was refused; Russia mobilised to support the Serbs; Germany mobilised to support the Austrians, and declared war on Russia on 1 August. The inflexible military strategy of Germany depended upon victory over France, the old enemy, in six weeks, and so Germany declared war on 3 August and attacked France through Belgium. Under a treaty of 1839 (see p. 185), Britain was bound to uphold Belgian neutrality, and in any case wished to keep the Channel ports out of German hands, and so entered the war on 4 August. These sombre and ominous events caused Grey to remark on the same day: 'The lights are going out all over Europe; we shall not see them lit in our lifetime.'

World War I, 1914–1918

As the Germans poured through Belgium, the British sent an Expeditionary Force of 130,000 men across the Channel. Both sides had ludicrously assumed that the war would be over by Christmas, but in the horrific conditions of mud, water and trench warfare, a relentless war of attrition started. Each side threw huge numbers of troops into all-out frontal assaults which more often than not produced little result. The names of the battlefields in France and Belgium have become legendary:

World War I: a machine-gun crew in action

Mons, Ypres, the Somme, Arras and Passchendaele. The pattern of attack for both sides was to shell the enemy's trenches and then send attacking troops 'over the top' through the shell-pitted 'No Man's Land'. They were weighed down with equipment and hindered by barbed wire; the advance was always slow and the defenders could easily machine-gun the oncoming waves of men. The statistics are terrible: at the battle of Verdun (1916) over 37 million shells were fired; at the battle of the Somme (1916) 420,000 British troops were killed or injured, 60,000 dying on the first day; 300,000 troops died at Passchendaele (1917).

Although the main fronts were close to the border between France and Belgium, allied troops were involved elsewhere. In 1915 a joint British, Australian and New Zealand force was sent to capture Constantinople (now Istanbul) and were then supposed to attack Germany's ally, Turkey. The force landed at Gallipoli against well-defended Turkish positions. The allied troops could not get far inland from the beaches and the disastrous expedition was abandoned in December 1915. The retreat was the only well-organised part of the whole campaign. Winston Churchill, first lord of the admiralty, was blamed for the Gallipoli failure and resigned.

Britain, as an island, relied heavily on the navy, which kept up a continual blockade of Germany. The only major naval engagement of the war occurred off Jutland in the North Sea in May 1916; even though both sides suffered heavy losses, the British achieved a long-term victory for the Germans retreated to harbour. A more serious danger to Britain came from the German submarines, called U-boats, which threatened merchant ships bringing vital supplies: in one month alone they sank a million tons of British shipping. Lloyd George, who had taken over from Asquith as prime minister of a coalition government in 1916, ordered armed convoys to escort the merchant ships; against all prediction they were a great success. World War I was also the time when aerial warfare developed greatly. Over the trenches air battles raged, and the Germans bombed English cities for the first time from their Zeppelin airships.

SOCIAL CONDITIONS

Despite the horrifically high number of casualties, the war continued to be supported by most British people; the whole nation felt involved in the war-effort. Railways, coal mines and shipping were all taken into state control, strikes were forbidden and, as the men were sent to the front, women replaced them in the factories. Before national conscription was introduced in 1916, and while military service was voluntary, crude but often powerful propaganda was used to recruit new troops: a poster showed a little girl asking her father, 'What did you do in the Great War, Daddy?' The most famous recruiting poster portrayed Lord Kitchener, the secretary of state for war, sternly pointing his finger at the viewer, with the words 'Your Country Needs You'. A few days after the poster had appeared, over 100,000 men had volunteered. Thousands of women also served at the front – usually in the medical field hospitals. The urgency of the war tore down the old values, for a woman's place was now as much working in the factories as waiting at home for her sons or husband to return. Left-wing critics of the war noted ironically that it had produced greater social reforms than all the campaigning by politicians and unions in the previous twenty-five years.

The Americans joined the allies in 1917, although Russia withdrew as a combatant after the October Revolution in the same year. The Germans, who feared the increasing number of American forces, launched a major attack against the British lines at the Somme in 1918; the allied forces were forced back forty miles before they recovered and then advanced. The allied offensive quickened, and when the German commander, Ludendorff, realised that defeat was inevitable he signed an armistice. The end of the war came at 11 am on 11 November 1918.

THE PRICE PAID

Whilst there was little physical destruction of towns and cities in Britain, the total number of dead was tragically high. It was estimated that 750,000 had died and over 1.5 million were wounded. A memorial was erected in every town and village of Britain to remember the local people who died. Every year on the Sunday nearest to 11 November, Remembrance Sunday is held to remember the dead and poppies are sold to raise funds for the injured of this and other wars. The poppy was the obvious symbol: it covered the fields of Flanders where so many had died.

The Economy Declines

Towards the end of the war the returning soldiers had been promised a country 'fit for heroes' and in the immediate aftermath the country prospered under Lloyd George's coalition government. Some social reforms were undertaken, such as an extension of unemployment benefit, but the most important was the extension of the franchise to women over the age of thirty and men over twenty-one.

But Britain's economic position in the world had declined, and continued to deteriorate throughout the interwar years. Countries which were once dependent upon British manufactured goods had now built their own factories. Several industries were especially affected. Before the war the Lancashire cloth industry exported over six million yards, but by 1924 this figure was down to 4.5 million yards. Coal, steel and ship-building suffered badly at the hands of foreign competitors; in 1921 alone 300 orders for ships from British yards were cancelled. The labour-intensive traditional industries were worst hit, and as exports and profits fell so unemployment rose. The slump of 1921 forced the unemployment total over two million, and throughout the interwar years it never fell below the million mark. Yet there was a safety net of sorts: the unemployment benefit, first introduced in 1911, was extended in 1920 and then further in 1922. Unemployment benefit, or 'dole', gave workers a tiny, but significant, income on which to survive whilst out of work. It has been argued that one reason why Britain did not embrace Fascism or Communism was because of the cushioning effect of the dole against starvation and outright despair.

Ireland, 1910–1923

Until World War I the chances of settling the political future of Ireland hinged upon the prospect of Home Rule, which would have given a measure of independence to southern Ireland at least. The Liberal government of Asquith vacillated, mainly because it feared a violent reaction from the Protestants in the six northern counties of Ireland. By 1914 the situation was so bad that a civil war in Ireland seemed far more likely than war in Europe. With the advent of war the Home Rule Bill was shelved – and with it the hopes and fears of the people of Ireland.

THE EASTER RISING OF 1916

Many Irishmen, however, saw Home Rule as a poor substitute for real independence. During the war, though many fought for Britain, others were determined to further the cause of Irish independence rather than wait for the possibility of Home Rule at the end of the war. At Easter 1916 a group of Republicans launched an uprising in an attempt to gain independence from a war-torn Britain. They seized several strong points in Dublin, the most famous being the General Post Office, and fought off the British troops for several days.

The Republicans had no chance of winning in the Easter Rebellion. Up to this point the moderates in Ireland had not supported the uprising, but the British treatment of the prisoners, which included shooting fifteen Republican leaders, sent a shock wave of horror through the country. People flocked to join the Republican party Sinn Fein (Ourselves alone) which worked with the Irish Republican Army (IRA) to force the British to leave Ireland.

YEARS OF CONFLICT, 1916–1923

Two years later, in 1918, Sinn Fein had grown so powerful that it won seventy-three of the 105 Irish seats at Westminster, and so decided to set up a separate assembly in Ireland rather than go to the British Parliament. The Irish Parliament, known as the Dail Eireann (Assembly of Ireland), simply ignored the British. Led by Eamon De Valera, the Dail organised its own government and administered the country in its own way. In England a Home Rule Bill was passed in 1920 by the Lloyd George government, a move by which it was hoped to win back moderate support to the British. The six predominantly Protestant northern counties were partitioned from the south and given their own Parliament at Stormont in Belfast. Sinn Fein, unsurprisingly, rejected the Home Rule Bill.

In the following years terrible atrocities were committed on both sides. The IRA, who had about 2,000 'soldiers', attacked British properties and personnel, while the British-backed Royal Irish Constabulary (RIC), reinforced by English recruits known as the Black and Tans, were equally vicious: in one episode they burnt a large part of the Irish city of Cork. By 1921 the situation had become so serious that Lloyd

George pushed through a new Home Rule Bill. But the measure was seen by most Irishmen as being too little too late, and in 1921 Sinn Fein won 124 out of the 128 seats in the elections. Lloyd George met De Valera, and in 1922 the Irish Free State was founded. Ireland was now granted 'dominion' status in the empire, equivalent to that held by Canada and the other self-governing colonies.

The emergence of the Irish Free State led to a bloody civil war in southern Ireland between those who supported the agreement and the IRA, who wished to include the six northern counties as well. Eventually the moderates triumphed and the country was pacified under the leadership of William Cosgrave, who led the Irish Free State from 1922 to 1932.

Politics: A Quiet Revolution

The politics of the interwar years in Britain were noted for their moderation. Coalitions between the main parties of Conservative, Labour and Liberal came and went as the public voted in governments unlikely to revolutionise the country. A few Communist MPs who wanted radical change were elected, but they altered little. However, a quiet revolution was heralded by the continuing rise of the Labour party.

THE LABOUR PARTY

After World War I the Liberal party became riven with factional in-fighting and they lost their standing in the polls after 1922. Labour replaced them as the second party in what seemed to be a two-party system. From its beginnings in the late nineteenth century the Labour party had now become a major political force; support came predominantly from trades unions, which sponsored MPs, from people of the depressed inner-city areas and from middle-class intellectuals. The Russian Revolution was a mixed blessing, for while it promised better things for the masses, the communist tendencies of some Labour MPs lost votes. In January 1924 the Labour party, led by James Ramsay MacDonald (1866–1937), formed its first government, with tacit Liberal support. Although it only lasted for ten months, the minority Labour administration had shown that it could govern responsibly. That it had been in office at all further emphasised that it had replaced the Liberal party as the second major political force.

The Conservatives won a landslide victory in the election of October 1924 and in the following five years the image of the prime minister, Stanley Baldwin (1867–1947), as a calm, honest man, contentedly puffing his pipe, reflected upon the Conservative government as a whole. The only major disturbance of these years was the General Strike of 1926.

THE 1926 GENERAL STRIKE

The idea of a general strike was first seriously considered by the trades unions in 1921, but it was triggered five years later by the treatment of the coal-miners. An already bad economic position suddenly worsened in 1925 with a drop in coal exports. The government refused to nationalise the industry and it was left to the pit-owners to decide the wages. In 1926 they announced that the miners must accept lower wages and work longer hours. Understandably the miners were enraged and antagonised, and they threatened to strike on 1 May 1926; the owners retaliated by locking up the mines on 30 April. The TUC, the ruling body of all unions, gave its support to the miners and in an impressive display of solidarity the road, rail, docks, printing, electricity, iron, steel and chemical industries showed virtually 100 per cent support. There was little violent class confrontation (except in some depressed industrial areas such as the East End of London) even though white-collar workers and students rushed to take over the duties of the strikers, such as driving trucks and trains. The government seized land and buildings and used troops to continue vital services. These measures convinced the union leadership that the government was not about to back down, and on 12 May the TUC called off the strike. The left-wingers of the Labour movement saw the chance of revolution slip away.

The miners, who accused the TUC of betrayal, continued their strike until December but in the end were forced back to work through hunger. The government claimed a victory and, with the introduction of anti-union laws, union membership fell from eight million to five million over the next few years. The prospect of violent revolution had been apparently banished.

THE ARTS

In Europe and America the growing challenge of the 'modern' led to revolutions in all forms of the arts. After World War I European 'Modernism' became largely, and understandably, disillusioned, though great works came out of the movement. The Dublin novelist James Joyce (1882–1941), whose *Ulysses* (1922) is undoubtedly the masterpiece of the age, and the English novelist, Virginia Woolf (1882–1941), both experimented with the 'stream of consciousness'. D.H. Lawrence (1885–1930) wrote about new depths of feeling, and E.M. Forster (1879–1970) in his *A Passage to India* was sensitively pessimistic about relationships – both personal and imperial.

The 'War Poets' of World War I had produced graphic and horrific images of the war in which they had fought. Siegfried Sassoon (1886–1967), Herbert Read (1893–1968) and Robert Graves (1895–1985) all survived, but Rupert Brooke (1887–1915) and Wilfred Owen (1893–1918) died along with the hundreds of thousands of 'ordinary' citizen soldiers. After the war the most influential poet was T.S. Eliot (1888–1965) whose *The Waste Land* (1922) used a succession of themes and images expressing the disillusionment of post-war Britain.

Much of the mood of the twenties was governed by the need to forget, a trend cleverly demonstrated in the novels of Evelyn Waugh (1902–66). In still lighter mood P.G. Wodehouse (1881–1975) wrote, among much else, of the butler Jeeves, the natural superior of his good-natured but incompetent master Bertie Wooster. The poet and dramatist Noel Coward (1899–1973) became the embodiment of a spirit of witty cynicism. The popularity of detective novels by such exponents as Agatha Christie (1890–1976) and Dorothy L. Sayers (1893–1957) demonstrated the same escapist need. The dark threats of the 1930s – totalitarianism, Nazism and Stalinism – brought a similar darkening in the literary response. George Orwell (1903–50) described social deprivation and the impoverished lives of ordinary people in *The Road to Wigan Pier* (1937), and much else. (After World War II his most famous novel *1984* describes a nightmare totalitarianism in a conquered Britain.) The poetry of W.H. Auden (1907–73), Stephen Spender (1909–   ) and Louis MacNeice (1907–63) combined personal lyricism and perspective realism.

In music, Edward Elgar (1857–1934), Ralph Vaughan Williams (1872–1958) and William Walton (1902–1983) found inspiration from traditional English folk music; Elgar, indeed, was considered the most English of all the composers. In sculpture, two of the great English exponents began their careers in this era and continued long after World War II: both Henry Moore (1898–1986) and Barbara Hepworth (1903–75) had their first exhibitions in 1928 and helped to revolutionise sculpture. Also continuing after the war L.S. Lowry (1887–1976) painted unsentimental industrial landscapes around Manchester.

New developments were also bringing entertainment to a much greater range of people. The cinema was an even greater attraction than hitherto, especially with the advent of sound. Before, during and after World War II the British film industry boomed, producing many films, some of them masterpieces. The British Broadcasting Corporation, the BBC, was established in 1926: now people could be entertained and informed instantly in their own homes.

The Crash of 1931 and the National Government

Despite the General Strike (see p. 216), Labour just won the 1929 election and governed with the informal support of a small number of Liberal MPs. Yet global events were overtaking them. In 1929 Wall Street, the financial centre of the United States, crashed and sent a economic shock wave around the world. In Germany desperation produced political extremism which polarised support between the Fascist or Communist parties. In Britain the Labour government soon believed, perhaps mistakenly, that it could not cope. Ramsay MacDonald, the prime minister, under some pressure from George V, formed a National Government which included Conservatives and Liberals. Much of the Labour party was alienated and accused MacDonald of betraying the cause of socialism; however, this middle-of-the-road approach to the national crisis was very popular with the voters, and the coalition National Government was returned overwhelmingly to power in 1931 and 1935.

At the height of the financial crisis of 1931 the situation was so tense that naval crews mutinied against salary cuts at Invergordon. The government took various measures to lessen the effect of the financial chaos, such as devaluing the pound (thereby making exports cheaper), imposing import duties, and increasing inflation. By the mid-1930s the situation was improving, though it is now widely believed that the remedies implemented by the National Government had less effect on the nation's economic recovery than was once supposed.

UNEMPLOYMENT AND EXTREMISM

However, there were still regions with very high unemployment. The long-established industries of coal, iron, steel and ship-building continued to suffer from foreign competition and lack of exports. In 1933 J.B. Priestley (1894–1984) wrote in his *English Journey*: 'One out of every two shops appeared to be permanently closed. Wherever we went there were men hanging about . . . hundreds and thousands of them. The whole town looked as if it had entered a perpetual penniless bleak Sabbath.' One of the most famous incidents of the Great Depression was the Jarrow March of 1936, when unemployed shipbuilders from Jarrow walked to London. These representatives of the unemployed received support along the route and helped to publicise their plight, but the government did little to help.

In some areas of deprivation political extremism flourished. The British Union of Fascists was led by Oswald Mosley (1896–1980), who had originally been a member of the Labour government but had left in 1930. Unlike Germany and Italy the Fascists did not achieve nationwide support in Britain; the government's policy of 'safety first' appealed to the majority of voters. The Fascist party lost any nationwide appeal it may have had when, in 1934, Fascist 'Black Shirts' brutally ejected hecklers during a rally at Olympia in London.

The Empire

Despite losing its economic dominance throughout the interwar years, Britain still had the largest empire in the world. It included the wealthy 'white dominions' of Canada, Australia, New Zealand and South Africa, as well as vast areas of Africa, India, Burma and South-East Asia, and had been greatly increased in size at the end of World War I when Iraq,

Palestine and Transjordan had been given to Britain to administer as a mandate by the League of Nations. In the Middle East, during World War I, Britain had supported the Arabs against the Turks. A key military and political leader of the Arabs had been a British intelligence officer T.E. Lawrence (1888–1935) who became world famous as Lawrence of Arabia. After the war the Turkish Empire had been divided up between Britain, France and several Arab rulers. Iraq eventually achieved independence in 1932. In Palestine the conflict of interests between Jewish immigrants and Arabs caused great tension, which finally exploded after World War II.

One of the major events for the empire in the interwar years was the evolution of the British Commonwealth. During the war the dominions had loyally supported Britain, but they had also pressed for a clearer recognition of their status as independent nations within the empire. At the Imperial Conference of 1926 dominion status was reappraised and the term 'the British Commonwealth' was agreed upon to describe the self-governing parts of the empire. The dominion countries were defined as free countries, equal to each other and Britain, and with control of their own internal and external affairs though still owing allegiance to the British crown.

The imperial country to give most concern to the British in the interwar years was India. Under the leadership of Mahatma Gandhi and Jawaharlal Nehru the Indian nationalist movement demanded independence. The British government accepted that some sort of self-government was desirable but implemented reforms slowly. Gandhi organised successful non-violent protests, which were in marked contrast to the Amritsar massacre of Indians by the British army in 1919. The pressure continued and by the 1935 Government of India Act the Indian Assembly gained control of everything except defence and foreign policy.

The Abdication of Edward VIII

With the death of George V in 1936 Edward VIII came to the throne. As a prince he had enjoyed action, especially horse-riding, and had left Oxford to serve in the Grenadier Guards. He had wanted to fight in the trenches during World War I but this had been forbidden in case he was captured by the Germans. He ironically styled himself 'Ambassador Extraordinary' for his foreign trips to India, the United States, Canada and Australia. However, it was for an American that he gave up the throne.

In 1931 Edward met Wallis Simpson, an American with her second divorce pending. Over the years Edward and Mrs Simpson fell in love and by 1934 he was determined to marry her; her second divorce was awarded in 1935, freeing her to marry again. As the coronation was being planned, Edward performed the responsibilities of king with increasing reluctance. The press at last began to publicise the affair and it became obvious that Edward had to choose between the throne and Mrs Simpson. He chose Mrs Simpson and on 10 December 1936 he signed the document of abdication. He and Mrs Simpson left the country and were married. Taking the title Duke of Windsor, the ex-king who had once seemed so full of promise was a somewhat pathetic figure, rejected by his mother, Queen Mary, and bitterly resentful that his wife, now Duchess of Windsor, was denied the title 'Her Royal Highness'. He had flirted with Fascism before his abdication, and afterwards was imprudent enough to be received by Hitler in Germany. During World War II he made some amends by becoming governor-general of the Bahamas. He died in 1972 after a belated reconciliation with the British royal family – something that was achieved only by the constructive good sense of his niece, Queen Elizabeth II.

George VI, 1936–1952

When the Duke of York was told of his elder brother's abdication he exclaimed, 'It isn't possible! It isn't happening!' As the second son of George V and Queen Mary, he was unready for the position of king – he had not even seen a state paper – but despite only three weeks in which to prepare, he kept the coronation date which Edward had planned.

George VI was born in 1895 and christened Albert Frederick Arthur George. Rather than become King Albert he decided to emphasise the links with the past by becoming George VI. In 1923 he had married Lady Elizabeth Bowes-Lyon (the present Queen Mother) and the marriage proved to be long and happy. They had two children, Princess Elizabeth, born in 1926, and Princess Margaret, born in 1930. From 1931 until 1936 George devoted himself to his family.

In 1936 this domestic serenity was shattered by Edward's abdication. George VI's first years were difficult, for war looked increasingly probable. Like many of his generation who had witnessed World War I (he had fought in the navy at Jutland) he wished to avoid another conflict and supported Neville Chamberlain (1869–1940), who had become Conservative prime minister on Stanley Baldwin's retirement in 1937, in his attempt to appease Nazi Germany. Once war had been declared, however, he did everything possible to boost the morale of the country, Empire and Commonwealth, insisting that the royal family, too, should be subjected to rationing and relative austerity. During the war he visited North Africa and Malta; to the latter he gave the George Cross for gallantry in withstanding repeated air attacks.

After the war the king continued to play an influential role as a monarch who did his duty and shared his people's trials. He developed close and supportive relationships with both the Labour and Conservative prime ministers of the post-war years, Clement Attlee (1883–1969) and Winston Churchill (1874–1965). In 1948 he became ill and eventually developed cancer of the lung. He never recovered his health but continued with his many official engagements which included the opening of the Festival of Britain in 1951 (see p. 232). He died in his sleep on 6 Februrary 1952.

The Background to World War II

THE GROWTH OF FASCISM

In the 1930s the doctrine of Fascism had become increasingly powerful. In the Far East, Japan increased its empire by invading Manchuria in 1931. In Germany Hitler rebuilt the armed forces and then planned a policy of territorial and political expansion within Europe, advancing into the demilitarised Rhineland in 1936, actively helping the Fascists to win the Spanish Civil War, and occupying Austria in March 1938. Other countries followed similar policies, notably Italy under Mussolini who marched into Abyssinia in 1935, enraging world opinion by the use of gas and warplanes against their ill-equipped opponents.

'PEACE IN OUR TIME'

The key-note of British foreign policy during the 1930s was 'appease-ment' – a policy which gave way to the demands of the aggressive powers in the hope of buying peace, or at least time. Any military reaction to aggression was left to the efforts of private organisations and was not equipped or financed by the British government. A large contingent of British volunteers, which included the writer George Orwell, joined the Communist-backed International Brigade to fight the fascist forces in the Spanish Civil War.

With hindsight the policy of appeasement seems disastrous, but at the time the horrors of World War I were still alive in people's minds. In addition, governments were reluctant to rearm because of the massive costs involved. Many people also feared the Communists more than the Fascists and at first welcomed the rise of the right in Central Europe as a buffer to a Russian communist threat. Appeasement was actively pursued by Neville Chamberlain: in 1938 he flew to Munich for a meeting with Hitler and Mussolini, and returned in triumph with an agreement which he said would bring 'peace in our time'. With the outbreak of war a year later this agreement, and Chamberlain's vision of peace, were widely criticised. However, the extra year of peace allowed Britain time to prepare for war. Even so, though the production of new planes such as the Spitfire and the Hurricane increased, by the time war came the British forces were under-trained and badly equipped. One example of England's inadequate preparation came in 1939 when an incredulous German military attaché reported that he saw troops carrying gas pipes to represent anti-tank rifles and holding blue flags to denote the trucks they were supposed to be riding in.

World War II, 1939–1945

As in August 1914, Britain declared war on Germany because of a German invasion – this time of Poland. On 1 September 1939 the Germans entered Poland and on 3 September Neville Chamberlain announced to the nation that Britain was now at war. France also declared war on Nazi Germany.

THE EARLY YEARS, 1939–1941

In the early weeks of the war the main event in Britain was the evacuation of tens of thousands of children from the cities and towns to the countryside, to avoid what were thought to be imminent mass air-raids. The absence of a German invasion of France and the sense of anti-climax were such that this period became known in Britain as the 'phoney war'. (Poland fell shortly after the German invasion.) Military action by Britain and France was negligible at first, with the exception of a British force fighting at Narvik in defence of Norway. But the political situation in Britain changed rapidly when Germany invaded France and the Low Countries in May 1940. Chamberlain was obliged to resign as prime minister and on 13 May a coalition government was

Winston Churchill

formed for the duration of the war under a new prime minister, Winston Churchill.

WINSTON CHURCHILL

Churchill's previous career as a minister had been erratic, and many remembered the disaster of Gallipoli in World War I (see p. 211); but now aged sixty-five he proved a remarkable wartime prime minister. He was a stirring speaker and a master of the memorable line: 'I have nothing to offer but blood, toil, tears and sweat' and, after the Battle of Britain, 'Never in the field of human conflict was so much owed by so many to so few'. His gruff voice, his self-confidence and the large cigars he smoked helped to make him a larger-than-life figure, and his determination to achieve victory rallied the country behind him. Among the other members of the Cabinet were the Labour leader, Clement Attlee, and the newspaper magnate Lord Beaverbrook, who increased the production of fighter aircraft.

DUNKIRK 1940

The comparative peace of the 'phoney war' was shattered in 1940 as the German forces swept through France. The inadequate equipment and training of British troops was no match for the Germans' method of Blitzkrieg, ('lightning war'). As the Germany Panzer tank divisions rolled through France and the Luftwaffe (the German air force) harried the allied ground forces, the troops of the British Expeditionary Force retreated to Dunkirk on the French coast. A massive rescue operation was organised in which naval ships and small private boats took allied troops off the beaches of France and transported them back to Britain. Between 27 May and 4 June 1940 over 340,000 men were rescued. The evacuation was seen both as a miracle and a victory: a victory snatched from the jaws of utter defeat. Even so the situation was perilous. The French surrendered on 22 of June, and Britain, with the distant but solid backing of the empire, now stood alone against the victorious Germans and their triumphant Blitzkrieg tactics. As Hitler began preparing for the invasion of Britain, Churchill was defiant: 'We shall defend our island, whatever the cost may be. We shall fight on the beaches, we shall fight on the landing grounds, we shall fight in the fields and in the streets, we shall fight in the hills. We shall never surrender.'

'THEIR FINEST HOUR': THE BATTLE OF BRITAIN 1940

With only the English Channel separating the Germans from England, much depended upon control of the air. If the Luftwaffe gained superiority a safe Channel crossing could be assured, despite the superiority of the Royal Navy; if not, then the Royal Air Force could cut the German supply lines. The heaviest fighting took place between 24 August and 6 September 1940: on 6 September alone the RAF lost 161 planes and the Luftwaffe 190. British resources were soon stretched to the limit as pilots were killed and could not be replaced, and fuel supplies and aircraft were destroyed. The situation became increasingly critical, since industrial production could not keep up with task of replacing fighter aircraft.

Britain's perilous position was underestimated by Goering, the commander of the Luftwaffe. As a reprisal for some daring British bombing raids on Berlin, he ordered that English cities should be bombed in an attempt to demoralise the population. As a result, the attacks upon the airfields dwindled and the RAF had a chance to rebuild. Moreover, the Germans failed to knock out the vital British radar network. On 15 September the Luftwaffe lost sixty planes compared to the twenty-six lost by the RAF. The RAF had won; lacking command of the skies, Hitler abandoned his invasion plans on 17 September. Though the situation was still bleak, the most dangerous time had been survived. Large-scale bombing raids by both sides continued throughout the war and many English cities were seriously damaged, notably London, Plymouth and Coventry. In Coventry the shell of the burnt-out cathedral has been left as a reminder of the raid which destroyed the heart of the city.

Japan entered the war with a sudden and lethal attack on the American naval base at Pearl Harbor on 7 December 1941, and the United States entered the war. Japan also attacked in the Far East and captured the British possessions of Malaya, Burma, Hong Kong and Singapore between December 1941 and March 1942. An attack on India seemed imminent, although it never materialised.

THE TURN OF THE TIDE

From 1941 the tide of war began to turn. In July of that year the German forces attacked Russia. Britain and Russia quickly became allies which meant that Hitler was now fighting on two fronts. Indeed, it was the Soviet Union's heroic resistance which finally broke the back of the German war machine and enabled the western allies to strike back at their enemies with greater confidence.

The first major allied successes occurred in North Africa. By 1942 the German Afrika Corps, led by Rommel, had advanced eastward across North Africa to within seventy miles of the Egyptian port of Alexandria. The allied Eighth Army, nicknamed the Desert Rats, led by General Montgomery, won the ensuing battle of El Alamein. This was the first major victory of the war and led to the retreat of the German forces from North Africa in 1943. Command of the North African coast allowed the allies to capture Sicily in 1943 and then to invade mainland Italy later in the same year. This led to the downfall of Mussolini, the Italian dictator, also in 1943. His successor signed an armistice and brought Italy into the war on the allied side. The German troops occupying Italy defended brutally and tenaciously, and there were major battles at Salerno, Anzio and Cassino in 1943 and 1944. Milan was not captured by the allies until 1945.

A plan for opening up another front by invading France was prepared, and on 6 June 1944 (D-Day) the allied forces landed on the Normandy coast. The logistics of 'Operation Overlord', as the invasion was officially known, were astounding: over 1,200 ships had been assembled, along with 10,000 planes and 156,000 troops; 132,500 troops landed from the sea, whilst 23,500 were either parachuted into France or arrived in troop gliders. As the allied forces had no harbour to unload supplies (the French port of Cherbourg was not captured until 26 June), they constructed floating ports, called Mulberry Harbours, and towed them across the English Channel to the Normandy coast.

The allied forces fought their way across France and through Belgium. They suffered some defeats, notably at Arnhem where an attempt to capture some vital bridges narrowly failed, and when the Germans later counter-attacked at the battle of the Bulge. But the pressure of the British, Americans and Free French from the west, and the Russians from the east, proved too much for the German forces. As Russian tanks neared Berlin, Hitler committed suicide on 30 April 1945. On 8 May 1945 VE-Day (Victory in Europe Day) was celebrated by jubilant crowds all over Britain. World War II officially ended on VJ-Day (Victory over Japan Day), 14 August 1945, after the surrender of the Japanese. Their capitulation had, however, been brought about by the total destruction of the cities of Hiroshima and Nagasaki in a few seconds by atomic bombs – events which meant that global history was beginning a new and dangerous era.

CHAPTER TEN

Contemporary England,
1945–2000

During the post-war years, until the late 1970s, several strong trends were evident in the development of England. The principal one was the concept of 'Consensus Government', which resulted in the two major parties, Labour and Conservative, having very similar policies. In the 1950s this was sometimes satirised by the press as Butskellism – a combination of the names of the then Conservative Chancellor of the Exchequer, R.A. Butler (1902–82), and the former Labour chancellor, and then leader, Hugh Gaitskell (1906–63).

Internationally, each successive government tried to keep up the image of the country as a 'Great Power'. In the closing stages of World War II Churchill had attended the Yalta summit between Russia, America and Britain in order to divide up the spoils of victory. When Attlee took over as prime minister he also promoted Britain's image as one of the 'Big Three' powers. Yet even then Britain was being eclipsed by other major world powers, and through the following decades its influence in the world steadily diminished, despite trying to convince itself to the contrary.

Labour in Power, 1945–1951

Even though no land battle had been fought on English soil, the country had suffered badly during World War II. Many cities had been severely damaged by bombing, merchant ships had been sunk, and the cost of the war had resulted in a war debt of £3,000 million. The gold reserves left in Britain were an insignificant £3 million.

After the war in Europe ended, the coalition government disbanded and a general election was held in July 1945. The Conservatives relied heavily upon Churchill's personality and 'war leader' image. His brilliant speeches attracted large crowds and he never missed an opportunity to attack the Labour party and its leader, Clement Attlee, variously describing him as a 'sheep in sheep's clothing' and 'a modest little man with plenty to be modest about'. It is a measure of Churchill's misjudgement that Attlee won the biggest victory in Labour's history by promising better conditions for those returning from the war. This victory confirmed Attlee as a shrewd politician and administrator behind his seemingly dull and modest exterior. He had, after all, been a successful deputy prime minister during the war. He survived several attempts to oust him from office and implemented one of the greatest changes that Britain has ever seen in a single Parliament.

NATIONALISATION AND THE WELFARE STATE

The Labour government set about reconstructing the nation. There were two main parts to its plan: the state control of industry and public utilities through the policy of nationalisation, and the creation of 'The Welfare State', so called as a deliberate contrast to Hitler's 'Warfare State'. Major industries and enterprises were successively nationalised: the Bank of England (1946), the coal industry (1946), electricity and gas (1947) and transport, comprising air transport (1946) and road, rail and waterways (1947). Thus roughly 20 per cent of all British industry was brought into public ownership between 1945 and 1950. Apart from heated debates concerning the nationalisation of the iron and steel industry, there was virtually no resistance from the Conservative opposition which had accepted the wartime need for central control of the economy.

In the social sector the most spectacular reform was the creation of the National Health Service (1946). For the first time, free medical advice and treatment was available to all at no cost, whether medicines, spectacles, or maternity and child welfare services. Nationwide care for the injured and seriously ill became available after hospitals were nationalised. At first there was huge opposition from doctors to the reforms (over 90 per cent threatened to boycott the scheme), but they were eventually accepted. The National Health Service became the bedrock of the Welfare State.

That these far-sighted policies were implemented at all was a tribute to the determination of a Labour government facing terrible economic conditions. The enormous war debt, owed mainly to the United States, resulted in new and more stringent financial measures, and 1947 proved to be a year of economic crisis. An exceptionally hard winter caused a fuel shortage, which hampered exports. Food was still severely rationed; the amount of food available for one person per week was meagre: 1 egg, 2 pints of milk, 1½ ounces of cheese and 13½ ounces of meat; in 1948 bread and potatoes were rationed for the first time. However, an important step on the road to recovery was taken in 1947 when the United States introduced the Marshall Plan to help European economic recovery. Seventeen countries took part, though Britain benefited most. Taken together with other measures, such as a devaluation of the pound, expanding world markets and the revival of the wartime spirit that 'Britain can take it', the balance of payments deficit shrank rapidly. By 1949 and 1950 rationing began to be abolished: rationing of clothes and restrictions on meals in restaurants both ended in 1950, and egg rationing in 1953, after twelve years. Meat rationing was the last to go, in 1954.

THE COLD WAR AND NATO

After the end of the war the goodwill that existed between Russia and the western powers quickly vanished. While touring America in 1946 Churchill made a famous speech emphasising the threat of communist expansionism; in his characteristically brilliant use of words he described how 'from Stettin in the Baltic to Trieste in the Adriatic an iron curtain has descended across the continent'. The bond between Europe and the United States had already been economically strengthened by the Marshall Plan (in which no communist country was involved) and the bond was militarily cemented in 1949 by the formation of the North Atlantic Treaty Organisation (NATO). For the first time the defences of Europe and North America were meshed together. The superpowers now faced each other across the continent of Europe, with the capitalist island of West Berlin proving to be a constant irritant to the Russians.

In 1948 Russia had tried to resolve the situation by blockading all overland routes to Berlin in order to force the West to withdraw from the city. Instead the West started an airlift of supplies to the beleaguered city. It was a calculated risk that the Russians would not shoot down the transport planes from Britain and elsewhere, and for ten months the airlift kept the population of Berlin warmed and fed. In May 1949 the Russians lifted the blockade by opening up the land routes to Berlin again.

The Cold War continued, with spies on both sides, the most famous Russian spies in Britain being Philby, Burgess and Maclean, who were finally exposed and defected to Russia.

'You've Never Had It So Good': Britain in the 1950s

After an indecisive general election in 1950, which returned Labour by a narrow margin, a further election was held in 1951 and gave the Conservatives a majority, although, by one of the freaks of the British voting system, Labour actually gained 230,000 more votes than the Conservatives. The Conservatives were to hold office for thirteen years.

Winston Churchill now became prime minister in his first and only peacetime government. However, the years since the war had taken their toll: he had suffered two strokes – he was to suffer two more in office – and according to his doctor 'his old capacity for work has gone and with it much of his self-confidence'. Yet the economic prospects were excellent, chiefly owing to an upturn in world trade. When the Conservatives came to power in 1951 the balance of payments deficit was £700 million; in 1952 there was a surplus of £300 million.

In 1951 the Festival of Britain was organised to symbolise the fact that Britain was emerging from the austerities of wartime, and to indicate to the world that Britain had recovered her old supremacy. It was held on the south bank of the Thames in London as a celebration of the new era and to mark the centenary of the Great Exhibition. A lasting reminder of the event is the Festival Hall, situated on the site of the exhibition.

Queen Elizabeth II and the Royal Family

When George VI died on 6 February 1952 he was succeeded by his daughter, Elizabeth II, who was crowned at Westminister Abbey on 2

Queen Elizabeth II and the Duke of Edinburgh

June the following year. The coronation was the first great state occasion to be televised, and city centres were deserted as families, friends and neighbours huddled round the 10-inch black and white screens. To cap the celebrations, news came through that Edmund Hillary and Sherpa Tenzing had conquered Everest. It seemed, indeed, as if a new and promising era had begun. Queen Elizabeth was only twenty-five when she came to the throne and was already a wife and mother. In November 1947 she had married Lieutenant Philip Mountbatten, who although a Greek prince was, like her, a great-great-grandchild of Queen Victoria; he was created Duke of Edinburgh. A year later Elizabeth gave birth to her first child, Prince Charles; they subsequently had three more children Princess Anne (born in 1950), Prince Andrew (1960) and Prince Edward (1964).

The royal family have become respected for the part they play in public life. They often tour the Commonwealth nations and the British Isles, and every social engagement is avidly reported by journalists. Even in their leisure pursuits, which are very varied, they are constantly in the public eye. The queen has her own racing stables; the Duke of Edinburgh is President of the World Wide Fund for Nature; Prince Charles speaks out on subjects like the environment and architecture; Princess Anne campaigns for the Save the Children Fund; Prince Andrew served in the 1982 Falklands campaign; and Prince Edward's main interests lie with the theatre. Leaving aside the adulation expressed for the royal family in the popular press and elsewhere, there is no doubt that the monarchy is well regarded by the vast mass of the British people.

NEW TOWNS: HOMES FOR THE MASSES

During Churchill's premiership, between 1951 and 1955, there was a major housing initiative by Harold Macmillan (1894–1986), an up-and-coming politician. One of the legacies of the war was the huge amount of bomb damage, homelessness and dereliction within the inner cities. Macmillan was determined to change this and surpassed his target of 300,000 houses a year by achieving 680,000 new houses in two years. Most of these houses formed 'New Towns', each containing a central shopping area around which were located industry and housing. Many of these new towns, such as Hemel Hempstead to the north and Crawley to the south, circled London, leaving the 'Green Belt' undeveloped in between.

New housing conditions, several cuts in income tax and the maintenance of full employment meant that the social structure began to change. The number of people rising out of the 'working-class' to consider themselves 'lower middle-class' rose dramatically, and after a few years the Conservative government could for the first time speak of a 'property-owning democracy'.

EDEN AND SUEZ, 1955–1957

By 1955 Churchill was eighty and in ill health. He was persuaded to resign and Macmillan commented, 'Now that he has really decided to go, we are all miserable.' The new prime minister, Sir Anthony Eden, called a general election, which the Conservatives won convincingly. Eden was at the height of his power; he had a reputation as an international statesman, had charm, and his 'training, knowledge and courage' were widely written about in the press. But within two years his reputation had been destroyed, largely due to the Suez fiasco of 1956.

In 1955 Colonel Nasser, the new leader of Egypt, nationalised the Suez Canal. Although he promised compensation to the British and French shareholders in the canal, Britain was concerned at the rise of Egyptian nationalism and the potential cutting of communications to the Far East. Eden described Nasser as 'having his thumb on our windpipe'. In October the Israelis launched an invasion of the Egyptian-owned Sinai Peninsula. Britain and France issued an ultimatum demanding that Egypt and Israel withdraw ten miles from the canal; Israel complied, but Egypt refused. In response, a joint Anglo–French force was organised and on 6 November it occupied Port Said, at the north end of the canal.

Although the invasion was initially successful, the basic question of how long the Anglo–French forces were to stay in the canal zone had not been considered in detail. Most of the world united against the action, with the Americans and Russians for once in accord and demanding a ceasefire. Britain and France withdrew from Egypt in humiliation, Nasser's prestige soared, and Eden was so exhausted that he resigned. Suez proved, if proof were needed, that Britain could no longer act as a world power.

The Macmillan Years, 1957–1964

Harold Macmillan, the Chancellor of the Exchequer during the Suez crisis, became the new Conservative prime minister. In many ways he was a political enigma: a skilful and ruthless politician with a taste for international politics, who at the same time had a reputation for caring for the ordinary people of the country. During his early years in office he became known by his opponents, and some admirers, as 'Super Mac', and he led the Conservatives to a very comfortable victory in the 1959 election.

Economically the 1950s had been a time of 'stop–go' policies, with British industry experiencing economic expansion, followed by contraction and then expansion again. Governments tended to initiate a 'go' phase just before a general election, as happened in 1959 when the Conservatives retained power. For the majority of the population the fifties and early sixties were a time of increasing prosperity. The austerities of the forties were swept away and, as wages rose nearly twice as fast as prices, consumer goods became affordable. Between 1951 and 1963 the number of cars owned increased dramatically from under three million to over seven million, and the number of televisions in use rose from 300,000 to over twelve million. People had more leisure time, as the working week was cut from forty-eight to forty-two hours in 1961. With the economy manageable, the main issues were defence and foreign policy.

DEFENCE: THE NUCLEAR ISSUE AND CND

Britain's nuclear policy dated back to 1946 when Attlee, without informing Parliament, had allowed work on a British atom bomb to begin. In 1952 the first British bomb had been tested. To its supporters the bomb was a symbol that Britain was still a major world power – and possibly a superpower. In Parliament Churchill's son, Randolph, asserted that Britain had the capacity to destroy twenty-four Russian cities, ending his speech with the statement: 'We are a world power again.' The nuclear deterrent also had economic implications as it was hoped that the armed forces could be reduced from 700,000 to 165,000 by 1962. At first all went well: the development of the Blue Streak missile meant that 13,000 troops were withdrawn from Europe.

However, opposition to the atom bomb was beginning to grow. The Labour party were divided over the value of nuclear weapons: many left-wing MPs and trade unions (who supported and helped to finance the Labour party) wanted to get rid of the deterrent, whilst the leadership supported the deployment of nuclear weapons. This split continued until the late 1980s. The Campaign for Nuclear Disarmament (CND) was started in 1957 with the stated aim of expelling nuclear weapons from Britain. The most celebrated CND events of the early years were the annual marches, starting in 1958, from London to the Aldermaston nuclear research establishment in Berkshire. Eventually the escalating costs of nuclear research caused the government to

The Aldermaston March

abandon the Blue Streak project in 1960, leaving a gaping hole in British defences. Prime Minister Macmillan therefore turned to the Americans to fill the gap. The Polaris missile – which could be fired from submarines – was adopted in 1962, with the proviso that the weapons should not be used without mutual American and British consent. Harold Wilson, who had become the Labour party leader in 1963 on the death of Hugh Gaitskell, retorted that the 'independent British deterrent' was neither independent nor British nor a deterrent.

The acceptance of the American Polaris missile resulted in Britain forging closer links with America than with Europe. The European countries, especially France led by General de Gaulle, found the Anglo–American relationship deeply suspicious: it was felt that America could influence European decisions through British diplomatic channels. In the early 1960s Britain had been trying to get into the European Economic Community (EEC), with behind-the-scenes American backing, but this was vetoed by de Gaulle, who was determined to give Europe a voice independent from America.

The Decline of Empire: The Growth of Commonwealth

Between 1945 and 1960 500 million people in former British dependencies became self-governing, with nearly all of the newly independent states becoming members of the British Commonwealth. Whilst it was seen by many as the loss of empire, others viewed the granting of independence as 'a major event in world history', and certainly the formation of the Commonwealth is unique amongst all the overseas empires. The growth of independence came in two main stages. The first, under the Labour government of 1945–51, included India, Pakistan, Burma, Sri Lanka and Palestine; the second, during the late fifties and early sixties, saw many African countries, the West Indies and imperial possessions in South-East Asia gain their independence.

INDIA AND PAKISTAN

India's nationalist campaign had somewhat abated during World War II, but with the return of peace the Indians reasserted their demands with vigour. Although Attlee wanted a delay in granting independence, several factors were against him: post-war reconstruction and the establishment of the welfare state were costly, and empire seemed increasingly irrelevant; Indian distrust of British intentions was mounting; and growing antagonism between Muslim and Hindu was expressed in the bloody Calcutta riots. The most expedient step was to divide India into two states. An Act of Parliament was rushed through in August 1947: the Muslim majority areas became Pakistan, whilst the Hindu majority areas became India. Four hundred million people had gained political independence. Millions of refugees crossed the borders of the new states to reach the country appropriate to their religion. Communal massacres accompanied these mass migrations, and in the Punjab alone over 250,000 people were slain. Despite the bloodshed accompanying partition, Britain's role was generally seen as benevolent and constructive, and the newly freed nations joined the rapidly expanding Commonwealth.

THE MIDDLE EAST

Palestine had been occupied by the British since 1919, but serious difficulties arose out of the growing hostilities between the Arabs and the Jews. After World War I increasing numbers of Jews had settled in Palestine, and during and after World War II this flow had become a torrent. The atrocities inflicted upon the Jews under the Nazis meant that the ideal of a 'national home' raised even stronger passions. In Palestine they started a terrorist campaign against the British occupying forces. The worst incident occurred in 1946 when ninety-six British soldiers died after a bomb attack. The violence continued unabated and Britain, under some pressure from the United States, decided to withdraw in 1948, leaving the Jews and Arabs to fight it out. A new state, Israel, was established as the British withdrew, and the surrounding Arab states launched an invasion which was successfully repelled by the Israelis. The British were generally criticised for the manner of their leaving, but a peaceful solution to the Arab–Jewish confrontation seemed beyond them.

THE WIND OF CHANGE: THE COMMONWEALTH IN THE LATE 1950s AND 1960s

In 1960 Harold Macmillan spoke of the 'wind of change' blowing through the African continent. Throughout the 1950s and into the 1960s Britain's African colonies had been rapidly advancing towards independence. This pressure, combined with the generally sympathetic attitude of the British government, led to a wholesale granting of independence. African countries who achieved their independence during this time included Nigeria, Ghana (formerly the Gold Coast), Uganda, Kenya and Tanzania. The majority of the transitions to independence were peaceful. However, in Kenya the Kikuyu people organised a secret society, the Mau Mau, and carried out attacks upon white settlers; only after a major anti-terrorist campaign by British forces did the situation become stable enough to allow Kenya to proceed to black majority rule.

South Africa continued to pose a threat to the unity of the Commonwealth. In 1909 a united South Africa had received dominion status which gave it virtual independence, although it still remained in the empire. The white minority, which formed 20 per cent of the population, felt increasingly threatened by the development of black African nationalism throughout the continent and were determined to preserve their power. They did so by implementing even more rigorously the policy of *apartheid* – the complete segregration of the races. Amidst mounting criticism from around the world, in 1960 South Africa voted to become a republic, but was then denied continuing membership of the Commonwealth on the grounds that *apartheid* was unacceptable.

The British withdrew from other parts of the world as well as Africa. The West Indian islands of Jamaica and Trinidad received independence in 1962, Malaya in 1957, Cyprus in 1960 and Malta in 1964. In all but a few instances, every country which gained independence joined the Commonwealth. The principal exceptions were Burma, which left the Commonwealth in 1948, the Irish Republic (1949), South Africa (1961) and Palestine. Of all the other overseas empires, none was translated into an organisation like the Commonwealth. It has no control over the member countries, has very little administrative machinery, and its existence rests upon a certain amount of mutual self-interest and upon the Commonwealth ideal, which Queen Elizabeth, its head, stated in 1953: 'The Commonwealth . . . is built on friendship, loyalty and the desire for freedom and peace.'

The Swinging Sixties: Freedom and Intolerance

Socially the sixties were the age of youth. The affluent society had arrived in the fifties and the post-war 'baby boom' meant that the number of young people rose dramatically. With the austerities of the war left behind the atmosphere became vibrant and exciting. The rules of the 'establishment' were reviled, and freedom and experimentation were seen as the way to happiness. For the first time the teenage years and early twenties were treated as an entity in their own right. New freedoms meant that the social behaviour became more daring, as exemplified by the sexual revolution which changed many people's attitudes to sex and marriage. Popular culture was also altered. The musical scene was changed for ever by such groups as The Beatles, The Rolling Stones and The Who. Television increased greatly in popularity; investigative documentaries highlighted social wrongs, and satirical programmes, which culminated in *Monty Python's Flying Circus* at the end of the decade and into the 1970s, turned accepted behaviour upside down. Kingsley Amis (1922–) also satirised the English way of life in literature. To the older generation clothes often seemed shocking, with the introduction of the sometimes unbelievably short mini-skirt, and the flowery shirts and open-toed sandals of the hippy culture. At the height of the excitement the major footballing achievement in English history occurred when England won the World Cup at Wembley in 1966, beating West Germany 4–2. The zenith of the sixties apparently had been reached for many English people.

Between the wars and into the 1950s 'culture' was thought to be the preserve of an élite minority and T.S. Eliot had written in 1939 that a mass culture leads to the depression of standards. However, attitudes were changing and the last great expression of the post-war mood of depression was the Irish playwright Samuel Beckett's (1906–89) play *Waiting for Godot* (1953). In 1956 a new era dawned with the first production of John Osborne's (1929–   ) *Look Back in Anger*. Other 'kitchen sink' dramas followed. The ordinary daily lives of people were presented to a mass audience and were accepted as 'culture'. Censorship began to be challenged: after a famous trial for obscenity D.H. Lawrence's novel *Lady Chatterley's Lover* became available, unexpurgated, to a mass audience. During the trial the forces of reaction were exposed to ridicule when the prosecuting counsel asked the jury if they would allow their servants to read the book. In the theatre many censorship restrictions were lifted, and although some remained for films there was a notable slackening off.

Yet the freedoms which were realised also had a negative side. The atmosphere of experimentation, especially amongst the young, led to a drug culture taking root, with the availability of such drugs as cannabis and the much stronger LSD (the capital letters of the Beatles' song 'Lucy in the Sky with Diamonds' can represent 'LSD'). Changes were also taking place in the urban landscape: high-rise tower blocks were believed to be the economical answer to the destruction of the slums in the major cities. Many new idealistic housing schemes were awarded prizes at the time, but the reality of life in a tower block was often very different to the architects' dreams. In 1968 a tower block in East London partially collapsed, and gradually exploitation and profiteering were exposed. The results of the planning blight of the sixties is all too visible in inner-city areas today.

In 1958 London saw the first race riots in Britain at Notting Hill, where violence broke out between West Indians and the local white population. During the late fifties and early sixties immigration had rapidly increased. Full employment in Britain created a labour shortage in the low-paid jobs which whites did not want, but which were eagerly filled by Indians, Pakistanis and West Indians who were entitled to full access to Britain on the independence of their countries. By 1961 113,000 immigrants had arrived in the United Kingdom. Many people objected to the new influx and they found a spokesman in the Conservative politician, Enoch Powell. In 1968 he spoke of the 'rivers of blood' that racial tensions would generate, and had to resign from the Conservative opposition front bench. At grass-roots level opposition was growing: in 1966 a number of ultra right-wing groups joined together to form the National Front.

POLITICS

By 1962 the Conservative government was facing economic decline and rising unemployment. On the international level Prime Minister Macmillan's initiatives had failed with both the Blue Streak nuclear development (see p. 236) and entry into the European Economic Community (see p. 237). Macmillan was worried enough to take ruthless measures and on 13 July 1962 sacked one-third of his cabinet in a political purging known as 'The Night of the Long Knives'. As a Liberal MP wryly commented: 'Greater love hath no man than this, that he lays down his friends for his life.' The following year the government was again rocked by the Profumo Scandal, which contained elements of sex, compromised national security and the Russian threat. The war minister, John Profumo, had been having an affair with a call-girl, Christine Keeler, who was also intimate with a Russian diplomat widely presumed to have been a spy. Macmillan was humiliated by the scandal, which convinced many that he was out of touch and not in control. In 1963 he expediently fell ill and resigned, to be replaced by Sir Alex Douglas-Home as the Conservative leader and prime minister.

Labour in Power, 1964–1970

Labour leader Harold Wilson (1916–1995) appealed to the public with his dry wit and easy television manner. Apparently a clever but bluff northerner, he seemed far more in tune with the national mood than the aristocratic Douglas-Home. In the general election of 1964 Wilson's emphasis on new technology, modernisation and growth gave the Labour party a tiny majority in Parliament, though in 1966 this was dramatically increased to just under one hundred.

Whilst society was distracted by the social changes of the sixties, the Labour government had some difficult economic problems to face. The main crises occurred over the value of sterling against other currencies, and over the growing balance of payment deficit. The remedies included increasing taxes, cutting expenditure on defence and house-building, devaluing the pound against the dollar, and attempting to impose a wage freeze upon the unions. This last one was a deeply unpopular measure which produced wild-cat strikes (strikes where employees simply walked out without any kind of ballot) and several industrial disputes; the worst strikes were among the dock-workers of London and Liverpool, which affected the balance of payments statistics. The strikes were economically damaging, but there was no danger of the government being ousted. Unlike France, those on strike did not join forces with the British students who demonstrated against the war in Vietnam and for other causes.

By the end of the decade the Labour government had had some success with the economy. One in five people owned a car – an increase of over three million cars – and the proportion of homeowners rose from 46 to 50 per cent; by 1970 over 90 per cent of householders owned a television. The age of affluence continued, but against all the opinion poll trends a Conservative government under Edward Heath (1916–) surprisingly won the 1970 general election. It has been rightly argued that, although prosperity increased under the Labour government, the rise had not been as fast as the politicians had promised and many voters expected, and so the electorate had become disillusioned.

NORTHERN IRELAND: THE START OF 'THE TROUBLES'

Southern Ireland, which had broken away from British rule in 1922 (see p. 213), had remained neutral in World War II and had declared itself an independent republic in 1949. In the six northern counties a different system had evolved, for there the Protestant majority wanted to remain part of the United Kingdom. For over half a century Northern Ireland had its own Parliament at Stormont, and sent twelve MPs to the UK Parliament in London. Northern Ireland politics up to the late 1960s were dominated by the 'Unionists' who wanted these close links to remain. Their most trenchant opponents were hard-line Catholics who wanted to join the two parts of Ireland into one nation. The most extreme Catholic group were the Irish Republican Army (IRA) which had sporadically committed outrages in the 1950s and 1960s.

By the late 1960s the situation had become dramatically worse. The Catholic minority in the north (about 30 per cent of the population) protested with increasing vigour about discrimination in housing, jobs and voting rights. From 1968 they began to campaign for full equality but the Protestants, fearful of their own privileged position, broke up the civil rights marches. By 1969 the violence had become so bad that Prime Minister Harold Wilson sent troops into Belfast and Londonderry to protect the Catholics from Protestant attacks.

The Turbulent Seventies

The years of Edward Heath's Conservative government (1970–4) were dominated by two main issues: entry into the EEC and the power of the trade unions. Attempts to get into the EEC were nothing new; the French president, de Gaulle, had vetoed British entry in 1963 and 1967, but in 1969 he resigned and the most obvious obstacle had been removed. As the possibility of entry to the EEC approached, a growing number of MPs – especially on the Labour side – became 'Anti-Marketeers', determined to keep Britain out of Europe. The issue dominated the politics of the early seventies, with passions roused on both sides, but on 1 January 1973 Britain entered the Common Market.

Meanwhile, the problems of the economy and of the trade unions were becoming acute. As the economic situation worsened – inflation increased, the economy stagnated and wage demands rose out of control – the government reacted in 1972 by imposing a 'freeze' on the price of goods, services, rents and wages for ninety days, which did nothing to endear it to the unions. Throughout that year the miners, railwaymen and dock-workers all flexed their industrial muscles by taking strike action.

THE 1974 MINERS' STRIKE

Further government measures included stringent monitoring of pay rises in 1973 which led to industrial action by many groups, especially the miners and the electricity power workers. To make matters worse, oil supplies were disrupted in 1973 by the Arabs, in retaliation for tacit support of Israel during the Arab–Israeli war. On 13 November 1973 the government declared a national emergency. Drastic energy-saving measures were imposed: electricity supplies were rationed, the maximum speed limit was reduced from 70 miles per hour to 50 in order to save petrol, television had to close down by 10.30, and industry could only work on three specified days a week. When domestic electricity was turned off, families huddled around gas or coal fires and lit the darkness with candles. Settlements and formulas were passed back and forth between the government and the TUC, but to no avail; in February 1974 the miners voted for an all-out strike. Heath decided to make an election issue out of the unions versus the government, and so the general election campaign started with the state of emergency still in force. Television times were lengthened to allow for political broadcasts.

LABOUR, 1974–1979

Although the Conservatives were generally expected to win the election, they gained fewer seats than Labour and resigned office. After 184 days a second election was held which gave Labour just a large enough majority to govern effectively. The same concerns were evident in the Labour administration as in the previous Conservative one. In 1975 a nationwide referendum was organised to decide once and for all whether Britain should stay in the EEC. Despite intense lobbying by anti-marketeers the final vote was 2–1 in favour of remaining a member.

An attempt at co-operation between the Labour party and the unions resulted in the social contract, an agreement which attempted to keep both wage increases and price rises low. In 1975 the inflation rate had risen to 24 per cent, but by the social contract and stringent pay controls it was down to 10 per cent by 1978. Even so the government's majority in Parliament had slipped to one.

Harold Wilson had resigned as prime minister in 1976 and been replaced by Jim Callaghan (1912–   ). He was obliged to come to an agreement with the Liberals, who had gained fourteen seats at the previous election. The Lib–Lab Pact prolonged the life of the Labour government for another two years. It also needed the support of Scottish and Welsh Nationalist MPs, and in return organised referenda to decide whether Scotland and Wales should have their own governments. The outcome was a resounding 'No' vote to devolution in Wales and a half-hearted 'Yes' vote in Scotland, so both schemes were abandoned.

It was widely expected that Callaghan would go to the polls in the autumn of 1978, as the economic situation was steadily improving, but he believed the outcome of the election would be uncertain and so delayed it. In the face of economic difficulties, wage rises were limited to 5 per cent and widespread strikes followed. The Conservative press termed the period 'the winter of discontent'. The election of 1979, precipitated by the government narrowly losing a vote of confidence in the Commons, brought the Conservatives back to power under their new and forceful leader, Margaret Thatcher (1925–   ).

NORTHERN IRELAND: THE TROUBLES CONTINUE

The 1970s saw the spread of violence within Northern Ireland and on to 'mainland' Britain. In Northern Ireland both Catholics and Protestants were guilty of atrocities against the other side. The Catholics, who had originally welcomed British troops, now saw them as an army of occupation; the first British soldier was killed in 1971 and by the end of the decade over 300 soldiers had died. The killings were not one-sided, and on one day in January 1972 British troops killed thirteen civilians, on what is remembered as 'Bloody Sunday'. There were various peace initiatives from London, but none worked. In 1972 the system of Home Rule for Northern Ireland ended and 'Direct Rule' from London was imposed. The IRA began to attack English targets, causing substantial loss of life at Aldershot barracks and in the Birmingham pub bombing.

The Thatcher Years, 1979–1990

Mrs Thatcher, Britain's first female prime minister, led the Conservatives to victory in three general elections (1979, 1984 and 1987) and her philosophies have dominated the 1980s. A central tenet of her policies was monetarism: the money supply was strictly controlled and public expenditure was cut back, with an associated emphasis on 'self help'. Business investment and competition were encouraged, and private enterprise was looked upon with favour. Several long-term monetarist trends continued through the 1980s: financial cuts in health, social services and education, and the polarisation of society, where the rich got richer and the poor poorer. The sharpening of the 'North–South Divide' became politically obvious – the Conservatives controlled the South (with the exception of parts of London) and East, and Labour controlled much of the North, the Midlands, Scotland and Wales

The introduction of monetarist policies caused mass unemployment (three million by 1981) and bankrupted many firms, although inflation fell after a steep initial rise. After three years in office the government had become deeply unpopular and was doing badly in local and by-elections. But salvation was to come from an unexpected quarter.

THE FALKLANDS WAR, 1982

On 2 April 1982 Argentine forces invaded the Falkland Islands. The Falklands lie 400 miles (640 kms) off the Argentinian coast and 8,000 miles (12,800 km) from Britain. Ownership of the islands had long been in dispute between Britain and Argentina, and the British government had many warnings of Argentinian intentions. The invasion force quickly overpowered the tiny British garrison and the two countries found themselves at war. A British task force was rapidly assembled and sent to recapture the islands. The fighting was concentrated into a few weeks: the main events were the sinking of the elderly Argentinian cruiser *General Belgrano*, the destruction of seven British ships, and the

British landings at Bluff Cove and Goose Green. On 14 June the Argentinians surrendered – barely two months after the invasion. The war resulted in 254 British deaths (750 Argentinians died) and cost about £700 million. In Britain the main effect was upon politics: the government's popularity soared as a result of the patriotic fervour inspired by the war.

THE CENTRE PARTIES

The general election of 1983 proved to be a landslide victory for the Conservatives. The 'Falklands factor' continued to give the image that the government was patriotic and tough, and opposition parties did little to improve their own standing.

Two years before, in 1981, a new opposition party, the Social Democratic Party (SDP) was formed, but despite initial success in recruiting new members it was not able to survive as a separate party and merged with the Liberal Party. The party had some spectacular successes and in the 1983 General Election received 8 million votes. Despite its apparent success the new party only gained 23 MPs. The Labour Party too had gained just over 8 million votes, but because of the nature of the voting system had gained 209 MPs in the new parliament.

Mrs Thatcher's Second Term, 1983–1987

THE 1984 MINERS' STRIKE

In Mrs Thatcher's first term of office the Falklands War had been a catalyst for government support. In her second term the miners' strike fulfilled a similar role. In 1983 the National Coal Board (NCB) was determined to close large numbers of uneconomic pits; the government, remembering that the miners brought down the Conservative administration of 1974, naturally supported the NCB. (There were later suspicions that the cabinet had planned the whole confrontation.) From 9 March 1984 a nationwide strike was started by the National Union of Mineworkers to protect mining jobs. Unfortunately for them, not all miners went on strike and the productive Nottingham-shire coalfields kept working. By May and June the dispute had grown bitter, with confrontations between the miners and the police. Mrs Thatcher called the miners 'the enemy within' – in contrast to the Argentine threat from overseas. It was a statement resented by the miners who were fighting for their jobs and communities. By March 1985 the impoverished miners had returned to work: the power of the miners unions had been broken.

THE CAMPAIGN FOR NUCLEAR DISARMAMENT

A more peaceful mass movement could be found in the spectacular resurgence of CND. It had remained an active organisation since the 1950s, but it took on a new lease of life after 1980 when the government, without informing Parliament, allowed land-based nuclear Cruise missiles to be sited at American air force bases in Britain. The main focal point of protest was the Greenham Common air base, where a group of protesting women camped permanently outside the gates. The missiles were finally removed from the bases in late 1989, and with their destruction, the lessening of the Russian threat and the rise of green issues, CND has become less prominent.

NORTHERN IRELAND

In 1985 an initiative, called The Anglo-Irish Agreement, was signed by Britain and the Irish Republic. The two countries agreed to confer over the problems of Northern Ireland and began to work together to combat terrorism. The Unionist parties denounced the move for giving too much power to the Irish Republic, but despite opposition and protest the agreement has survived. The single worst act of violence in Britain at that time came in 1984 when the IRA bombed the Grand Hotel in Brighton where the Conservatives were holding their annual conference. Mrs Thatcher narrowly missed being killed, several Conservative ministers were injured, and several people died. Thus the terrorists came perilously close to dramatically changing the course of English history.

Contemporary Britain

In 1987 Mrs Thatcher won her third consecutive general election with a large majority (Conservative 380 seats, Labour 229, Alliance 22). After the election Labour won back voters, at the expense of the SDP and Liberals, with support for nuclear weapons and banning the left-wing Militant tendency organisation. Voters now considered Labour as sensible and moderate. The SDP and Liberals realised that they could no longer survive as separate parties, and so combined to form the Liberal Democrats, led by Paddy Ashdown.

Mrs Thatcher continued her policies of tight economic control, the privatisation of industry and the 'reorganisation' of the welfare state. Since 1979 massive privatisation schemes have been successfully launched: notably for British Gas, British Telecom, the Water Authorities, British Airways and the electricity industry. These and other sales, of what the former Tory premier Harold Macmillan called, in a critical speech, 'the family silver', have boosted the government's short-term revenue dramatically and have seen a marked increase in the number of shareholders in Britain, from 7 to 20 per cent. The irony was, however, that opinion polls continually revealed that only a minority of the population supported these and other Thatcherite policies.

The 1980s were also marked by a mixture of new unrest and new prosperity. The nation was shocked by the violence witnessed during the miners' strike in 1984, the continued IRA bombings, and riots in the deprived inner-city areas of Liverpool, London and elsewhere in 1981, and in the prisons, especially Strangeways in Manchester in 1990. So-called England football supporters also rioted in England and in Europe. Despite these outbreaks, for the majority of the population, and especially for those in work, the 1980s have been a decade of prosperity. Home ownership rose dramatically (mainly as a result of selling off council houses), as did the number of people owning cars (up from 19 million to 25 million between 1979 and 1990) and televisions (up from 1.8 million to 3.79 million between the same years). More people than ever before have a higher standard of living. But there are also many more people living below the poverty line than before Conservative rule.

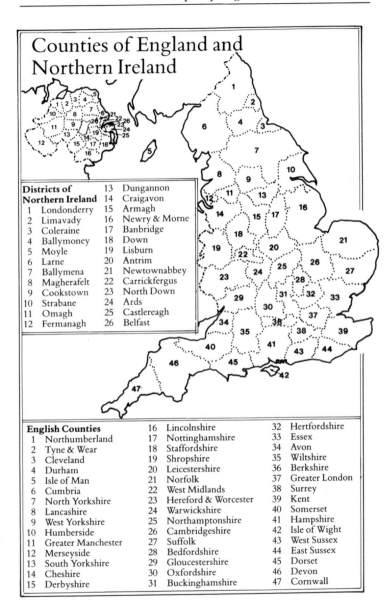

Counties of England and Northern Ireland

Districts of	13	Dungannon
Northern Ireland	14	Craigavon
1	Londonderry	15	Armagh
2	Limavady	16	Newry & Morne
3	Coleraine	17	Banbridge
4	Ballymoney	18	Down
5	Moyle	19	Lisburn
6	Larne	20	Antrim
7	Ballymena	21	Newtownabbey
8	Magherafelt	22	Carrickfergus
9	Cookstown	23	North Down
10	Strabane	24	Ards
11	Omagh	25	Castlereagh
12	Fermanagh	26	Belfast

Districts of
Northern Ireland
1 Londonderry
2 Limavady
3 Coleraine
4 Ballymoney
5 Moyle
6 Larne
7 Ballymena
8 Magherafelt
9 Cookstown
10 Strabane
11 Omagh
12 Fermanagh
13 Dungannon
14 Craigavon
15 Armagh
16 Newry & Morne
17 Banbridge
18 Down
19 Lisburn
20 Antrim
21 Newtownabbey
22 Carrickfergus
23 North Down
24 Ards
25 Castlereagh
26 Belfast

English Counties
1 Northumberland
2 Tyne & Wear
3 Cleveland
4 Durham
5 Isle of Man
6 Cumbria
7 North Yorkshire
8 Lancashire
9 West Yorkshire
10 Humberside
11 Greater Manchester
12 Merseyside
13 South Yorkshire
14 Cheshire
15 Derbyshire
16 Lincolnshire
17 Nottinghamshire
18 Staffordshire
19 Shropshire
20 Leicestershire
21 Norfolk
22 West Midlands
23 Hereford & Worcester
24 Warwickshire
25 Northamptonshire
26 Cambridgeshire
27 Suffolk
28 Bedfordshire
29 Gloucestershire
30 Oxfordshire
31 Buckinghamshire
32 Hertfordshire
33 Essex
34 Avon
35 Wiltshire
36 Berkshire
37 Greater London
38 Surrey
39 Kent
40 Somerset
41 Hampshire
42 Isle of Wight
43 West Sussex
44 East Sussex
45 Dorset
46 Devon
47 Cornwall

MRS THATCHER'S RESIGNATION

At the beginning of 1990 it was inconceivable that Mrs Thatcher should not lead the Conservatives into the next general election, as to many voters she was synonymous with the Conservative party itself.

However, during 1990, public opinion turned against her. The Community Charge or 'Poll Tax' was implemented in England and became very unpopular. High inflation and interest rates caused the Government increasing discomfort, as did Conservative divisions over Europe. Michael Heseltine challenged her leadership in 1990 and she failed by just four votes to win outright. She was persuaded to resign on the 22 November. She had dominated the government by her force of character and her conviction politics for the previous eleven years, and had made the 1980s the Thatcher Era.

Opinions about the Thatcher years are divided. Her opponents pointed to the uncaring side of her policies – the widening gap between the rich and the poor, the growing problem of homelessness, the unpopular changes to the National Health Service and educational system, the recalculation of the unemployment figures apparently to disguise the number of unemployed and the emphasis placed upon profit and materialism. Her supporters saw her as the saviour of Britain, breaking the power of the unions and the left-wing dominated local councils, forcefully promoting Britain's interests in Europe and around the world – there was a close relationship between Mrs Thatcher and Presidents Reagan and Gorbachev – encouraging free enterprise, rejuvenating and remodelling British industry, and, in the words of a former minister, proving that 'the impossible is possible'.

John Major, the Chancellor of the Exchequer, was elected as the new prime minister. One of his first duties was the connection of English and French sides of the Channel Tunnel. A regular rail service started in 1995, against a background of mounting debt. It is an amazing feat of engineering and England became physically joined to Europe for the first time in 10,000 years.

1991: THE GULF WAR

An immediate problem for Major was the situation in the Gulf region. Iraq invaded Kuwait in August 1990 and Mrs Thatcher sent British troops into Saudi Arabia as part of the United Nations multi-national task force. The RAF was involved with bombing raids. At sea the Royal Navy was employed in operations and mine-sweeping, and British troops and tanks were an integral part of the attack upon the Republican guard on the Iraq/Kuwait border. The battle lasted for only 100 hours before the Iraqis surrendered. The war resulted in 17 British deaths: a tragedy for individual families but remarkably few for the scale of the operation.

VICTORY AND RECESSION

In Parliament the Gulf War produced a consensus of opinion amongst the political parties, which was also evident during an IRA bombing campaign. On the 7 February the IRA attempted to bomb the War Cabinet by a mortar attack: one bomb landed in the garden of 10 Downing Street and shattered the windows. However, there was no political harmony concerning the economy. The recession, which was apparent in the last part of 1990, deepened throughout 1991 and 1992.

The royal family had a particularly stark year in 1992: the Queen described it as her *annus horribilis*. All three of her married children divorced or separated: Princess Anne was divorced from Captain Mark Phillips; the queen's second son, Andrew, Duke of York, separated from his wife Sarah, and Prince Charles, the Prince of Wales, separated from his wife Diana – the most significant constitutionally. The year culminated in the queen agreeing to pay taxes for the first time and a disastrous fire at her private residence, Windsor Castle. The only alleviating factor was the marriage of Princes Anne to Commander Timothy Lawrence. As head of the Church of England, the queen also witnessed the decision to allow women to be ordained to the priesthood – which was passed by just two votes.

In April 1992, against all opinion poll predications, the Conservatives won the general election, albeit with a greatly reduced majority (Conservatives 306, Labour 271, Liberal Democrats 20). After the election the Government's popularity plummeted. The Conservative's image of prudent financial policies was shattered when it was forced out of the European Exchange Rate Mechanism (ERM) in 1992 and the conduct of its own MPs in taking bribes and the associated sleaze indicated a party ill at ease with itself.

Perhaps the Conservative Government's most important achievement was the ceasefire in Northern Ireland. The 'Troubles' had lasted for 25 years and had left thousands killed or injured in Northern Ireland, with sporadic bombing campaigns in England. Between December 1993 and August 1994 the IRA detonated 35 bombs in England. The ceasefire started on 1 September 1994 and led to Bill Clinton visiting the province.

The Labour Government 1997–

During its time in opposition the Labour Party had transformed itself, first under the leadership of John Smith, who died in 1994, and then Tony Blair. The party changed from a basically left-wing ideology to a more main-stream and centrist party. Whilst the Conservative Party's fortunes declined, Labour's opinion poll ratings soared. On 1 May Labour won a landslide election victory (Labour 419, Conservatives 165, Liberal Democrats 46). Eighteen years of Conservative Government had come to an end with a crushing defeat; John Major resigned and William Hague was elected as leader of the Conservative Party.

Within months of the victory, the nation was gripped by grief at the death of Diana, Princess of Wales (1961–1997), in a horrific car crash in Paris. On the day of her funeral the nation came to a complete standstill. A lasting legacy is the public desire for the Royal Family to change and become less formal in its approach.

Once in power, Labour set about radical reform of the government of the United Kingdom. Both Scotland and Wales voted for their own parliaments which started in 1999. Within Parliament Labour proposed a radical shakeup of the House of Lords. In Northern Ireland the 1998 'Good Friday Agreement' has meant lasting peace with the subsequent elections bringing the two sides together. The horrific car bomb at Omagh, the worst atrocity of the 'Troubles', further increased desire for peace on all sides.

Environmental concerns have concentrated on air pollution and attempting to control the number of cars on the roads. On a longer time-scale the Greenhouse effect and atmospheric warming are a more ominous element of the permanent feature of British small talk: the weather.

Yet despite all the difficulties, traumas and violent episodes, England has remained a basically peaceful country throughout its long history. The present problems faced by the government have uncanny echoes from the past – from the Peasants' Revolt of 1381 against the poll tax to struggles of every government this century to solve the difficulties resulting from economic decline. What is remarkable about England is the traditional stability and permanence of institutions. Instead of the violent revolutions witnessed in Europe and elsewhere, the English people have generally proved that changes can be made peacefully. Despite – or perhaps because of the Civil War of the 1640s, the monarchy, Parliament and the people have existed together more or less peacefully for centuries.

The English love of tradition, ceremony and structure is partly derived from the essential continuity of England's history, and is partly a cause of that continuity with its attendant institutional stability. The English have generally had little time for theory or for violent innovation. They remain essentially peaceful, law-abiding and tolerant, good at making things work, persistent in desiring compromise rather than confrontation. Although they once ruled a quarter of the human race, and dominated the world's export trade, those days are long past. Despite their membership of the Economic Community and the building of the Channel tunnel, the English remain rather insular and aloof, as if the possession of so beautiful and varied a country as England was sufficient cause for contentment.

Rulers and Monarchs

Anglo-Saxon Kings

Alfred the Great   *871–99*
Edward   *899–924*
Athelstan   *924–39*
Edmund   *939–46*
Edred   *946–55*
Edwy   *955–59*
Edgar   *959–75*
Edward the Martyr   *975–79*
Aethelred the Unready   *979–1016*
Cnut   *1016–35*
Harold I   *1037–40*
Harthacnut   *1040–42*
Edward the Confessor   *1042–66*
Harold II   *1066*

The House of Normandy

William I (the Conqueror)   *1066–87*
William II (Rufus)   *1087–1100*
Henry I   *1100–35*
Stephen   *1135–54*

The House of Plantagenet

Henry II   *1154–89*
Richard I (the Lionheart)   *1189–99*
John   *1199–1216*

Henry III   *1216–72*
Edward I   *1272–1307*
Edward II   *1307–27*
Edward III   *1327–77*
Richard II   *1377–99*

The House of Lancaster

Henry IV   *1399–1413*
Henry V   *1413–22*
Henry VI   *1422–61*

The House of York

Edward IV   *1461–83*
Edward V   *1483*
Richard III   *1483–85*

The House of Tudor

Henry VII   *1485–1509*
Henry VIII   *1509–47*
Edward VI   *1547–53*
Mary   *1553–58*
Elizabeth I   *1558–1603*

The House of Stuart

James I   *1603–25*
Charles I   *1625–49*

The Commonwealth and Protectorate

Oliver Cromwell
  (Protector)   *1653–58*
Richard Cromwell   *1658–59*

The House of Stuart (Restored)

Charles II   *1660–85*
James II   *1685–88*
William III and Mary   *1689–94*
William III   *1694–1702*
Anne   *1702–14*

The House of Hanover

George I   *1714–27*
George II   *1727–60*
George III   *1760–1820*
George IV (Regent from
  1811)   *1820–30*
William IV   *1830–37*

The House of Saxe-Coburg-Gotha

Victoria   *1837–1901*
Edward VII   *1901–10*

The House of Windsor

George V   *1910–36*
Edward VIII   *1936*
George VI   *1936–52*
Elizabeth II   *1952–*

Prime Ministers, 1721–1997

Robert Walpole   *Apr 1721*
Henry Pelham   *Aug 1743*
Earl of Wilmington   *Feb 1742*
Duke of Newcastle   *Mar 1754*
Duke of Devonshire   *Nov 1756*
Duke of Newcastle   *July 1757*
Earl of Bute   *May 1762*
George Grenville   *Apr 1763*
Marquess of Rockingham   *July 1765*
Earl of Chatham (Pitt the
   Elder)   *Jul 1766*
Duke of Grafton   *Oct 1768*
Lord North   *Jan 1770*
Marquess of Rockingham   *Mar 1782*
Earl of Shelburne   *Jul 1782*
Duke of Portland   *Apr 1783*
William Pitt
   (the Younger)   *Dec 1783*
Henry Addington   *Mar 1801*
William Pitt
   (the Younger)   *May 1804*
Lord Grenville   *Feb 1806*
Duke of Portland   *Mar 1807*
Spencer Perceval   *Oct 1809*
Earl of Liverpool   *Jun 1812*
George Canning   *Apr 1827*
Viscount Goderich   *Aug 1827*
Duke of Wellington   *Jan 1828*
Earl Grey   *Nov 1830*
Viscount Melbourne   *Jul 1834*
Duke of Wellington   *Nov 1834*

Sir Robert Peel   *Dec 1834*
Viscount Melbourne   *Apr 1835*
Sir Robert Peel   *Aug 1841*
Lord John Russell   *Jun 1846*
Earl of Derby   *Feb 1852*
Earl of Aberdeen   *Dec 1852*
Viscount Palmerston   *Feb 1855*
Earl of Derby   *Feb 1858*
Viscount Palmerston   *Jun 1859*
Earl Russell   *Oct 1865*
Earl of Derby   *Jul 1866*
Benjamin Disraeli   *Feb 1868*
William Ewart Gladstone   *Dec 1868*
Benjamin Disraeli   *Feb 1874*
William Ewart Gladstone   *Apr 1880*
Marquess of Salisbury   *Jun 1885*
William Ewart Gladstone   *Feb 1886*
Marquess of Salisbury   *Jul 1886*
William Ewart
   Gladstone   *Aug 1892*
Earl of Rosebery   *Mar 1894*
Marquess of Salisbury   *Jun 1895*
Arthur James Balfour   *Jul 1902*
Sir Henry Campbell-
   Bannerman   *Dec 1905*
Herbert Henry Asquith   *Apr 1908*
David Lloyd George   *Dec 1916*
Andrew Bonar Law   *Oct 1922*
Stanley Baldwin   *May 1923*
James Ramsay MacDonald   *Jan 1924*
Stanley Baldwin   *Nov 1924*

James Ramsay MacDonald   *Jun 1929*
Stanley Baldwin   *Jun 1935*
Neville Chamberlain   *May 1937*
Winston Churchill   *May 1940*
Clement Attlee   *Jul 1945*
Winston Churchill   *Oct 1951*
Sir Anthony Eden   *Apr 1955*
Harold Macmillan   *Jan 1957*

Sir Alec Douglas-Home   *Oct 1963*
Harold Wilson   *Oct 1964*
Edward Heath   *Jun 1970*
Harold Wilson   *Mar 1974*
James Callaghan   *Apr 1976*
Margaret Thatcher   *May 1979*
John Major   *Nov 1990*
Tony Blair   *May 1997*

Chronology of Major Events

1066	Edward dies, Harold II becomes king. The Norman invasion. Battle of Hastings: Harold killed, William the Conqueror becomes king
1069–70	Harrying of the north
1086	*Domesday Book* survey carried out
1138–53	Civil war in England
1152	Henry of Anjou (later Henry II) marries Eleanor of Aquitaine
1154	Death of Stephen, accession of Henry II
1162	Thomas Becket becomes Archbishop of Canterbury
1170	Murder of Becket
1189–94	Richard I on crusade and held captive in Germany
1215	Magna Carta; civil war in England
1216	Accession of Henry III
1264	Henry III captured at the battle of Lewes, Simon de Montfort the effective ruler
1265	de Montfort killed at battle of Evesham
1272	Accession of Edward I
1282–84	Edward's conquest of Wales
1296	Edward invades Scotland
1297	Rebellion by William Wallace in Scotland
1307	Accession of Edward II
1314	Scottish victory at Bannockburn
1337	The Hundred Years War begins
1346	English victory at Crecy
1347	English capture Calais
1348	The Black Death reaches England
1356	English victory at Poitiers
1381	The Peasants' Revolt
1397–99	Richard II's 'tyranny'
1399	Henry IV deposes Richard II
1400	Chaucer dies
1413	Accession of Henry V
1415	English victory at Agincourt
1419–20	English conquest of Normandy
1422	Accession of Henry VI
1445	Henry VI marries Margaret of Anjou
1455–85	The Wars of the Roses
1461–85	Period of Yorkist ascendancy
1477	William Caxton's first printed book in England
1483	The death of Edward V
1485	The battle of Bosworth; Richard III dies; accession of Henry VII and establishment of Tudor dynasty

1509	Accession of Henry VIII
1513	English victory over the Scots at Flodden
1515	Thomas Wolsey appointed Lord Chancellor
1527	Catherine of Aragon divorce crisis begins
1533	Henry VIII marries Anne Boleyn
1534	Act of Supremacy
1536	Dissolution of the Monasteries; the Pilgrimage of Grace
1536/1543	Union of England and Wales
1547	Accession of Edward VI
1549	First Book of Common Prayer
1553	Accession of Mary Tudor
1555–8	Persecution of Protestants
1558	Accession of Elizabeth I
1587	Execution of Mary Queen of Scots
1588	Spanish Armada
1601	Accession of James I; English and Scottish crowns united
1605	Gunpowder Plot
1611	The Authorised Version of the Bible published
1617–28	Ascendancy of George Villiers, Duke of Buckingham
1620	Pilgrim fathers sail to America
1625	Accession of Charles I
1628	Parliament publishes 'Petition of Right'
1629–40	Charles I governs without Parliament
1640	Long Parliament summoned
1642–49	Civil War
1649	Execution of Charles I
1649–53	The Commonwealth
1649–50	Cromwell in Ireland
1653–60	The Protectorate
1658	Oliver Cromwell dies; succeeded by his son Richard
1660	Restoration of Charles II
1662	Church of England restored
1665	Great Plague
1666	Great Fire of London
1678	Titus Oates and Popish Plot
1679–81	The Exclusion Crisis; Whig and Tory parties emerge
1685	Accession of James II; Monmouth's rebellion fails
1688	The Glorious Revolution
1690	Battle of the Boyne; William III defeats James II in Ireland
1694	Death of Mary; Bank of England founded
1702	Accession of Anne
1704	Battle of Blenheim
1707	Union of England and Scotland

1714	Accession of George I
1715	Jacobite rebellion by 'the Old Pretender' fails
1720	The South Sea bubble
1738	John Wesley's 'conversion'; start of Methodism
1742	Fall of Walpole as prime minister
1745–46	Jacobite Rebellion by 'Bonnie Prince Charlie' fails
1746	Battle of Culloden, last battle on British soil
1759	Capture of Quebec
1773	Boston tea party
1775–81	American War of Independence
1788	Australian penal settlements established
1789	French Revolution
1801	Union with Ireland
1803–15	War against Napoleon
1805	Battle of Trafalgar
1815	Battle of Waterloo
1819	Peterloo massacre
1825	Stockton to Darlington railway, the first regular railway service
1832	Great Reform Bill
1837	Accession of Queen Victoria
1839	Chartist riots
1844	Irish potato famine starts
1846	Repeal of the Corn Laws opens the way for establisment of free trade
1851	Great Exhibition
1854–56	Crimean War
1858	Indian Mutiny
1861	Death of Albert, the Prince Consort
1867	Dominion of Canada established
1875	Disraeli buys Suez Canal shares (canal opened in 1869)
1876	Victoria proclaimed Empress of India
1882	British forces invade and occupy Egypt
1885	Death of General Gordon at Khartoum
1886	Issue of Home Rule for Ireland splits the Liberal party
1899–1902	Boer War; Britain has now acquired a huge African empire, running from the Cape to Egypt and from West Africa to Kenya
1901	Death of Victoria, accession of Edward VII
1905–15	Reforming Liberal government in power; Liberal landslide in 1906 election
1906	Labour party formed
1910	George V becomes king and emperor

1914	Britain enters World War I
1916	Battle of the Somme
1917	Battle of Passchendaele
1918	End of World War I (11 November)
1919	Gandhi begins all-India civic disobedience campaign
1922	Establishment of the Free Irish State
1924	First Labour government
1926	General Strike; dominion status defined, confirming the existence of a self-governing 'Commonwealth' and a dependent 'Empire'
1931	Financial crisis
1936	Abdication of Edward VIII; accession of George VI
1939	Britain enters World War II
1940	Churchill becomes prime minister; British withdrawal from Dunkirk; Battle of Britain, defeat of German invasion plan
1943	Successful allied North Africa campaign
1944	Normandy Landings: D-Day
1945	End of war; landslide Labour victory heralds foundation of the welfare state; Attlee becomes prime minister
1947	Independence for India and Pakistan
1948	National Health Service set up
1949	Britain joins NATO
1951	Festival of Britain; Conservatives win general election; Churchill becomes prime minister
1952	Accession of Elizabeth II
1955	Churchill resigns; Eden prime minister
1956	Anglo–French invasion of Suez
1957	Macmillan becomes prime minister
1958	Campaign for Nuclear Disarmament (CND) founded
1963	Douglas-Home becomes prime minister
1964	Labour wins the general election; Wilson becomes prime minister
1966	Labour returned with a landslide victory
1969	The start of 'The Troubles' in Northern Ireland
1970	Conservatives win general election; Heath becomes prime minister
1973	Britain enters the EEC
1974	National miners' strike; Labour win two general elections; Wilson prime minister
1976	Callaghan becomes prime minister
1978–9	'Winter of Discontent' convinces many that the trade unions have become too powerful

1979	Conservatives win general election; Mrs Thatcher becomes prime minister, committed to the 'free market' and 'monetarism'
1981	Social Democrat party founded after split in the Labour party
1982	Falklands War
1983	Conservatives returned to office with large majority; Cruise missiles installed
1984–85	Miners' strike
1987	Conservatives win third term of office
1989	Community Charge (Poll Tax) introduced in Scotland
1990	Community Charge introduced in England; Mrs Thatcher replaced by John Major as prime minister; Britain joined with France by the Channel tunnel
1991	Gulf War
1992	Conservatives win fourth term in office, the recession deepened. The Queen's *annus horribilis*
1993	The recession continued. IRA atrocities in England
1994	Ceasefire in Northern Ireland
1995	John Major resigned and was re-elected
1997	Labour win general election with a landslide victory. Diana, Princess of Wales, died in a horrific car crash.
1998	The 'Good Friday Agreement' brought peace to Northern Ireland. Scotland and Wales vote for devolution and separate Parliament.

Major Battles fought in Britain

MOUNT BADON c. 500
Romano–British army, supposedly led by Arthur, defeated the invading Saxons.
The site of the battle is unknown.

EDINGTON 878
King Alfred, who had fled to Athelney, gathered a force and decisively defeated
the Vikings. This was the first of a succession of victories which enabled Wessex
to conquer most of England.

BRUNANBURGH 937
Athelstan, king of the English, defeated a combined army of Norwegians and
Scots.

MALDON 991
A Viking force defeated the men of Essex. The battle has become famous
because of the Anglo-Saxon poem, *The Battle of Maldon*.

STAMFORD BRIDGE 25 September 1066
Fought near York between King Harold and a combined army of the king of
Norway and Tostig, Earl of Northumbria, Harold's brother. Harold destroyed
the invading army, but then had rapidly to march south to face William at
Hastings.

HASTINGS 14 OCTOBER 1066
The most famous battle in English history. The invading Duke of Normandy,
William the Conqueror, defeated the ruling English king, Harold. The actual
site is at Battle.

LEWES 14 MAY 1264
The baron Simon de Montfort defeated the forces of Henry III and became the
effective ruler of England.

EVESHAM 4 AUGUST 1265
Henry III's son, the future Edward I, defeated Simon de Montfort and regained the crown for Henry.

STIRLING BRIDGE 11 SEPTEMBER 1297
The Scottish hero William Wallace defeated the English army and encouraged Scottish independence.

FALKIRK 22 JULY 1298
William Wallace was defeated by Edward I. The battle was noted for the heavy and effective use of the long bow for the first time.

BANNOCKBURN 23–24 JUNE 1314
A two-day battle in which Robert the Bruce defeated and humiliated the English forces led by Edward II.

SHREWSBURY 21 JULY 1403
Henry IV defeated an uprising by the combined forces of Owen Glendower and the Earl of Northumberland. The earl's son, Harry Percy, or 'Hotspur', was killed in the battle.

Wars of the Roses

ST ALBANS (FIRST BATTLE) 22 MAY 1455
First battle of the wars and a victory for the Yorkists over the Lancastrians.

WAKEFIELD 30 DECEMBER 1460
Heavy Yorkist defeat in which Richard, Duke of York, was killed.

TOWTON 29 MARCH 1461
Yorkist victory by Edward IV over the Lancastrian forces. The bloodiest and most decisive of all the battles in the Wars of the Roses.

BARNET 14 APRIL 1471
Edward IV returned from exile in France, where he had been since October 1470, and defeated the Lancastrians in battle. A major player in the wars, Warwick 'the Kingmaker', was killed.

BOSWORTH 22 AUGUST 1485
Second most famous battle on English soil and effectively the end of the Wars of the Roses. Henry Tudor defeated Richard III, who was killed, and founded the House of Tudor.

FLODDEN 9 SEPTEMBER 1513
An invading Scottish force, led by James IV, was heavily defeated by the English army. James and virtually a whole generation of Scottish nobility were killed.

SPANISH ARMADA 1588
The most famous naval battle fought off the English coast. The English forces attacked the more numerous Spanish ships in the English Channel. The wind then blew the Spanish ships past their destination, and they were forced to sail round the north of Scotland, past Ireland and back to Spain.

The First Civil War, 1642–45

EDGEHILL 23 OCTOBER 1642
First major battle of the Civil War. The result was indecisive: the Royalist troops forced the Parliamentarian army to withdraw and so left the road to London open, but the capital remained a Parliamentary stronghold.

MARSTON MOOR 2 JULY 1644
The Royalist army, led by Prince Rupert, had recently broken the siege of York, but was defeated as it attempted to bar the way of the Parliamentarian army. The north of England was now lost to the king.

NASEBY 14 JUNE 1645
The last major battle of the first Civil War, where the Royalist forces were decisively beaten by Sir Thomas Fairfax and the New Model Army.

Charles II's Civil War, 1650–51

DUNBAR 3 SEPTEMBER 1650
The Scottish army, which supported Charles II and the Scottish Church, was defeated by Cromwell's forces.

WORCESTER 3 SEPTEMBER 1651
An attempt by the future Charles II to gain the English throne was routed by Cromwell's army. Charles fled to France.

SEDGEMOOR 6 JULY 1685
The Duke of Monmouth, Charles II's illegitimate son, was defeated by the forces of James II.

Glorious Revolution 1688

A successful overthrow of James II by William of Orange. Noted because of the lack of military conflict.

THE BOYNE 1 JULY 1690
William III defeated James II in Ireland and so secured Protestantism in northern Ireland.

The Jacobite Risings

PRESTON 12–14 NOVEMBER 1715
The Jacobite army briefly captured Preston but were defeated by the English.

SHERIFFMUIR 13 NOVEMBER 1715
An indecisive battle between the Jacobite forces, led by the Earl of Mar, and the English. The Scots retreated and the rebellion faded away.

PRESTONPANS 21 SEPTEMBER 1745
Jacobite victory over the English, which helped to secure Scotland for the Jacobite cause.

CULLODEN 16 APRIL 1746
The last battle fought on British soil. The 'Young Pretender', Charles Stuart, was defeated by the Duke of Cumberland, whose actions earned him the title of 'Butcher' Cumberland. Prince Charles was forced to flee and the Jacobite threat was effectively ended.

Selected List of Castles
Palaces and Houses

Castles

Aberystwyth (Dyfed)   *13th century*
Alnwick (Northumberland)   *12th century*
Arundel (West Sussex)   *11th century*
Beaumaris (Anglesey)   *13th century*
Berkhamsted (Hertfordshire)   *11th century*
Bodiam (East Sussex)   *14th century*
Caernarfon (Gwynedd)   *12th century*
Caerphilly (Mid Glamorgan)   *12th century*
Carlisle (Cumbria)   *11th century*
Conwy (Gwynedd)   *13th century*
Corfe (Dorset)   *11th century*
Denbigh (Clwyd)   *13th century*
Dover (Kent)   *Roman*
Egremont (Cumbria)   *12th century*
Framlingham (Suffolk)   *12th century*
Harlech (Gwyned)   *13th century*
Launceston (Cornwall)   *11th century*
Lewes (East Sussex)   *12th century*
Ludlow (Shropshire)   *11th century*
Portchester (Hampshire)   *Roman*
Richmond (North Yorkshire)   *11th century*
Rochester (Kent)   *11th century*
Scarborough (North Yorkshire)   *12th century*
Shrewsbury (Shropshire)   *11th century*

Skipton (North Yorkshire)   *12th century*
Tower of London   *11th century*
Warwick (Warwickshire)   *14th century*
Windsor (Berkshire)   *12th century*
York (North Yorkshire)   *11th century*

Palaces and Houses

Blenheim (Oxfordshire)   *18th century*
Brighton Pavilion (East Sussex)   *18th century*
Castle Howard (North Yorkshire)   *18th century*
Charlecote Park (Warwickshire)   *16th century*
Chatsworth (Derbyshire)   *16th century*
Hampton Court Palace, London   *16th century*
Hardwick Hall (Derbyshire)   *16th century*
Harewood House (West Yorkshire)   *18th century*
Hatfield House (Hertfordshire)   *17th century*
Holkham Hall (Norfolk)   *18th century*

Ickworth (Suffolk) *18th century*
Kensington Palace, London *17th century*
Knole House (Kent) *15th century*
Longleat House (Somerset) *16th century*

Osborne House (Isle of Wight) *19th century*
Sandringham House (Norfolk) *19th century*
Woburn Abbey (Bedfordshire) *17th century*

Selected Cathedrals, Abbeys and Priories (from oldest dated remains)

(R) = the building is ruined, but substantial and impressive ruins remain

Beverley Minster (Humberside)   *13th century*
Bolton Priory (North Yorkshire)   *12th century*   (R)
Byland Abbey (North Yorkshire)   *12th century*   (R)
Canterbury Cathedral (Kent)   *11th century*
Carlisle Cathedral (Cumbria)   *11th century*
Coventry Cathedral 1 (West Midlands)   *11th century*   (R)
Coventry Cathedral 2 (West Midlands)   *20th century*
Durham Cathedral (County Durham)   *11th century*
Ely Cathedral (Cambridgeshire)   *11th century*
Exeter Cathedral (Devon)   *13th century*
Fountains Abbey (North Yorkshire)   *12th century*   (R)
Furness Abbey (Cumbria)   *12th century*   (R)
Glastonbury Abbey (Somerset)   *13th century*   (R)
Gloucester Cathedral (Gloucestershire)   *11th century*
Hexham Abbey (Northumberland)   *12th century*
Jervaulx Abbey (North Yorkshire)   *12th century*   (R)
Kirkham Priory (North Yorkshire)   *12th century*   (R)
Kirkstall Abbey (North Yorkshire)   *12th century*   (R)
Lichfield Cathedral (Staffordshire)   *13th century*
Lincoln Cathedral (Lincolnshire)   *11th century*
Lindisfarne Priory (Northumberland)   *11th century*   (R)
Liverpool Cathedral (Merseyside, Anglican)   *20th century*
Liverpool Metropolitan Cathedral (Merseyside, Catholic)   *20th century*
London, St Paul's Cathedral   *17th century*
London, Westminster Abbey   *13th century*
Norwich Cathedral (Norfolk)   *11th century*
Oxford Cathedral (Oxfordshire)   *12th century*
Peterborough Cathedral (Cambridgeshire)   *12th century*
Reading Abbey (Berkshire)   *12th century*   (R)
Rievaulx Abbey (North Yorkshire)   *12th century*   (R)
Ripon Cathedral (North Yorkshire)   *12th century*

Rochester Cathedral (Kent)   *11th century*
St Albans Cathedral (Hertfordshire)   *11th century*
Salisbury Cathedral (Wiltshire)   *13th century*
Selby Abbey (North Yorkshire)   *13th century*
Southwark Cathedral, London   *13th century*
Southwell Minster (Nottinghamshire)   *12th century*
Tewkesbury Abbey (Gloucestershire)   *11th century*
Tynemouth Priory (Tyne and Wear)   *11th century*   (R)
Walsingham Priory (Norfolk)   *11th century*   (R)
Wells Cathedral (Somerset)   *12th century*
Whitby Abbey (North Yorkshire)   *13th century*   (R)
Winchester Cathedral (Hampshire)   *11th century*
Worcester Cathedral (Worcestershire)   *11th century*
York Minster (North Yorkshire)   *11th century*

Selected Reading on English History

BELOFF, M. *Wars and Welfare* (London, 1984)

BROOKE, C. *The Saxon and Norman Kings* (Glasgow, 1963)

CAMPBELL, J. (ed.) *The Anglo-Saxons* (Oxford, 1982)

CHRISTIE, I.R. *Wars and Revolutions* (London, 1982)

COWARD, B. *The Stuart Age* (London, 1980)

FRASER, A. (ed.) *The Lives of the Kings and Queens of England* (London, 1974)

FRERE, S. *Britannia* (London, 1987)

FULFORD, R. *Hanover to Windsor* (Glasgow, 1960)

GASH, N. *Aristocracy and People* (London, 1979)

GUY, G. *Tudor England* (Oxford, 1988)

HALLAM, E. (ed.) *The Plantagenet Chronicles* (London, 1986)
　　　　　　(ed.) *Chronicles of the Age of Chivalry* (London, 1987)
　　　　　　(ed.) *The Chronicles of The Wars of the Roses* (London, 1988)

HILL, C. *Reformation to Industrial Revolution* (Harmondsworth, 1967)

HOBSBAWM, E.J. *The Age of Empire, 1875–1914* (London, 1968)

KEE, R. *Ireland, A History* (London, 1980)

KENYON, J.P. *The Stuarts* (Glasgow, 1958)

LAING, L. and J. *The Origins of Britain* (London, 1980)

LOADES, D. (ed.) *The Chronicles of the Tudor Kings* (London, 1990)

MEDLICOTT, W.N. *Contemporary England, 1914–1964* (London, 1976)

MORGAN, K.O. *The Oxford Illustrated History of Britain* (Oxford, 1984)
　　　　　　The People's Peace (Oxford, 1990)

MORRIS, C. *The Tudors* (Glasgow, 1955)

PLUMB, J.H. *The First Four Georges* (Glasgow, 1956)

PORTER, B. *The Lion's Share* (London, 1984)

READ, D. *England 1868–1914* (London, 1974)

SAVAGE, A. *The Anglo-Saxon Chronicles* (London, 1982)

SEYMOUR, W. *Battles in Britain, 1066–1746* (London, 1979)

SPECK, W.A. *Stability and Strife* (London, 1977)

TAYLOR, A.J.P. *English History 1914–1945* (Harmondsworth, 1970)

THOMSON, D. *England in the Nineteenth Century* (Harmondsworth, 1950)

WALLACE, M. *A Short History of Ireland* (Newton Abbot, 1973)
WILLIAMSON, J.A. *The Tudor Age* (London, 1979)
WOOD, A. *Nineteenth Century Britain 1815–1914* (Harlow, 1982)

Historical Gazetteer

Anglesey (Gwynedd) A Welsh island, famous as a stronghold of Celtic druids until they were defeated by the Romans. The island also contains prehistoric burial mounds, and Beaumaris, one of Edward I's castles. **13, 17**

Avebury (Wiltshire) The village is partially situated in a huge prehistoric henge monument, which includes several stone circles. **8**

Bath (Avon) The hot springs enabled the Romans to build magnificent baths; archaeological excavations have uncovered the Roman Great Bath. In the 18th century Bath was transformed by new buildings and much Georgian architecture still remains. **16, 18, 33, 40**

Battle (East Sussex) The actual site of the battle of Hastings, 6 miles north of Hastings. **39–40**

Berwick-upon-Tweed (Northumberland) Near the English/Scottish border the town was constantly battered by sieges. By 1482 it was finally in English hands. It has geometric city walls, built between 1558 and 1569, which followed the best theories of defence during the Renaissance. **67**

Birmingham (West Midlands) Sec-ond largest city in Britain. Grew to be an important industrial city in the Industrial Revolution and has some impressive Victorian buildings and parks. **148, 168, 170, 203**

Brighton (East Sussex) Rose to prominence in the 18th century as a seaside town. The Prince Regent, later George IV, built the Royal Pavilion there, and others followed the example with elegant squares and superb houses. **171–172, 178**

Bristol (Avon) One of the wealthiest and most important towns in England during the middle ages, which also flourished in the 18th and 19th centuries by its trade with the New World. **4, 52, 71, 125, 148, 169, 174**

Cambridge (Cambridgeshire) Site of Roman, Saxon and medieval towns, but most famous for its university; the first recorded instance of teaching at the site is in 1231. The first college was Peterhouse in 1284; now there are 31. King's College Chapel is one of England's finest buildings. **63, 84, 94, 95, 125**

Canterbury (Kent) The Romans founded a settlement and St Augustine arrived there on the first mission from Rome in 597. Later Canterbury became an archbishopric: the archbishop is the primate of the English Church. The most famous archbishop was probably Thomas Becket and after his murder the cathedral became the major English pilgrimage centre of the middle ages: the destination for the pilgrims in Chaucer's *Canterbury Tales*. The Black Prince and Henry IV have tombs in the cathedral. **24–25, 33, 45, 51, 54–55, 58, 61, 72, 100**

Cardiff (South Glamorgan) The capital of Wales, it is the cultural and economic capital of the principality.

Chester (Cheshire) Famous as a Roman town it now has one of the most complete medieval city walls in England and many fine medieval buildings. **77**

Colchester (Essex) Founded by the Belgic tribe but captured by the Romans and used as the centre of the Imperial cult. It was destroyed by Boudicca in AD 61. Roman remains can still be seen. **13, 15, 20, 45**

Coventry (West Midlands) Industrial city with a modern centre, as it was rebuilt after devastating bombing raids during 1940. The shell of the old cathedral, and the new cathedral alongside, are the major attractions. **77, 226**

Dover (Kent) Historic gateway to Europe, it has one of the largest medieval castles in Europe. The town suffered heavily from bombing in World War II.

Durham (County Durham) The city has one of the finest Norman cathedrals in the country, which in the middle ages was the seat of the powerful Bishop of Durham. Next to the cathedral is the castle, both standing on a wooded peninsula and almost surrounded by the River Wear. **25, 31, 61**

Eton (Berkshire) Contains Eton College, the most famous English boys' school, which was founded in 1440 by Henry VI. **84**

Exeter (Devon) Originally a Roman town, and since the middle ages the seat of the Bishop of Exeter. **16, 89**

Glastonbury (Somerset) Site of an Iron Age lake village and a medieval abbey, now ruined, associated with King Arthur. The abbey stands upon the famous Glastonbury Tor. **11, 33**

Hastings (East Sussex) An important medieval port. The battle of 1066 was in fact fought at Battle (see above).

Lancaster (Lancashire) An important medieval port and city, which gave its name to the royal House of Lancaster. Few medieval remains survive.

Leeds (West Yorkshire) Important manufacturing town which flourished during the industrial revolution, and whose fortunes were based on the woollen industry. **63, 203**

Lincoln (Lincolnshire) The town is dominated by the cathedral, which stands upon a chalk ridge rising out of the flat lands of Lincolnshire. In the middle ages it was a port and an important centre for the wool trade. **16, 32, 62, 66**

Lindisfarne (Northumberland) St Aidan, a missionary from Iona in Scotland, founded a bishopric on the island in AD 635. It became the major Celtic missionary centre in the north of England but was sacked by the Vikings in 793. In 1083 a priory was founded on the site, the ruins of which can still be seen. (The island is reached by a causeway which floods at high tide.) **25, 27**

Liverpool (Merseyside) Grew to prominence as part of the 'Golden Triangle' of Atlantic trade in the 17th and 18th centuries, and later became an industrial city. From the port tens of thousands of Irish emigrants left for North America. In the 1960s the city underwent a remarkable revival, expressed in popular music; the most famous group was The Beatles. **4, 63, 169, 208, 243**

London Capital of England and the United Kingdom and the most important city since Roman times. The present population is over 9 million. Some of the most important features are:

The British Museum. Founded in 1753, it contains an immense number of objects, ranging from British prehistory to Chinese and Japanese art and objects. Some of the highlights are the objects from Sutton Hoo, the Elgin Marbles and the Rosetta stone. **10, 21**

Buckingham Palace. London residence of the monarchy (not open to the public). Building started in 1703 and much extended, especially for George IV between 1825 and 1830. A popular daily event is the changing of the guard at 11.30 am. **171, 178**

The City. Once the financial centre of the empire, and still of great significance. The City has sometimes supported radical political causes, for example it backed Parliament against the king in 1642.

Downing Street. Since the 18th century the home of the prime minister, although most of the building is given over to offices and working space.

Fleet Street. At one time dominated by newspaper publishing. Although many national newspapers have now moved to the outskirts of London, the term is still used to describe the world of newspapers and journalism.

Greenwich. A few miles down the Thames from the Tower of London. It is the site of the Old Royal Observatory, founded in 1675 by Charles II. On the river is the *Cutty Sark*, a fast 19th-century clipper sailing ship that carried cargo to Australia.

Houses of Parliament – see *Palace of Westminster*

Kensington. Contains many fine museums, including the Geological Museum, the Natural History Museum, the Science Museum, and the Victoria and Albert Museum. The land was bought with the profits from the Great Exhibition. Nearby is the Albert Hall, named after the Prince Consort and in Kensington Gardens stands the Albert Memorial, a heavy and sombre expression of Queen Victoria's devotion to her husband. **182**

Kew. Famous for the botanical gardens there, which were opened in 1841.

National Gallery. Built in the 1830s, it now houses one of the world's great art collections.

Piccadilly Circus. A famous junction of three routes, with a statue of Eros in the centre.

St Paul's Cathedral. Designed by Sir Christopher Wren and built between 1675 and 1710, after the original was destroyed in the Great Fire of London. It contains many tombs and monuments, including those of Wren, Nelson, Wellington and Dr Johnson, and even George Washington. A most notable feature is the Whispering Gallery with its remarkable acoustics. **136**

Tate Gallery. Contains the most important collection of British art, including works by Hogarth, Gainsborough, Constable and Turner.

Tower Bridge. Built between 1885–94, it is the only bridge across the Thames that can be raised to allow ships through underneath.

Tower of London. The central keep, called the White Tower, was built about 1078 by William the Conqueror. Contains the Crown Jewels, and collections of armour and heraldry. It has housed many important prisoners, including Princess Elizabeth, later Queen Elizabeth I. **46**

Trafalgar Square. Laid out in 1830 as a memorial to Admiral Nelson's victory in 1805 against the French. **165–166**

Palace of Westminster. Contains the House of Lords and the House of Commons, which were rebuilt after a fire in 1834. At the north end is St Stephen's Tower, which is popularly named Big Ben after the 13-ton bell in the tower. **203**

Westminster Abbey. Most ancient of London's churches and the site of royal coronations since William the Conqueror in 1066. The present abbey was largely rebuilt in the 13th and 14th centuries. Many famous memorials and tombs are in the abbey, including royalty (e.g. Edward the Confessor and Henry III), Winston Churchill and the Wesleys. **38, 44, 60–61, 66, 84**

Maiden Castle (Dorset) The largest and most impressive prehistoric hill fort in England. It was stormed by the Roman general, and later emperor, Vespasian in AD 43. **13**

Manchester (Greater Manchester) The cotton textile boom of the industrial revolution in the 18th century caused Manchester's rapid growth; in 1894 the Manchester ship canal turned the city into a major inland port. It was the centre for the Anti-Corn Law League movement in the 1840s. The city has some impressive Victorian buildings, especially the town hall, but also some uninspiring post-war development. The City Art Gallery has a fine collection of paintings by Turner and the Pre-Raphaelites. **168, 173, 180, 183, 203**

Newcastle upon Tyne (Tyne and Wear) The present city was founded by the Normans and has a medieval castle and cathedral, but most of the streets were laid out in the 19th century. It contains heavy industry, including chemical works and shipbuilding.

Norwich (Norfolk) Founded by the Saxons as a trading settlement. It has a magnificent cathedral, started in 1096. The castle is also Norman and contains a museum of the area, including artefacts from the prehistoric mineshafts at Grimes Graves. **27, 128**

Nottingham (Nottinghamshire)   The Danes occupied the town in 868 and it became the capital of the Danelaw. By popular tradition Robin Hood was supposed to have been in conflict with the sheriff of Nottingham in the middle ages. In 1642 Charles I raised his standard there, which marked the start of the Civil War. Nottingham became one of the earliest industrial towns and was the scene of Luddite riots between 1811 and 1816. **32, 57, 87, 174**

Offa's Dyke   An earth rampart built by Offa, King of Mercia, who reigned from 784 to 796. Originally it was over 150 miles in length and ran just inside the present Welsh border; 80 miles still exist, and a well-preserved section can be seen near Knighton (Powys). **26**

Oxford (Oxfordshire)   One of the oldest and most celebrated university towns in Europe. The first mention of the town occurs in 912. The university dates back to the 12th century and in 1214 it received its first official privilege. There are many fine medieval colleges clustered within the city centre. During the 20th century some manufacturing industry developed, particularly car production begun by William Morris, later Lord Nuffield. **63, 94, 95, 105, 125, 127, 129, 137, 139, 148**

Plymouth (Devon)   An important port in the seafaring history of Britain (Francis Drake returned to Plymouth in 1580 after circumnavigating the world). It was extensively damaged by bombing during World War II. **125**

Portsmouth (Hampshire)   England's most important naval port. Portches-ter castle nearby has the most complete set of Roman walls in northern Europe. The naval base has been the departure point of fleets for centuries, including those for the D-Day landings and the Falklands campaign. The naval museum includes the *Mary Rose*, Henry VIII's flagship which was raised from the seabed in 1982, Nelson's flagship *Victory*, and a D-Day exhibition.

St Albans (Hertfordshire)   The present town stands near the Roman town of Verulamium. St Albans was named after the first Christian martyr in England and the cathedral was built on the supposed site of his death. It has the longest nave in England. The city was the site of two battles in the Wars of the Roses. **12, 14, 15, 16, 18, 19, 63**

Salisbury (Wiltshire)   The original city lay two miles north at the easily defendable site of Old Sarum. In the 13th century the bishop moved to the present-day, prosperous lowland site. The medieval cathedral was conceived and built as a whole between 1220 and 1258 and is one of the most stylistically pure in England. The city still contains many medieval houses. **62, 63**

Stoke (Staffordshire)   Centre of the pottery industry during the 18th and 19th centuries. It became a centre of the provincial Methodism so vividly portrayed in the novels of Arnold Bennett.

Stonehenge (Wiltshire)   Probably the most famous and impressive stone circle in England. Despite knowledge of its complex construction, there is no consensus concerning its original purpose. **8–10**

Stratford-upon-Avon (Warwick-shire) An attractive market town famous as the place where William Shakespeare was born and where he returned to spend his last years. The church has a memorial to England's greatest poet and playwright in the chancel. The Royal Shakespeare Company (RSC) has several theatres in the town. **112, 114**

Warwick (Warwickshire) Medieval walled city dominated by the impressive castle. The castle belonged to the Earl of Warwick (Warwick the Kingmaker) who played such a crucial part in the Wars of the Roses.

Winchester (Hampshire) The Romans extended the previous Celtic site into one of the largest towns of Britain. It was the capital of the Anglo-Saxon kings and many were crowned there as well as London. Its importance continued throughout the middle ages, mainly because the royal treasury was there, but it declined during the 16th and 17th centuries. **44, 48**

Windsor (Berkshire) The elegant town is dwarfed by Windsor Castle.

The castle was started by William the Conqueror, enlarged by Edward III in the mid-1300s and refined by George IV between 1824 and 1837. Nearby is Windsor Great Park. It is still an important royal residence. **70, 171, 178**

York (North Yorkshire) The cathedral is called York Minster. York is, after Canterbury, the junior of the two archbishoprics of England. The city was founded by the Romans as the second most important military and civilian centre, after London, in the province. Its importance continued in Anglo-Saxon and Viking times as a royal and trading centre. (The Jorvik Viking Centre gives an accurately reconstructed view of the Viking town.) The Minster was built throughout the middle ages. In the city there are still many medieval buildings and winding streets. In more recent times it has become an important railway centre; the National Railway Museum is situated there. **15–16, 18, 24, 30, 32, 45, 49, 55, 56, 77, 94, 169**

Index